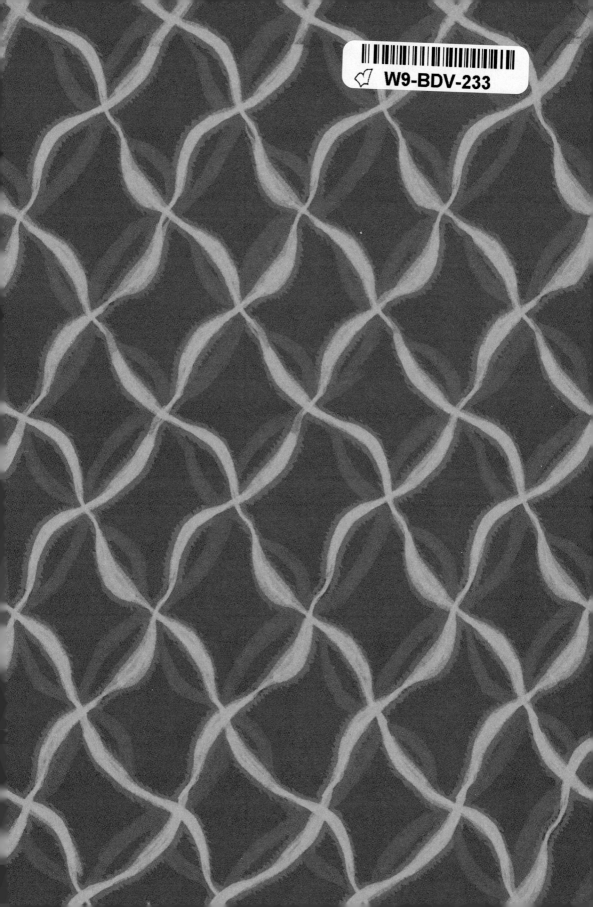

AYA

Marguerite Abouet & Clément Oubrerie

Drawn & Quarterly

Montréal

Previously published in French by Gallimard Jeunesse (ISBN 2-07-057311-7) as
part of the Joann Sfar edited Bayou collection.

Library and Archives Canada Cataloguing in Publication
Abouet, Marguerite, 1971- ; Aya / Marguerite Abouet ; illustrator: Clément
Oubrerie ; translator: Helge Dascher. Translation of: Aya de Yopougon.
ISBN 1-894937-90-2
1. Côte d'Ivoire--Comic books, strips, etc. 2. Teenage girls--Côte d'Ivoire--
Comic books, strips, etc. I. Oubrerie, Clément; II. Dascher, Helge, 1965- III.
Title. PN6790.I93A26 2007 741.5'96668 C2006-905291-3

Translation by Helge Dascher. Lettering by Tom Devlin.

Drawn & Quarterly, Post Office Box 48056, Montreal, Quebec, Canada H2V 4S8
www.drawnandquarterly.com

First hardcover edition: February 2007.
Printed in Singapore.
10 9 8 7 6 5 4 3 2 1

Distributed in the USA and abroad by:
Farrar, Straus and Giroux
19 Union Square West, New York, NY 10003
Orders: 888.330.8477

Distributed in Canada by:
Raincoast Books
9050 Shaughnessy Street, Vancouver, BC V6P 6E5
Orders: 800.663.5714

Distributed in the UK by:
Publishers Group UK
8 The Arena, Mollison Avenue, Enfield, Middlesex, EN3 7NL
tel: +44 (0) 208 216 6070

PREFACE

by Alisia Grace Chase, PhD

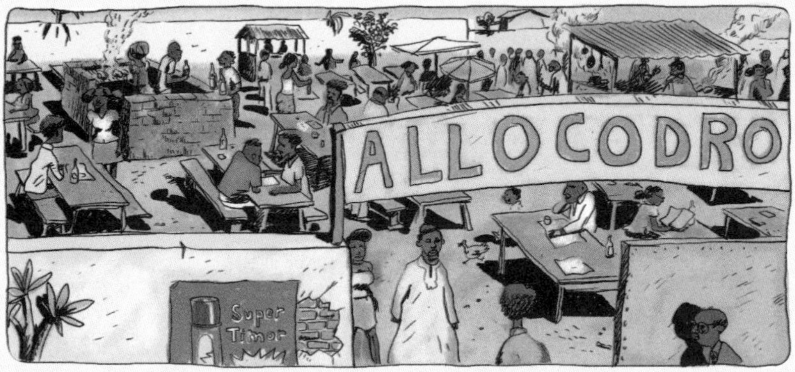
ALLOCODRO
Super Timor

The amorous hi-jinks narrated in *Aya* seem so familiar, so nearly suburban in their post-adolescent focus on dance floor flirtations, awkward first dates, and finding just the right dress for a friend's wedding, that to many western readers it may be difficult to believe they take place in Africa. As young Ivorian Myriam Montrat wrote about her homeland in the 1988 essay, *From the Heart of an African*, "The vision of Africa in the American mind is shaped by films, music, art, entertainment and the news media...(but) only the news media have the mission to inform. With regard to Africa, the media fail in this mission." Inarguably, the western world is becoming increasingly aware of the myriad cultures on this massively diverse continent, but swollen bellied children, machete wielding *janjaweeds*, and too many men and women dying of AIDS continue to comprise the majority of visual images that dominate the Western media.

In the Nineteen Seventies, however, one exceptional African nation belied the news channels' unremittingly tragic narratives and unsettling images: the Ivory Coast. A French colony for nearly eighty years, the nation was granted independence in 1960, and under the thirty-year leadership of its charismatic president, Félix Houphouët-Boigny, *Côte d'Ivoire* flourished. Instead of concentrating on industrial growth or the more immediate promise of petroleum, as its West African neighbors did, the new government hedged its bets on its 16 million hectares of virgin forest, and Houphouët-Boigny encouraged industrious migrants to clear it by liberally declaring, "the land belongs to the one who cultivates it." This political master-stroke, as historian Catherine Boone has called it, resulted in a rapidly expanding economy based upon small-scale production of coffee, cocoa, timber, and other agricultural staples such as bananas. In the two decades following independence, the Ivory Coast's economic growth was unsurpassed in the sub-Saharan region, and statistically undeniable: the GNP rose by more than 7% annually. During the time in which Aya's story takes place, the index of production was the highest in Africa, and what was commonly referred to as the "Ivorian miracle" resulted in unprecedented wealth.

The glamorous capital of Abidjan, often referred to as the "Paris of West Africa," was proof of this success, and not only because of a bridge named after Charles de Gaulle. Chic restaurants, elegant hotels, and world-class golf courses were only a few of this coastal city's many amenities. More than forty thousand French nationals provided economic stability, as "*la présence française*" tended to encourage foreign investment, and perhaps more influentially, granted the city incomparable cultural cachet. Abidjanaise French was the preferred language, patisseries and fried plantains peacefully coexisted, and *les filles Africaines* were more than familiar with the latest couture of Catherine Deneuve. Life seemed promising enough to be pedestrian; Bintou's hip-bumping moves in the open-air *maquis* and Adjoua's make-out sessions at the "1000 Star Hotel" were commonplace teenage pleasures that took place in such working class suburbs as Yopougon. The University of Abidjan flourished, with thousands of students graduating each year, and successfully finding jobs in government or other viable private sectors. Aya's dream of becoming a doctor, while dismissed by her conservative father, was very much a possibility. It was truly, as some wistfully refer to it, *la belle époque*.

Looking back on it, however, many economists wonder if this miracle was only a mirage, and the term "growth without development" is now more commonly accepted to describe this phenomenal period. Houphouët-Boigny's savvy *laissez-faire* policies tended to absorb rather than mobilize any opposition to his rule, and while this one party domination may have left the farmers free to cultivate land as they wished, it also left them politically disenfranchised. Not surprisingly, the real beneficiaries of the Ivorian miracle in the Seventies were not the industrious peasants whose crops were responsible for the country's gains, but an urban-based elite, characters not unlike the boss of Aya's father, a man who freely and frequently drops the names of both Houphouët-Boigny and French president Giscard D'Estaing. More problematically, because much of the gain was due more to a rise in the number of smallholders rather than an increase in farm size or individual production, once export prices for key crops declined, the country suffered a serious recession. As the economy began to stagnate in the Eighties, social unrest ensued. Student and worker strikes were commonplace; French companies began to pull out, and as dwindling resources began to affect all segments of society, blame and anger began to be directed towards the remaining French nationals and non-Ivorian Africans. These conflicts escalated after Houphouët-Boigny's death, when his successor, Henri Konan Bédié, resorted to divisive ethnic politics and xenophobia.

The last decade within the Ivory Coast has been dominated by a virulently Franco-phobic generation weaned not on the burgeoning potential of a newly independent nation, but on bloody coups and seemingly endless civil war. Sadly, the easy banter afforded by Aya and her girlfriends now seems a nostalgic anomaly, as the once glittering city of Abidjan falls further into decline. But Marguerite Abouet's gently comic narrative, her sexily piquant recipes, her advice on how to roll one's *pagne* (and one's *tassaba!*), coupled with Clément Oubrerie's vividly colored drawings, remind us of art's power to make another time and place come alive. Brilliantly, *dêh!*

FOR MARGAUX AND EMMANUEL
☆ ☆

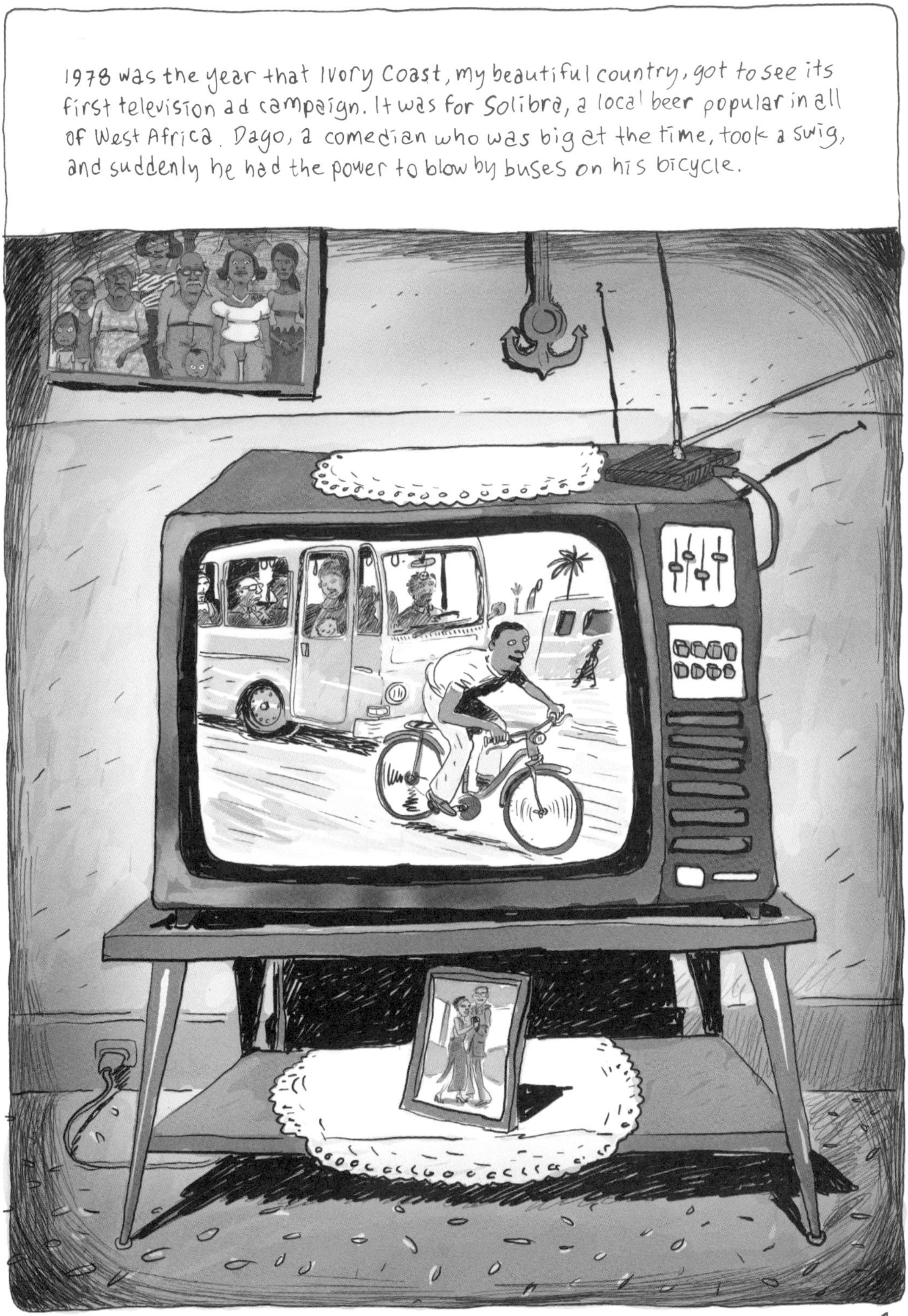
1978 was the year that Ivory Coast, my beautiful country, got to see its first television ad campaign. It was for Solibra, a local beer popular in all of West Africa. Dago, a comedian who was big at the time, took a swig, and suddenly he had the power to blow by buses on his bicycle.

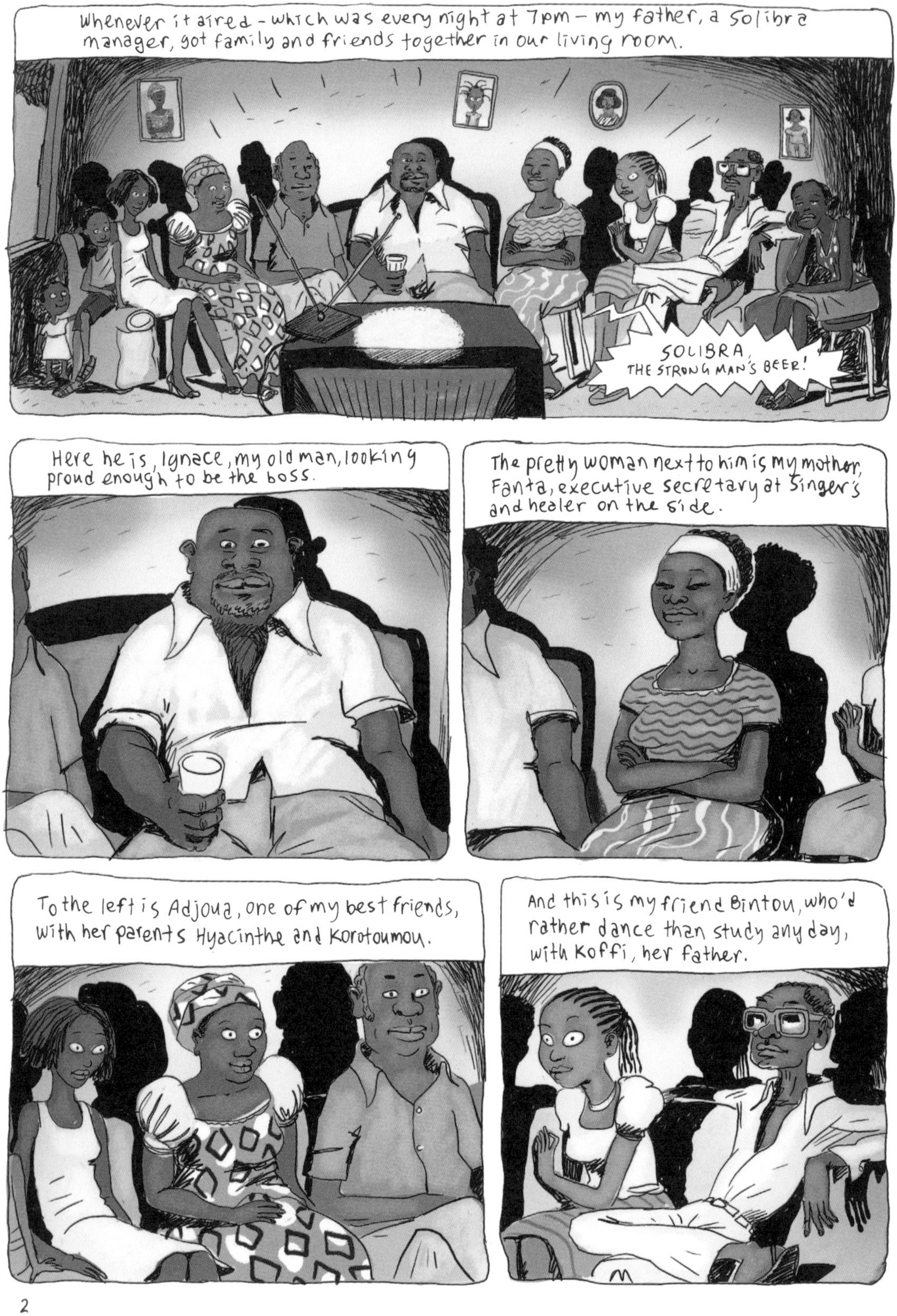

Whenever it aired – which was every night at 7pm – my father, a Solibra manager, got family and friends together in our living room.
SOLIBRA, THE STRONG MAN'S BEER!
Here he is, Ignace, my old man, looking proud enough to be the boss.
The pretty woman next to him is my mother, Fanta, executive secretary at Singer's and healer on the side.
To the left is Adjoua, one of my best friends, with her parents Hyacinthe and Korotoumou.
And this is my friend Bintou, who'd rather dance than study any day, with Koffi, her father.

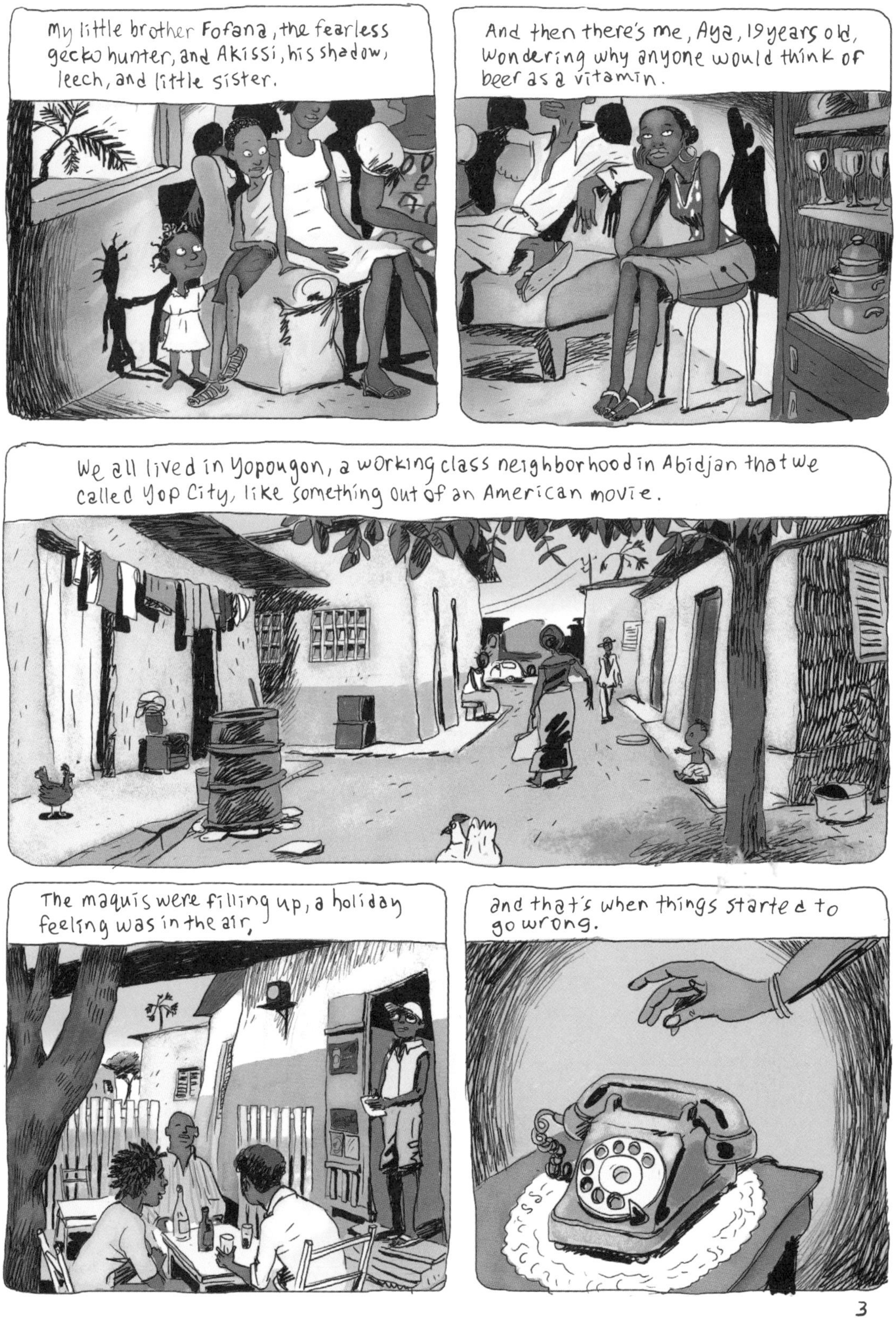
My little brother Fofana, the fearless gecko hunter, and Akissi, his shadow, leech, and little sister.
And then there's me, Aya, 19 years old, wondering why anyone would think of beer as a vitamin.
We all lived in Yopougon, a working class neighborhood in Abidjan that we called Yop City, like something out of an American movie.
The maquis were filling up, a holiday feeling was in the air,
and that's when things started to go wrong.

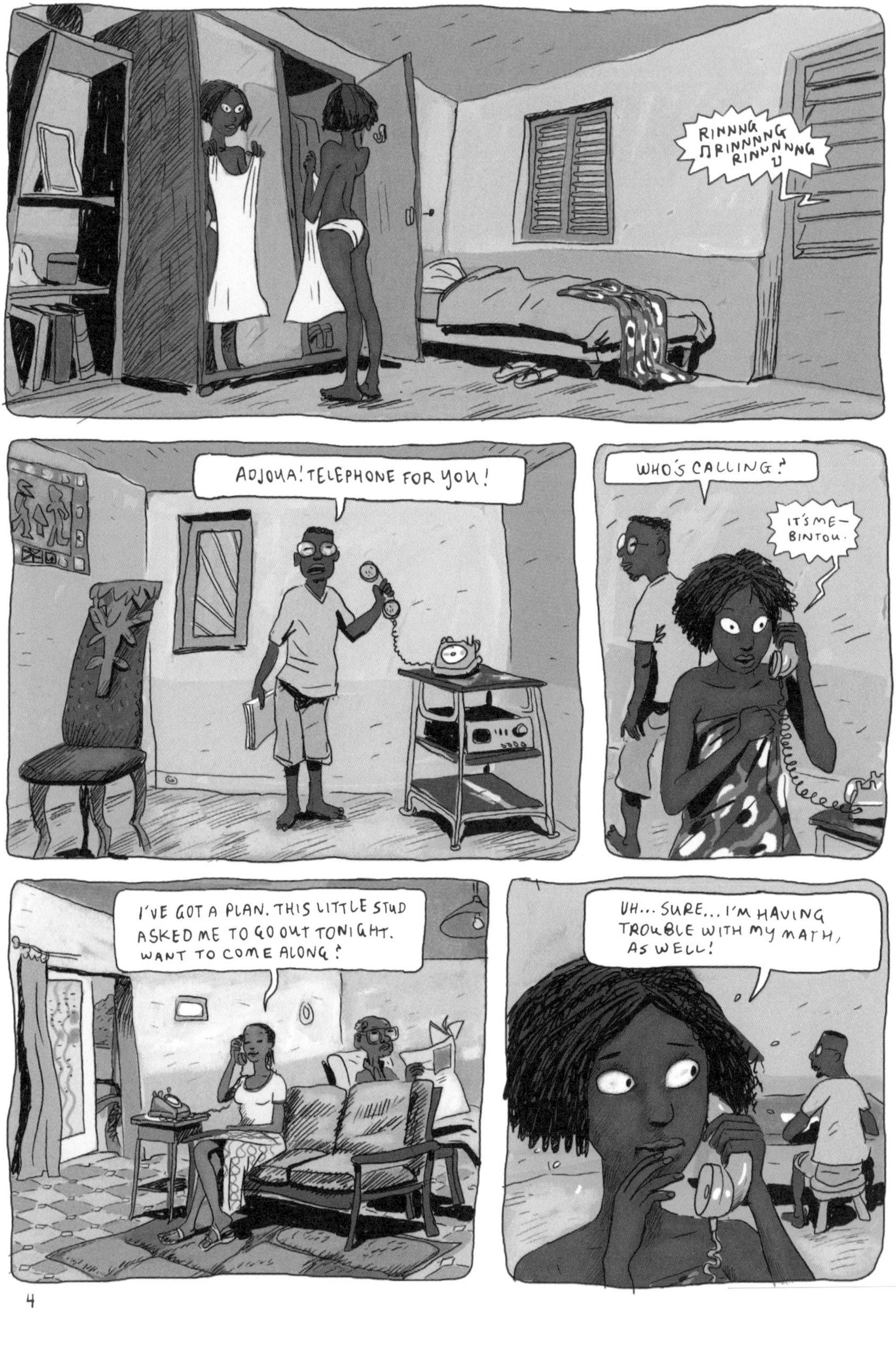
RINNNG RINNNNNG RINNNNNG
ADJOUA! TELEPHONE FOR YOU!
WHO'S CALLING?
IT'S ME- BINTOU.
I'VE GOT A PLAN. THIS LITTLE STUD ASKED ME TO GO OUT TONIGHT. WANT TO COME ALONG?
UH... SURE... I'M HAVING TROUBLE WITH MY MATH, AS WELL!

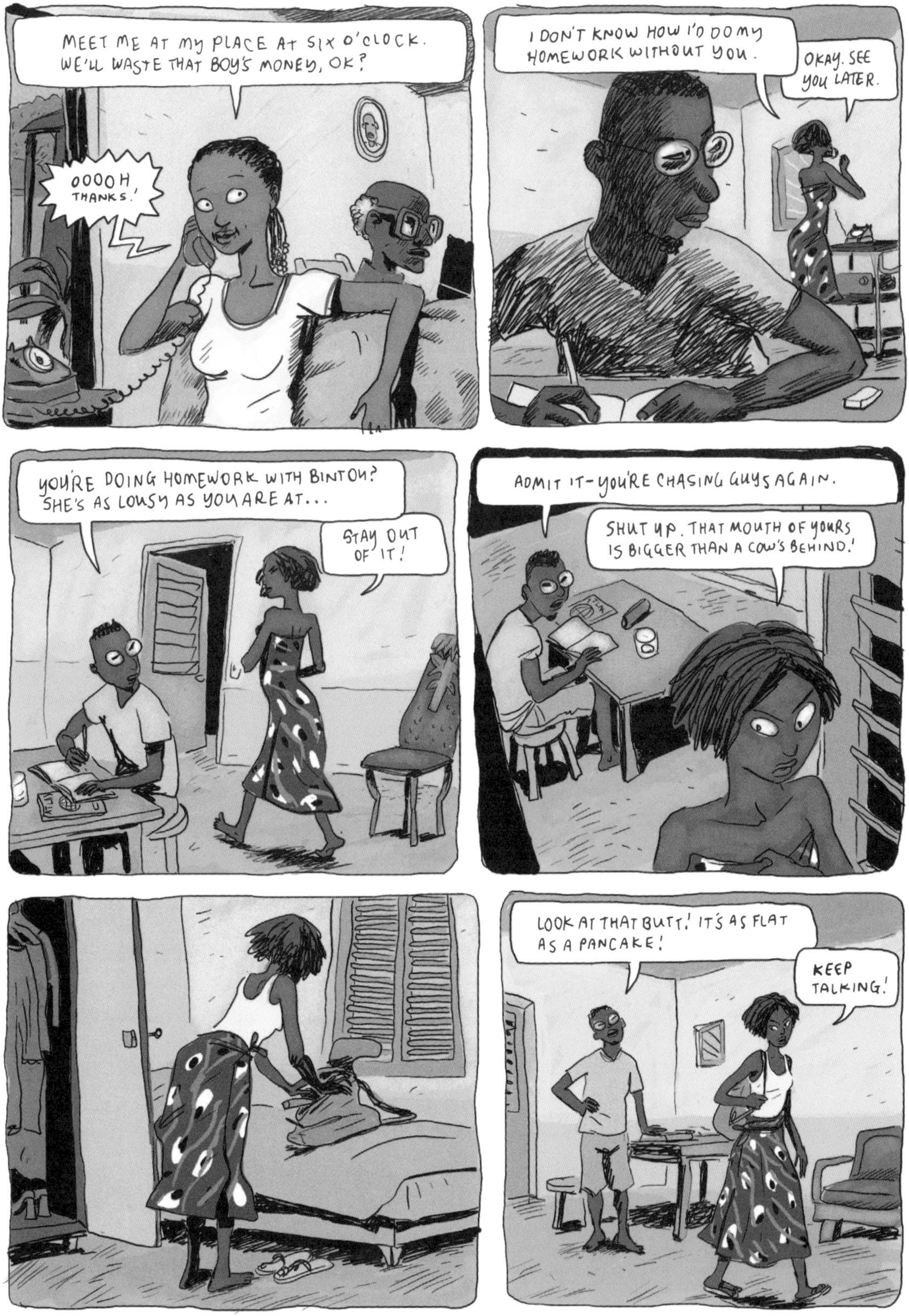
MEET ME AT MY PLACE AT SIX O'CLOCK. WE'LL WASTE THAT BOY'S MONEY, OK?
OOOOH THANKS!
I DON'T KNOW HOW I'D DO MY HOMEWORK WITHOUT YOU.
OKAY. SEE YOU LATER.
YOU'RE DOING HOMEWORK WITH BINTOU? SHE'S AS LOUSY AS YOU ARE AT...
STAY OUT OF IT!
ADMIT IT—YOU'RE CHASING GUYS AGAIN.
SHUT UP. THAT MOUTH OF YOURS IS BIGGER THAN A COW'S BEHIND!
LOOK AT THAT BUTT! IT'S AS FLAT AS A PANCAKE!
KEEP TALKING!

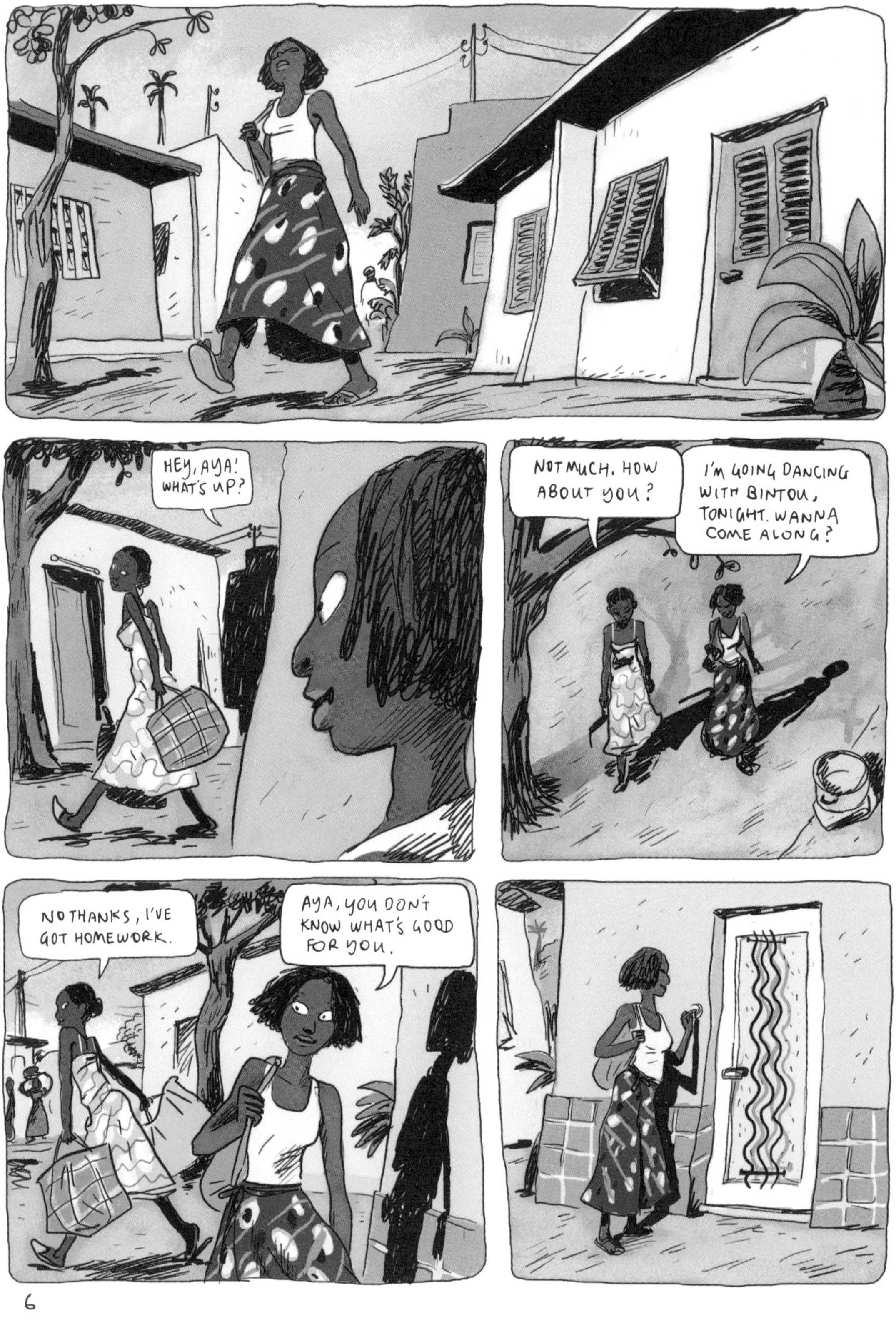
HEY, AYA! WHAT'S UP?
NOT MUCH. HOW ABOUT YOU?
I'M GOING DANCING WITH BINTOU, TONIGHT. WANNA COME ALONG?
NO THANKS, I'VE GOT HOMEWORK.
AYA, YOU DON'T KNOW WHAT'S GOOD FOR YOU.

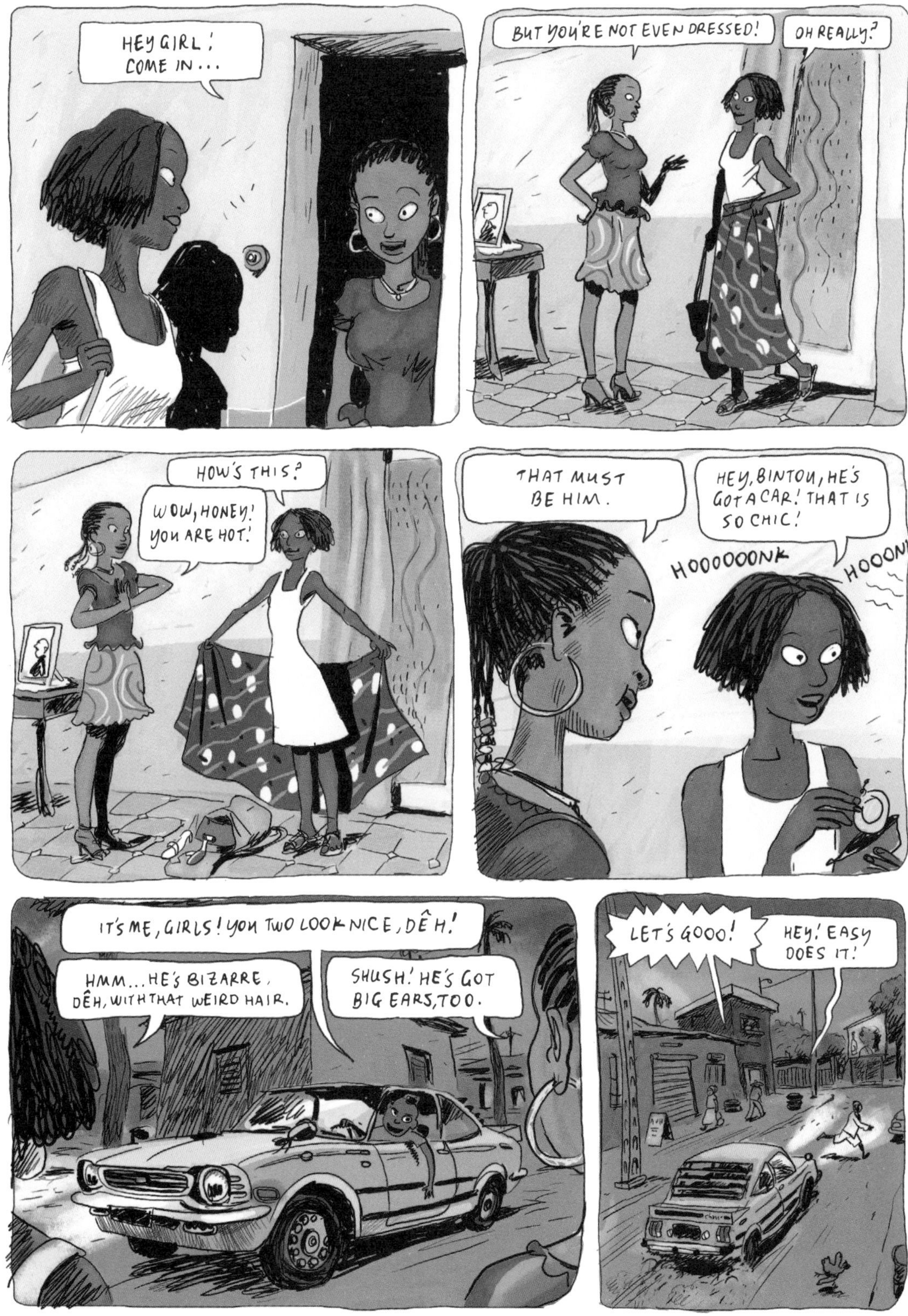
HEY GIRL! COME IN...
BUT YOU'RE NOT EVEN DRESSED!
OH REALLY?
HOW'S THIS?
WOW, HONEY! YOU ARE HOT!
THAT MUST BE HIM.
HEY, BINTOU, HE'S GOT A CAR! THAT IS SO CHIC!
HOOOOOONK
HOOONK
IT'S ME, GIRLS! YOU TWO LOOK NICE, DÊH!
HMM... HE'S BIZARRE, DÊH, WITH THAT WEIRD HAIR.
SHUSH! HE'S GOT BIG EARS, TOO.
LET'S GOOO!
HEY! EASY DOES IT!

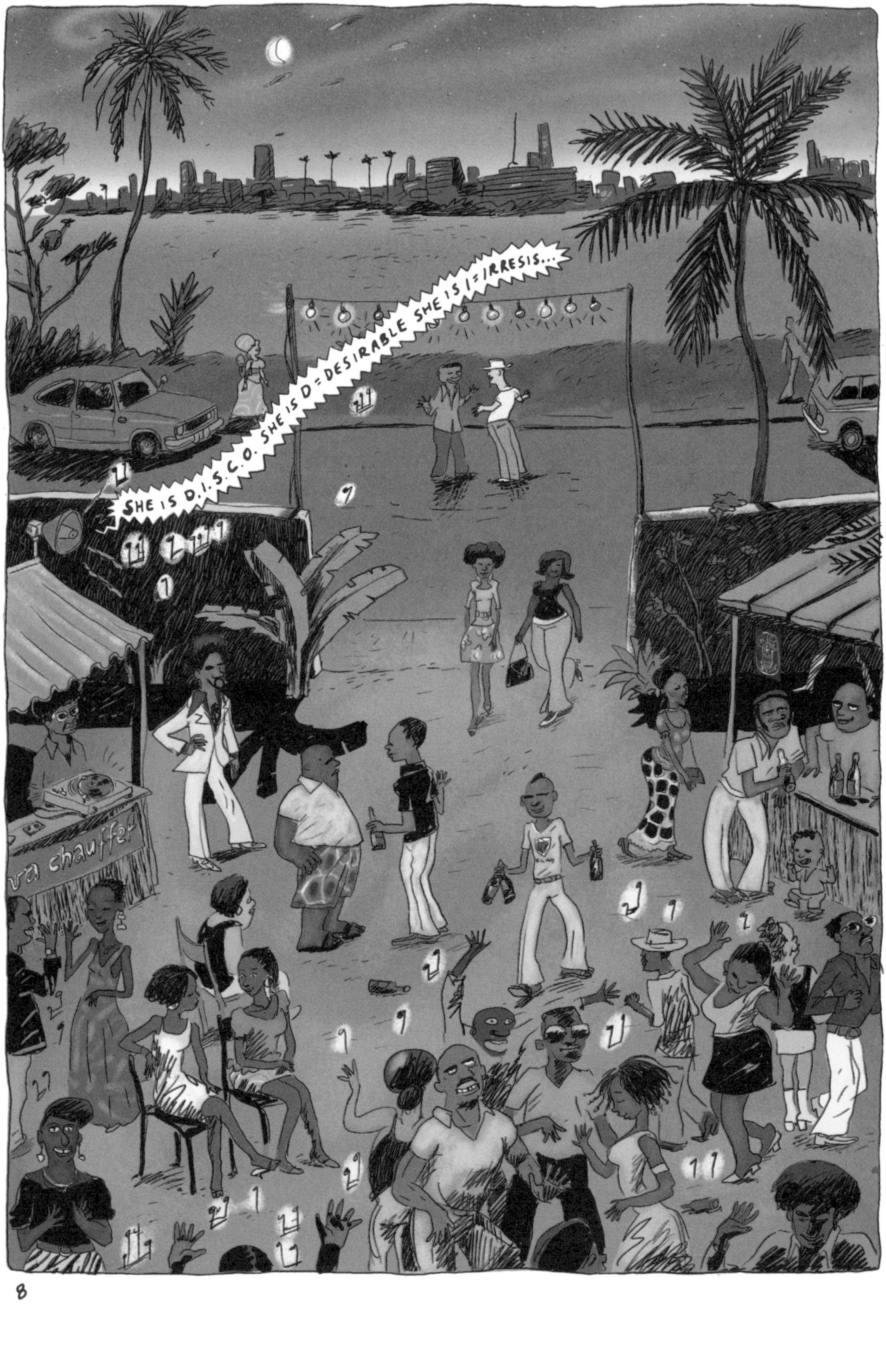
SHE IS D.I.S.C.O. SHE IS D=DESIRABLE SHE IS I=IRRESIS...
va chauffer

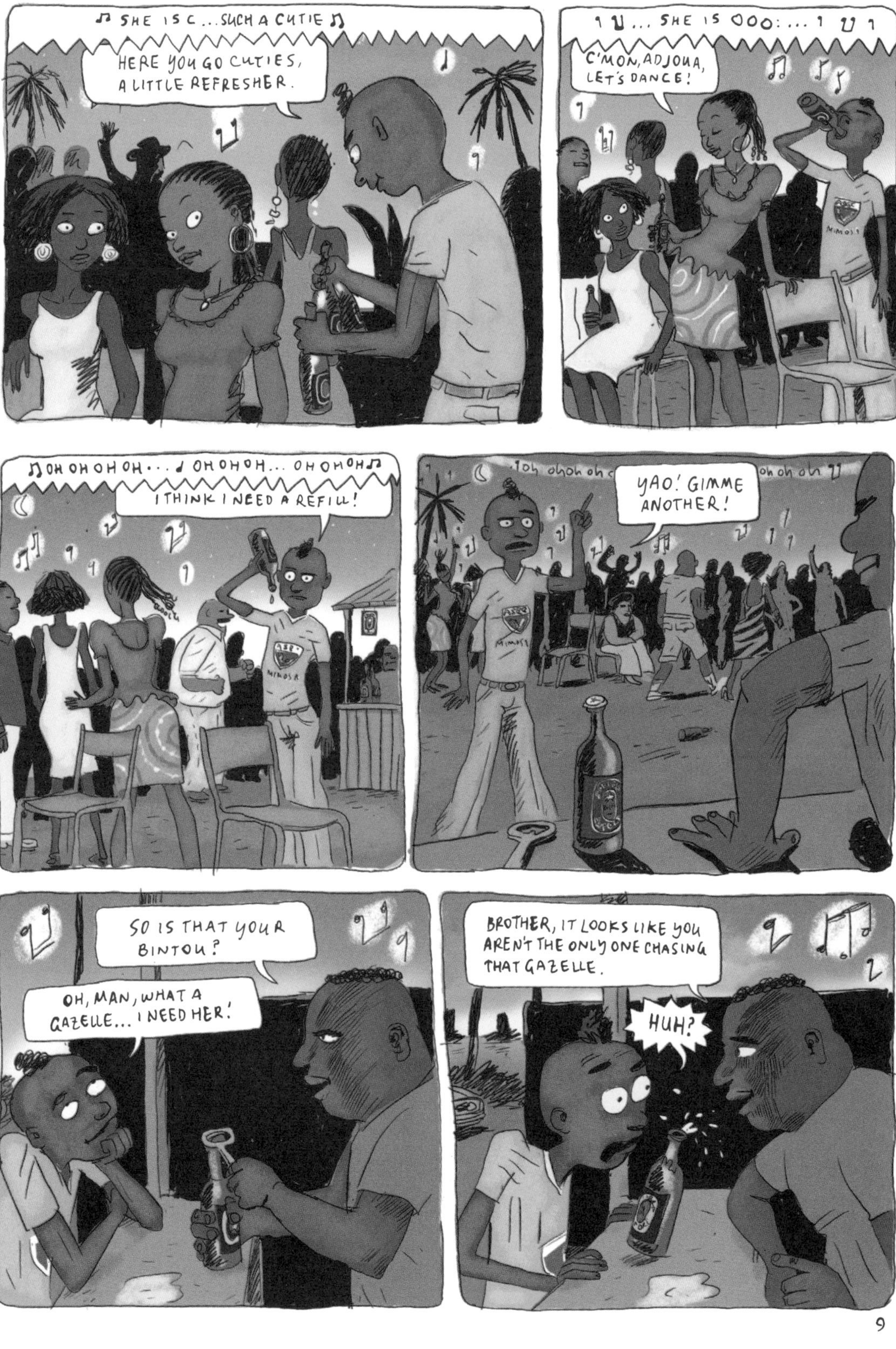
SHE IS C... SUCH A CUTIE
HERE YOU GO CUTIES, A LITTLE REFRESHER.
... SHE IS OOO: ...
C'MON, ADJOUA, LET'S DANCE!
OH OH OH OH... OH OH OH... OH OH OH
I THINK I NEED A REFILL!
YAO! GIMME ANOTHER!
SO IS THAT YOUR BINTOU?
OH, MAN, WHAT A GAZELLE... I NEED HER!
BROTHER, IT LOOKS LIKE YOU AREN'T THE ONLY ONE CHASING THAT GAZELLE.
HUH?

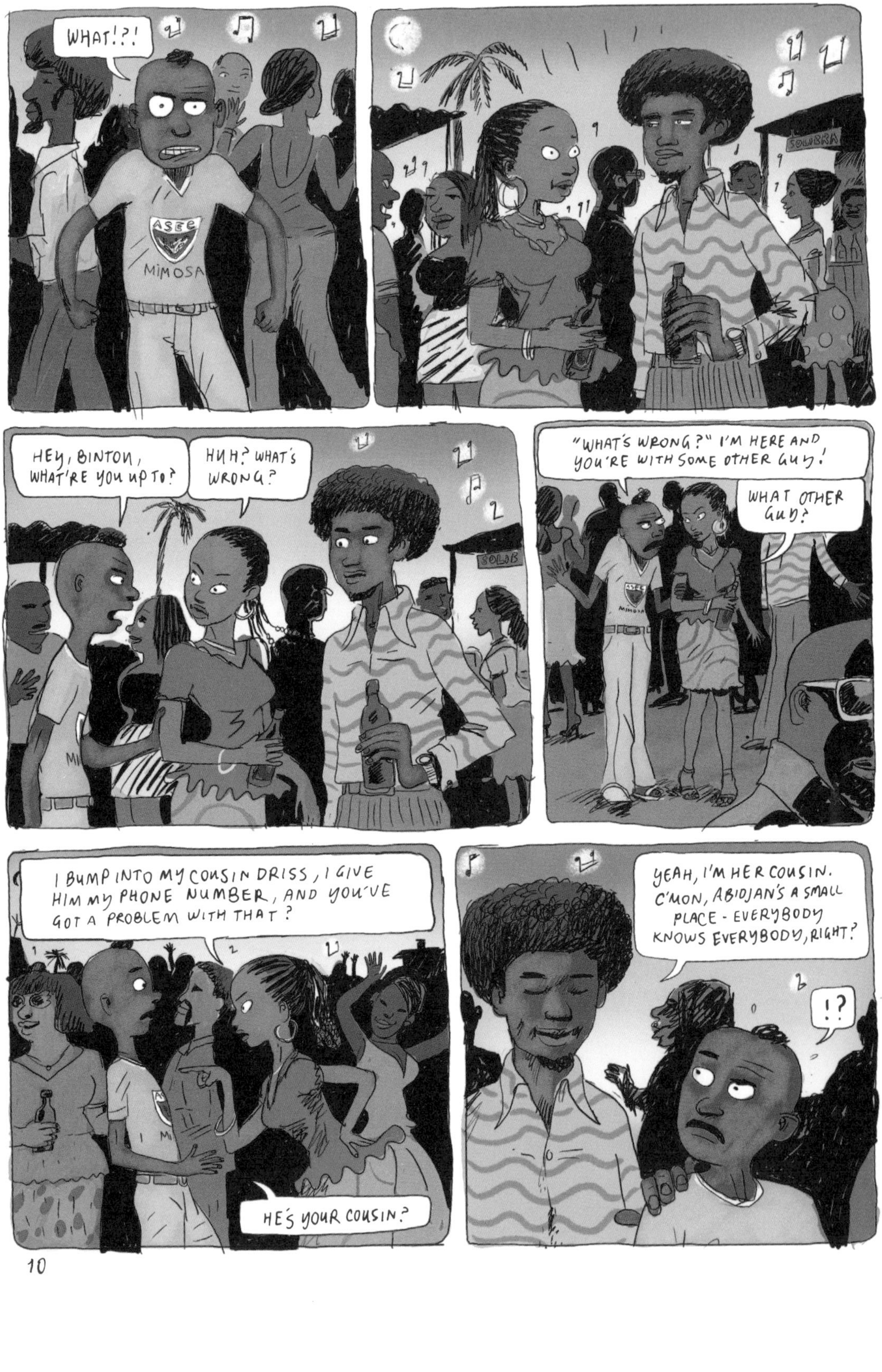
WHAT!?!
ASEC
MIMOSA
SOLIBRA
HEY, BINTOU, WHAT'RE YOU UP TO?
HUH? WHAT'S WRONG?
"WHAT'S WRONG?" I'M HERE AND YOU'RE WITH SOME OTHER GUY!
WHAT OTHER GUY?
I BUMP INTO MY COUSIN DRISS, I GIVE HIM MY PHONE NUMBER, AND YOU'VE GOT A PROBLEM WITH THAT?
HE'S YOUR COUSIN?
YEAH, I'M HER COUSIN. C'MON, ABIDJAN'S A SMALL PLACE - EVERYBODY KNOWS EVERYBODY, RIGHT?
!?

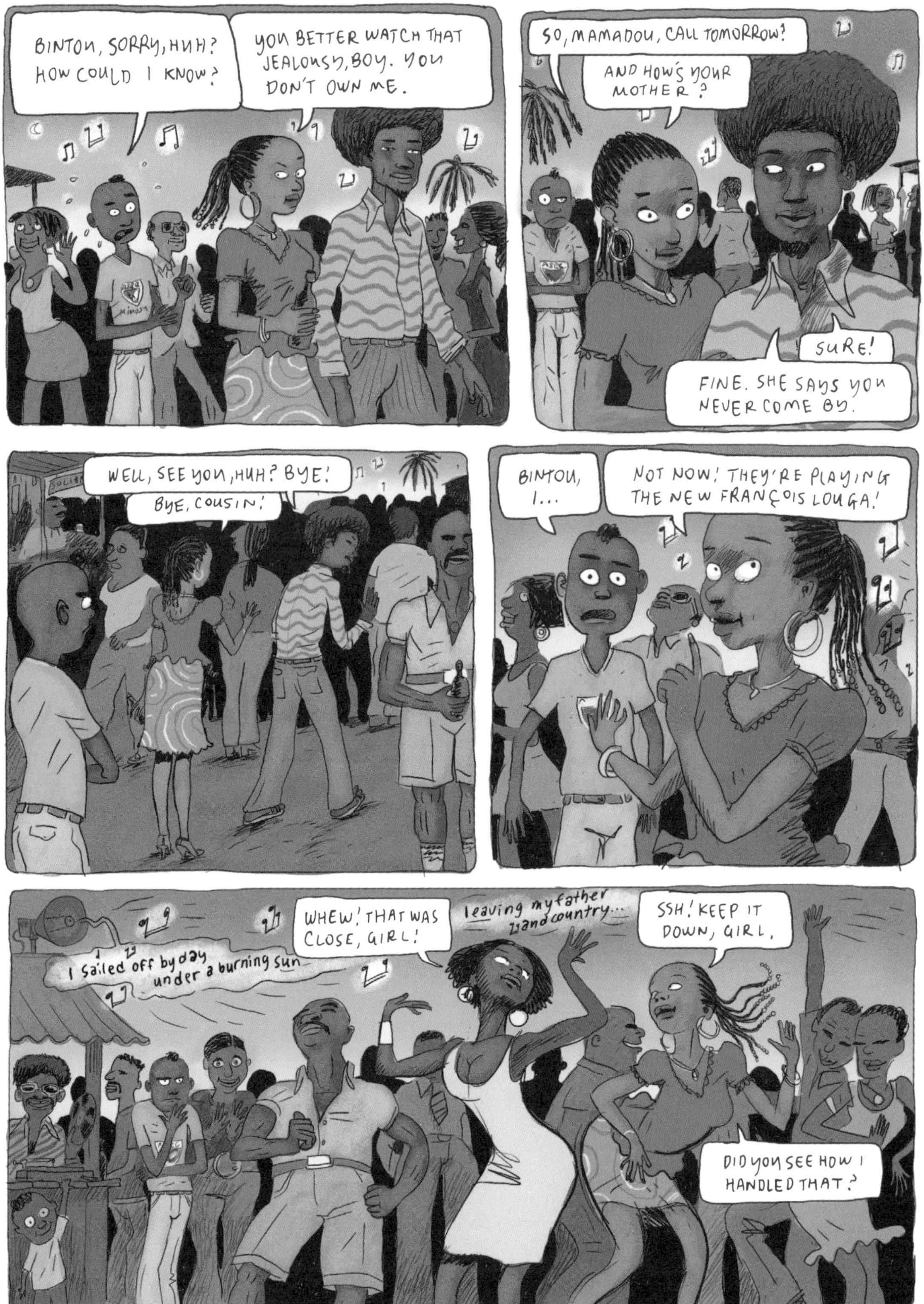
BINTOU, SORRY, HUH? HOW COULD I KNOW?
YOU BETTER WATCH THAT JEALOUSY, BOY. YOU DON'T OWN ME.
SO, MAMADOU, CALL TOMORROW?
AND HOW'S YOUR MOTHER?
SURE!
FINE. SHE SAYS YOU NEVER COME BY.
WELL, SEE YOU, HUH? BYE!
BYE, COUSIN!
BINTOU, I...
NOT NOW! THEY'RE PLAYING THE NEW FRANÇOIS LOUGA!
I sailed off by day under a burning sun
WHEW! THAT WAS CLOSE, GIRL!
leaving my father land country...
SSH! KEEP IT DOWN, GIRL.
DID YOU SEE HOW I HANDLED THAT?

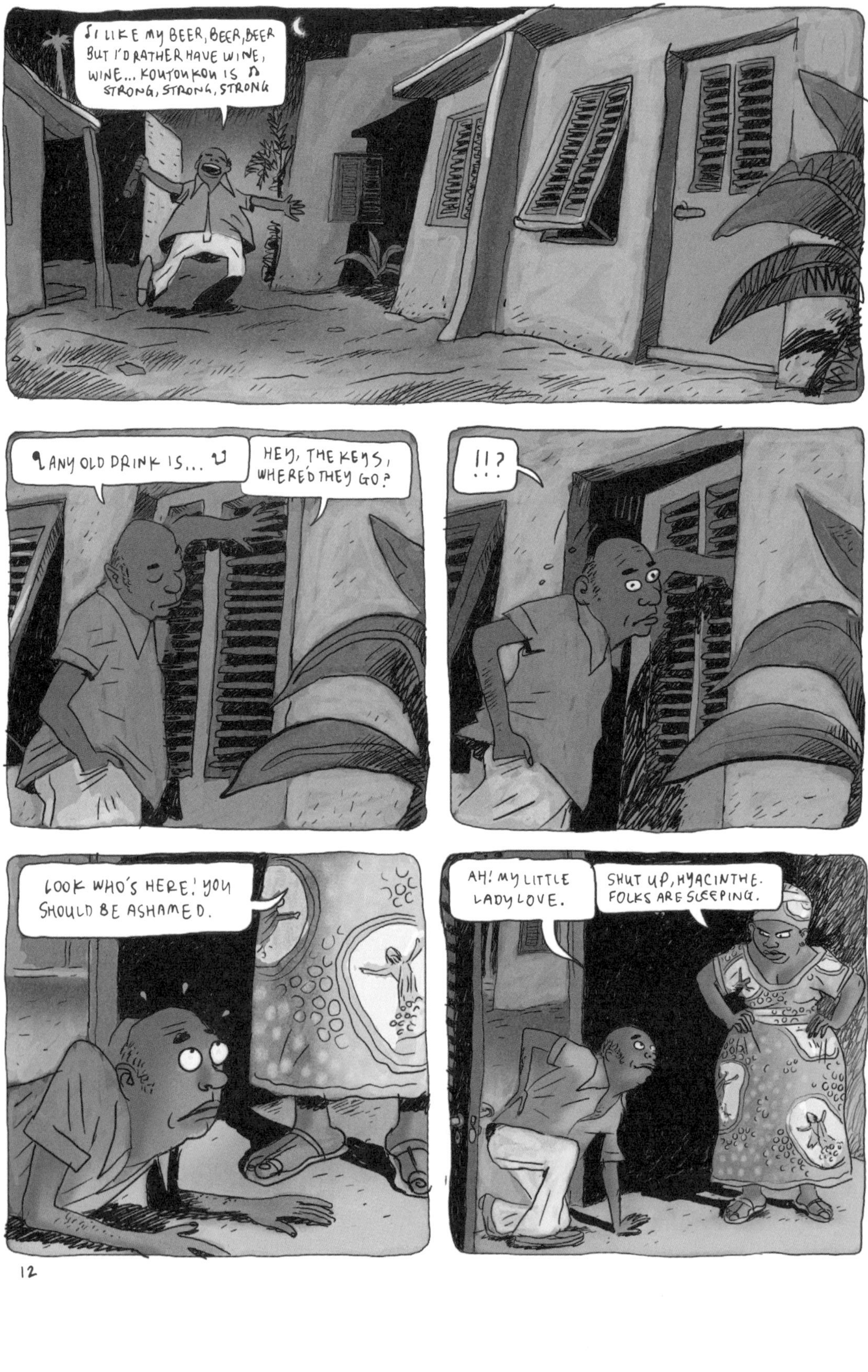
♪ I LIKE MY BEER, BEER, BEER BUT I'D RATHER HAVE WINE, WINE... KOUTOUKOU IS ♫ STRONG, STRONG, STRONG
♪ ANY OLD DRINK IS... ♪
HEY, THE KEYS, WHERE'D THEY GO?
!!? ...
LOOK WHO'S HERE! YOU SHOULD BE ASHAMED.
AH! MY LITTLE LADY LOVE.
SHUT UP, HYACINTHE. FOLKS ARE SLEEPING.

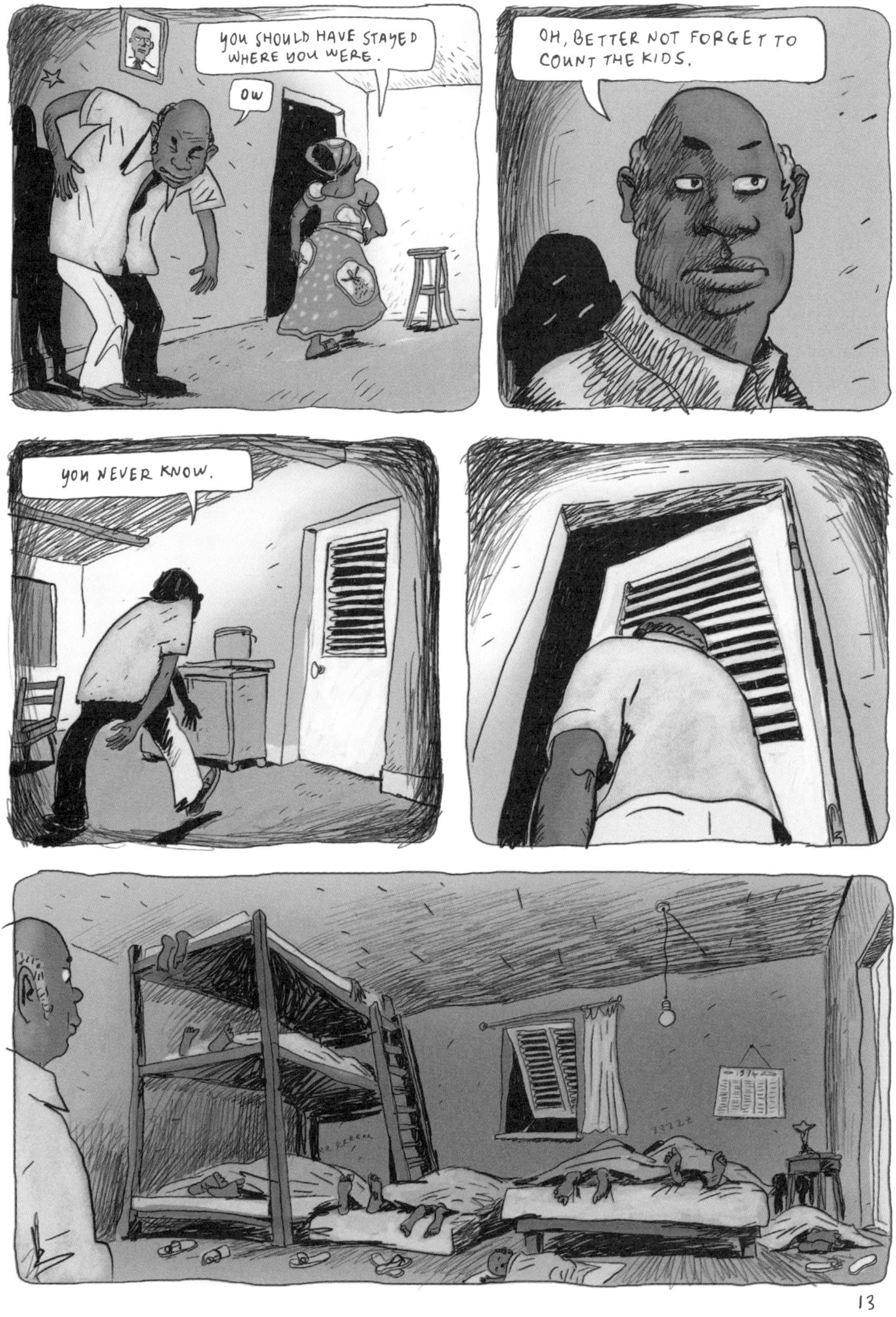

YOU SHOULD HAVE STAYED WHERE YOU WERE.
OW
OH, BETTER NOT FORGET TO COUNT THE KIDS.
YOU NEVER KNOW.

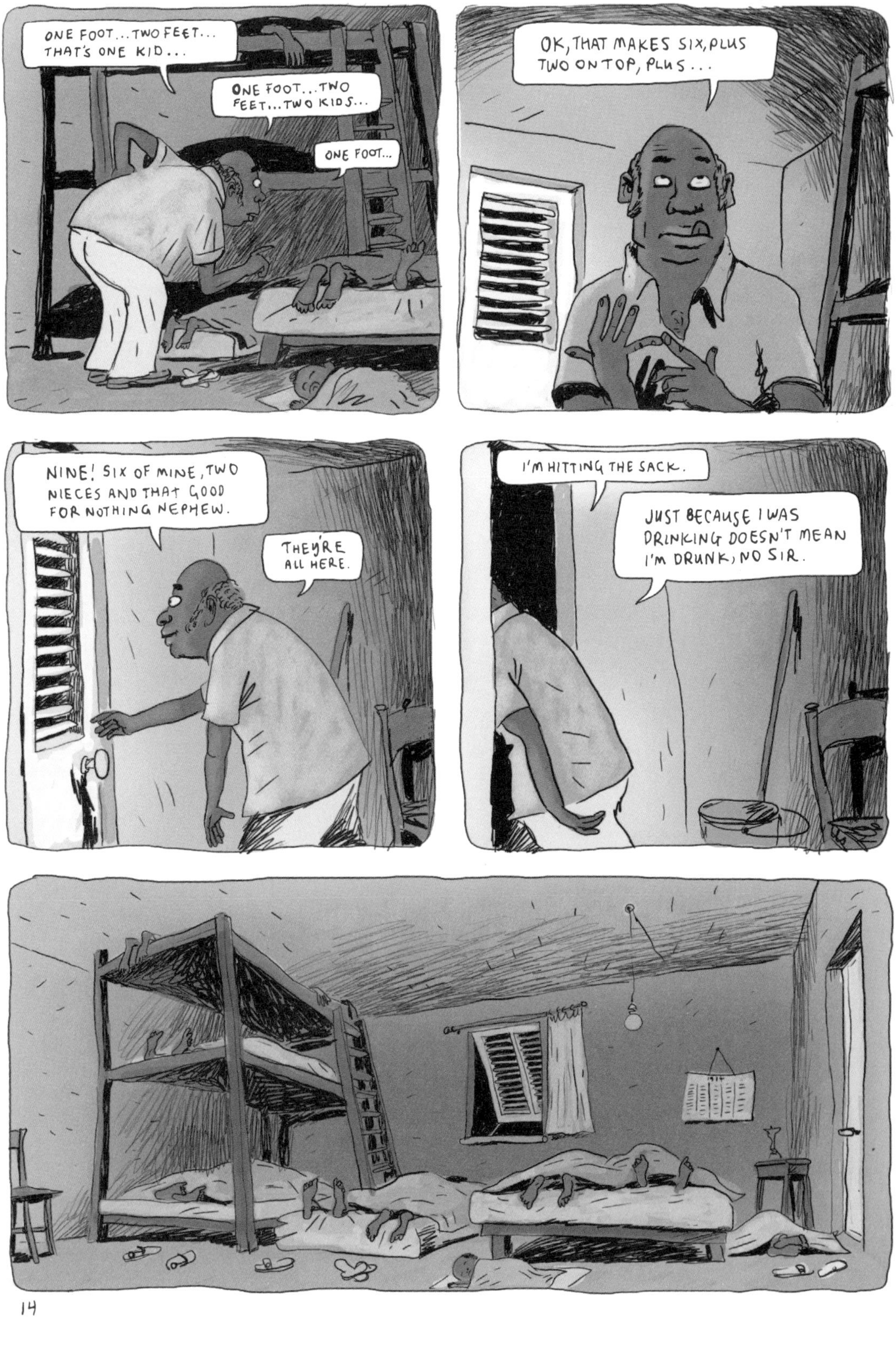
ONE FOOT... TWO FEET... THAT'S ONE KID...
ONE FOOT... TWO FEET... TWO KIDS...
ONE FOOT...
OK, THAT MAKES SIX, PLUS TWO ON TOP, PLUS...
NINE! SIX OF MINE, TWO NIECES AND THAT GOOD FOR NOTHING NEPHEW.
THEY'RE ALL HERE.
I'M HITTING THE SACK.
JUST BECAUSE I WAS DRINKING DOESN'T MEAN I'M DRUNK, NO SIR.

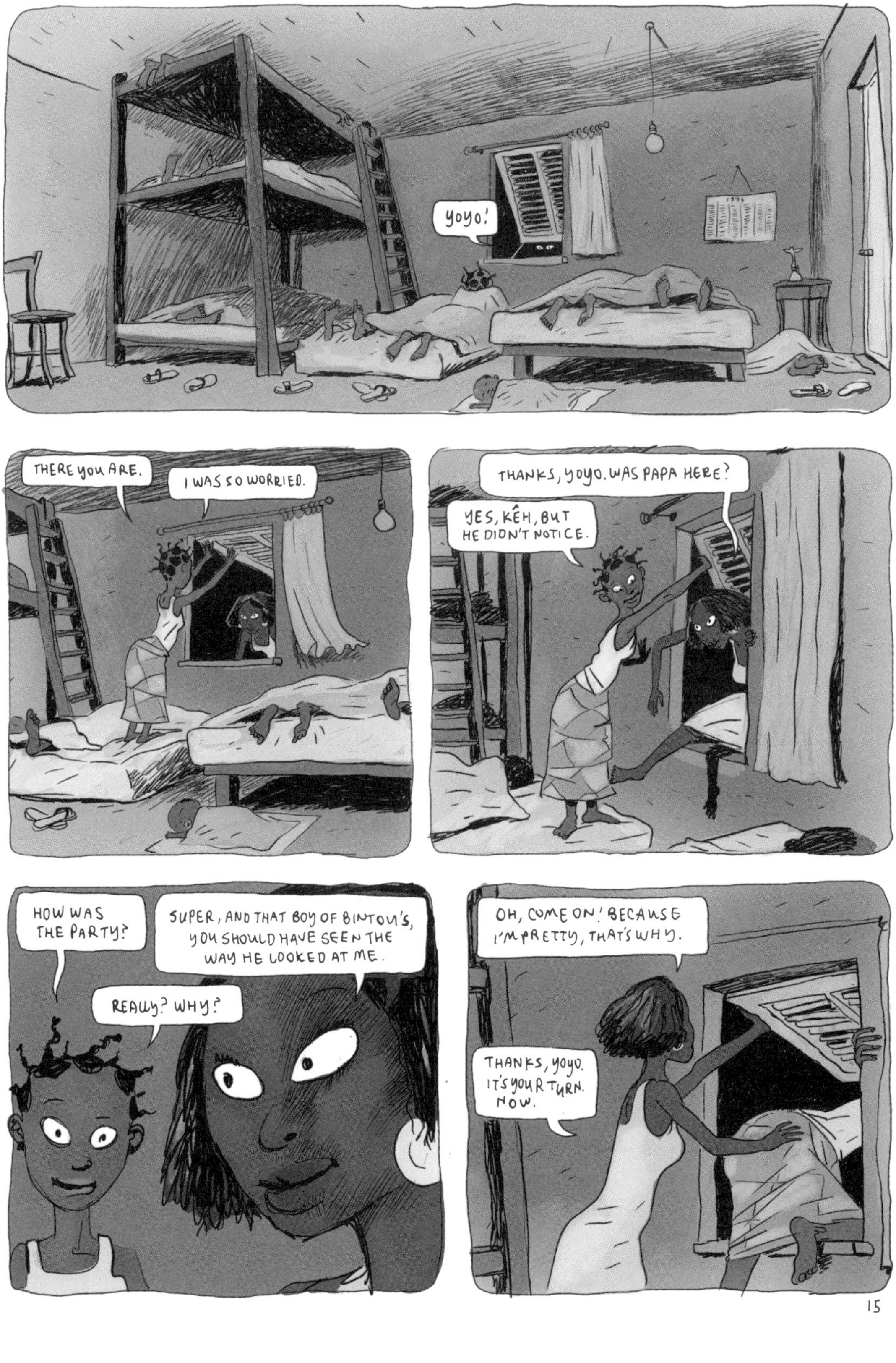
YOYO!
THERE YOU ARE.
I WAS SO WORRIED.
THANKS, YOYO. WAS PAPA HERE?
YES, KÊH, BUT HE DIDN'T NOTICE.
HOW WAS THE PARTY?
SUPER, AND THAT BOY OF BINTOU'S, YOU SHOULD HAVE SEEN THE WAY HE LOOKED AT ME.
REALLY? WHY?
OH, COME ON! BECAUSE I'M PRETTY, THAT'S WHY.
THANKS, YOYO. IT'S YOUR TURN NOW.

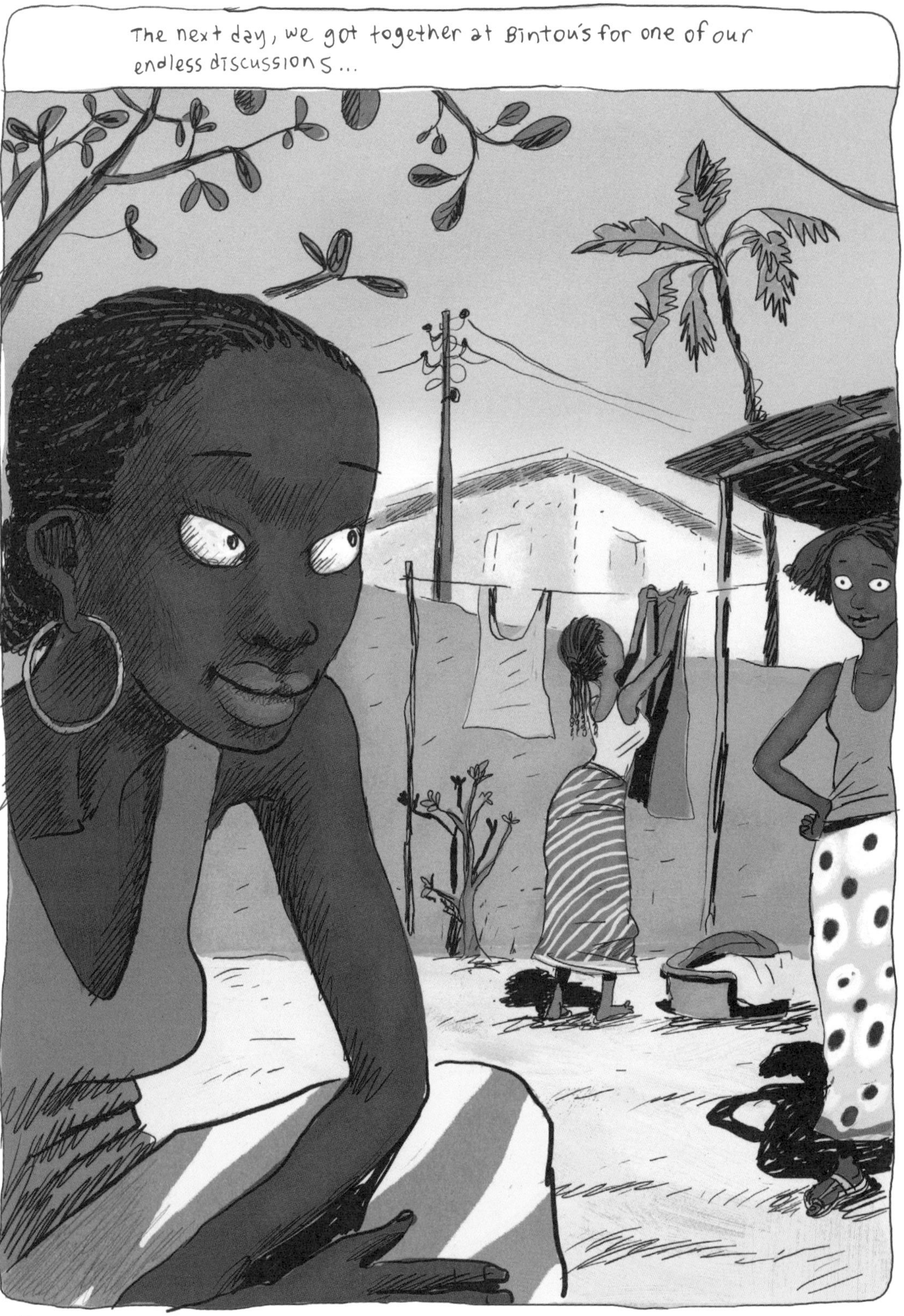
The next day, we got together at Bintou's for one of our endless discussions...

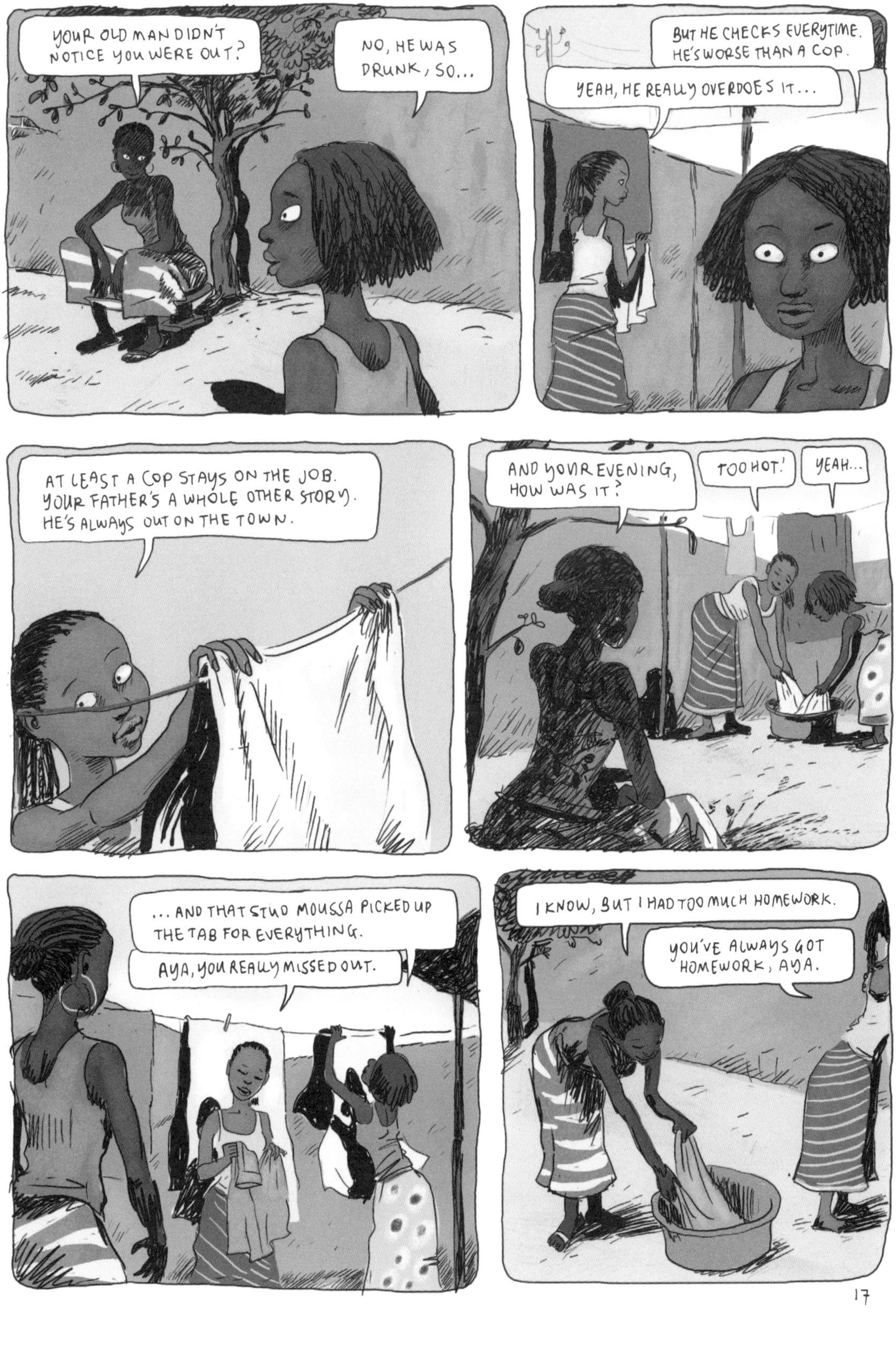
YOUR OLD MAN DIDN'T NOTICE YOU WERE OUT?
NO, HE WAS DRUNK, SO...
BUT HE CHECKS EVERYTIME. HE'S WORSE THAN A COP.
YEAH, HE REALLY OVERDOES IT...
AT LEAST A COP STAYS ON THE JOB. YOUR FATHER'S A WHOLE OTHER STORY. HE'S ALWAYS OUT ON THE TOWN.
AND YOUR EVENING, HOW WAS IT?
TOO HOT!
YEAH...
... AND THAT STUD MOUSSA PICKED UP THE TAB FOR EVERYTHING.
AYA, YOU REALLY MISSED OUT.
I KNOW, BUT I HAD TOO MUCH HOMEWORK.
YOU'VE ALWAYS GOT HOMEWORK, AYA.

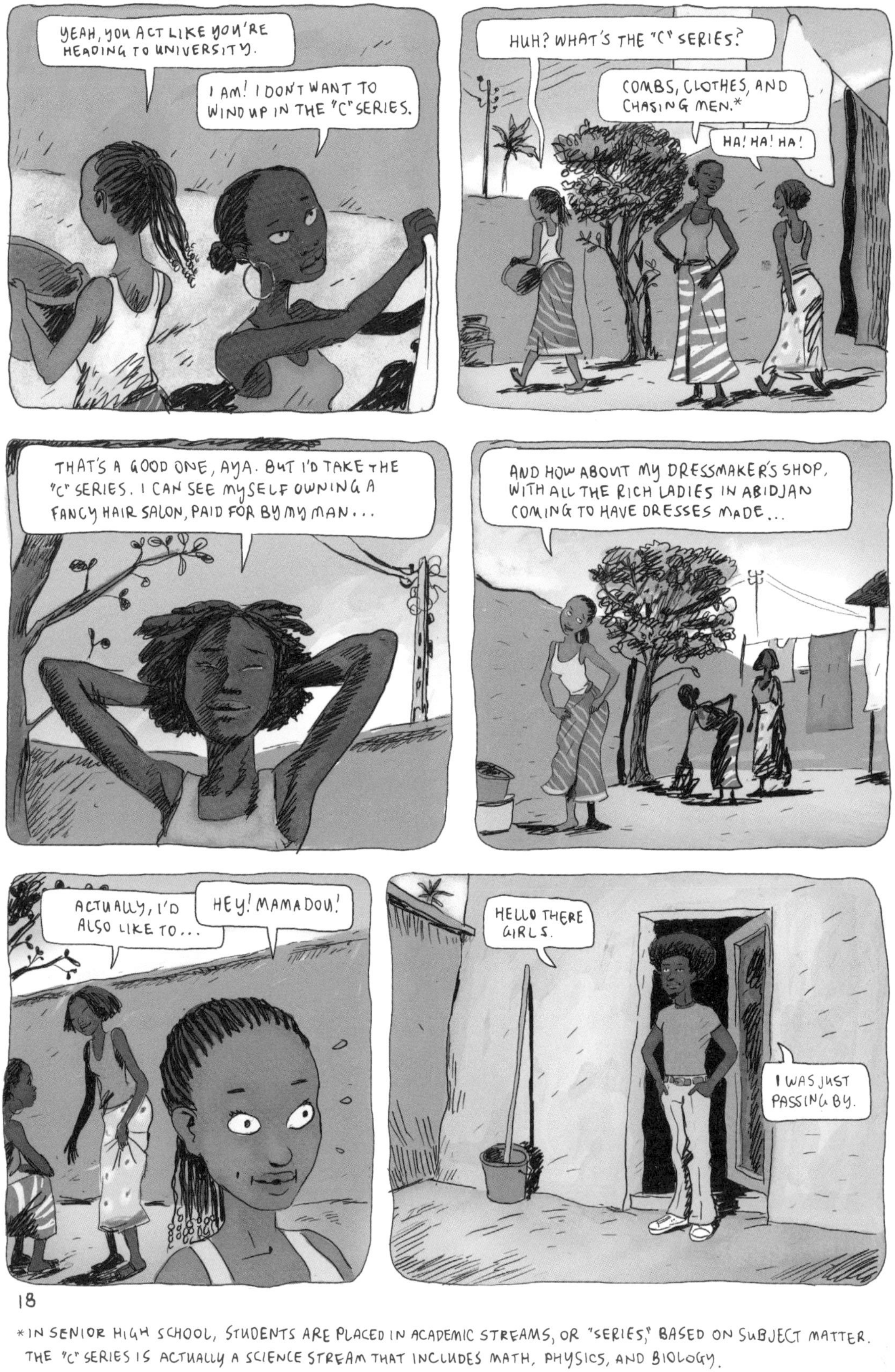
YEAH, YOU ACT LIKE YOU'RE HEADING TO UNIVERSITY.
I AM! I DON'T WANT TO WIND UP IN THE "C" SERIES.
HUH? WHAT'S THE "C" SERIES?
COMBS, CLOTHES, AND CHASING MEN.*
HA! HA! HA!
THAT'S A GOOD ONE, AYA. BUT I'D TAKE THE "C" SERIES. I CAN SEE MYSELF OWNING A FANCY HAIR SALON, PAID FOR BY MY MAN...
AND HOW ABOUT MY DRESSMAKER'S SHOP, WITH ALL THE RICH LADIES IN ABIDJAN COMING TO HAVE DRESSES MADE...
ACTUALLY, I'D ALSO LIKE TO...
HEY! MAMADOU!
HELLO THERE GIRLS.
I WAS JUST PASSING BY.

*IN SENIOR HIGH SCHOOL, STUDENTS ARE PLACED IN ACADEMIC STREAMS, OR "SERIES," BASED ON SUBJECT MATTER. THE "C" SERIES IS ACTUALLY A SCIENCE STREAM THAT INCLUDES MATH, PHYSICS, AND BIOLOGY.

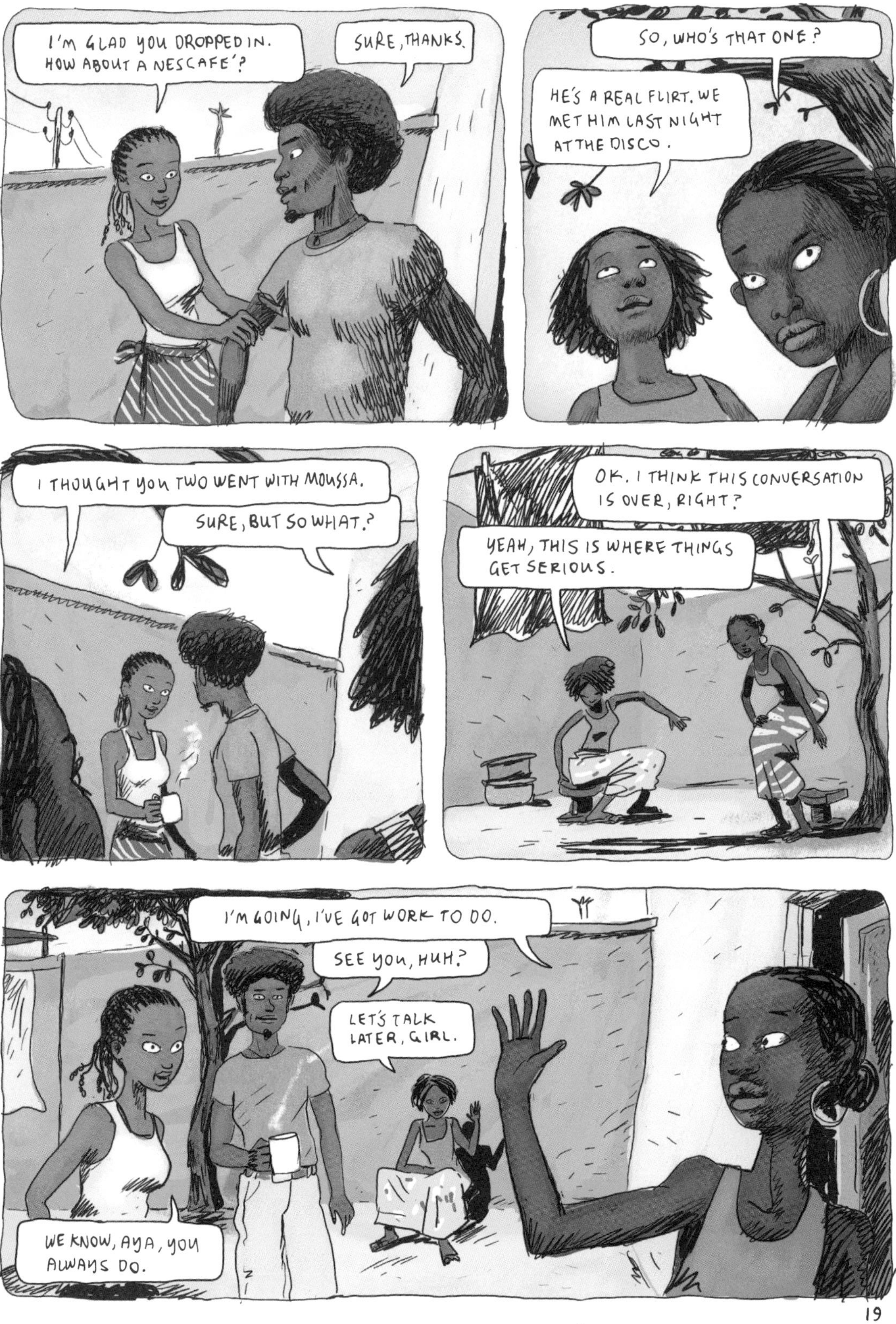
I'M GLAD YOU DROPPED IN. HOW ABOUT A NESCAFE'?
SURE, THANKS.
SO, WHO'S THAT ONE?
HE'S A REAL FLIRT. WE MET HIM LAST NIGHT AT THE DISCO.
I THOUGHT YOU TWO WENT WITH MOUSSA.
SURE, BUT SO WHAT?
OK. I THINK THIS CONVERSATION IS OVER, RIGHT?
YEAH, THIS IS WHERE THINGS GET SERIOUS.
I'M GOING, I'VE GOT WORK TO DO.
SEE YOU, HUH?
LET'S TALK LATER, GIRL.
WE KNOW, AYA, YOU ALWAYS DO.

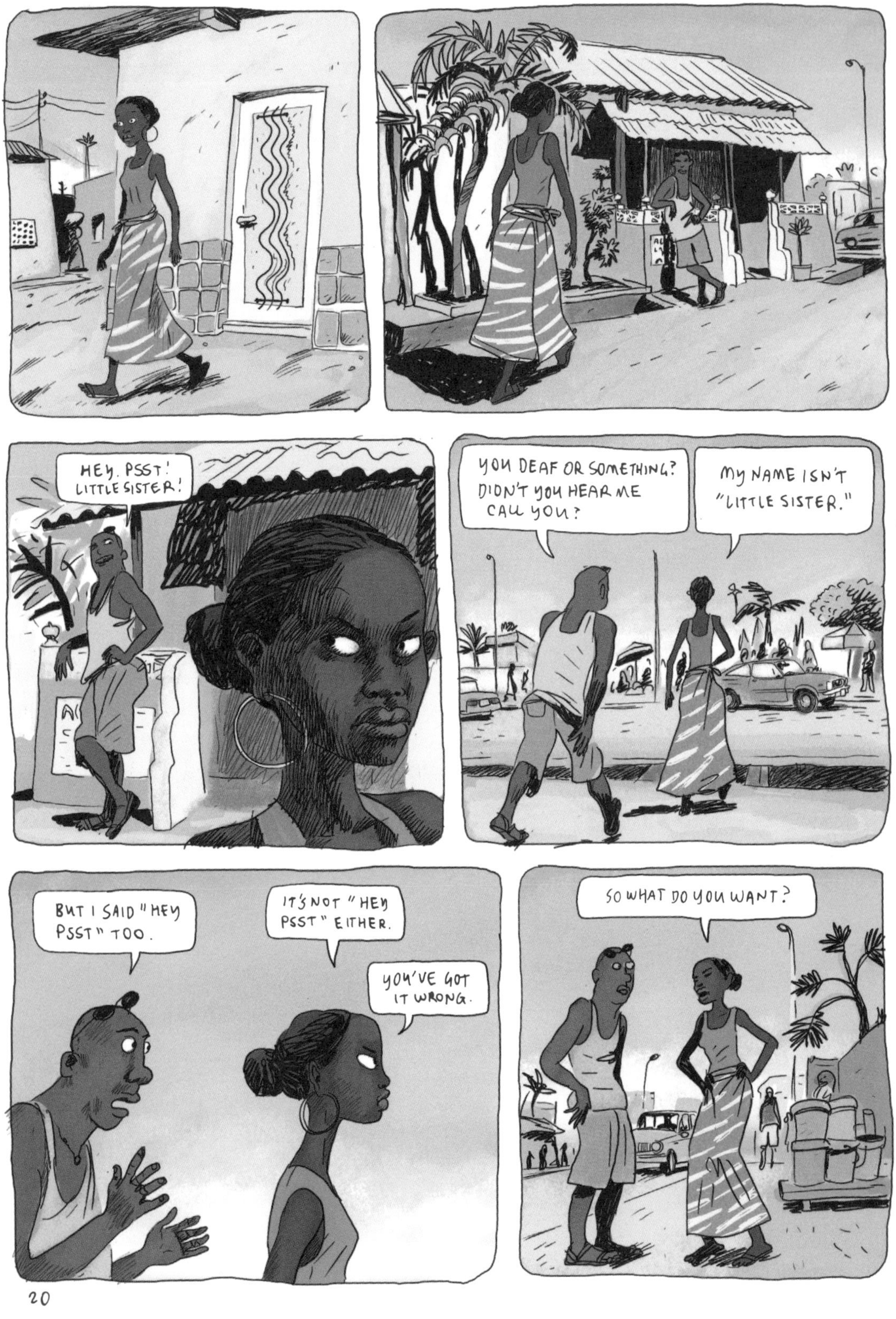
HEY. PSST! LITTLE SISTER!
YOU DEAF OR SOMETHING? DIDN'T YOU HEAR ME CALL YOU?
MY NAME ISN'T "LITTLE SISTER."
BUT I SAID "HEY PSST" TOO.
IT'S NOT "HEY PSST" EITHER.
YOU'VE GOT IT WRONG.
SO WHAT DO YOU WANT?

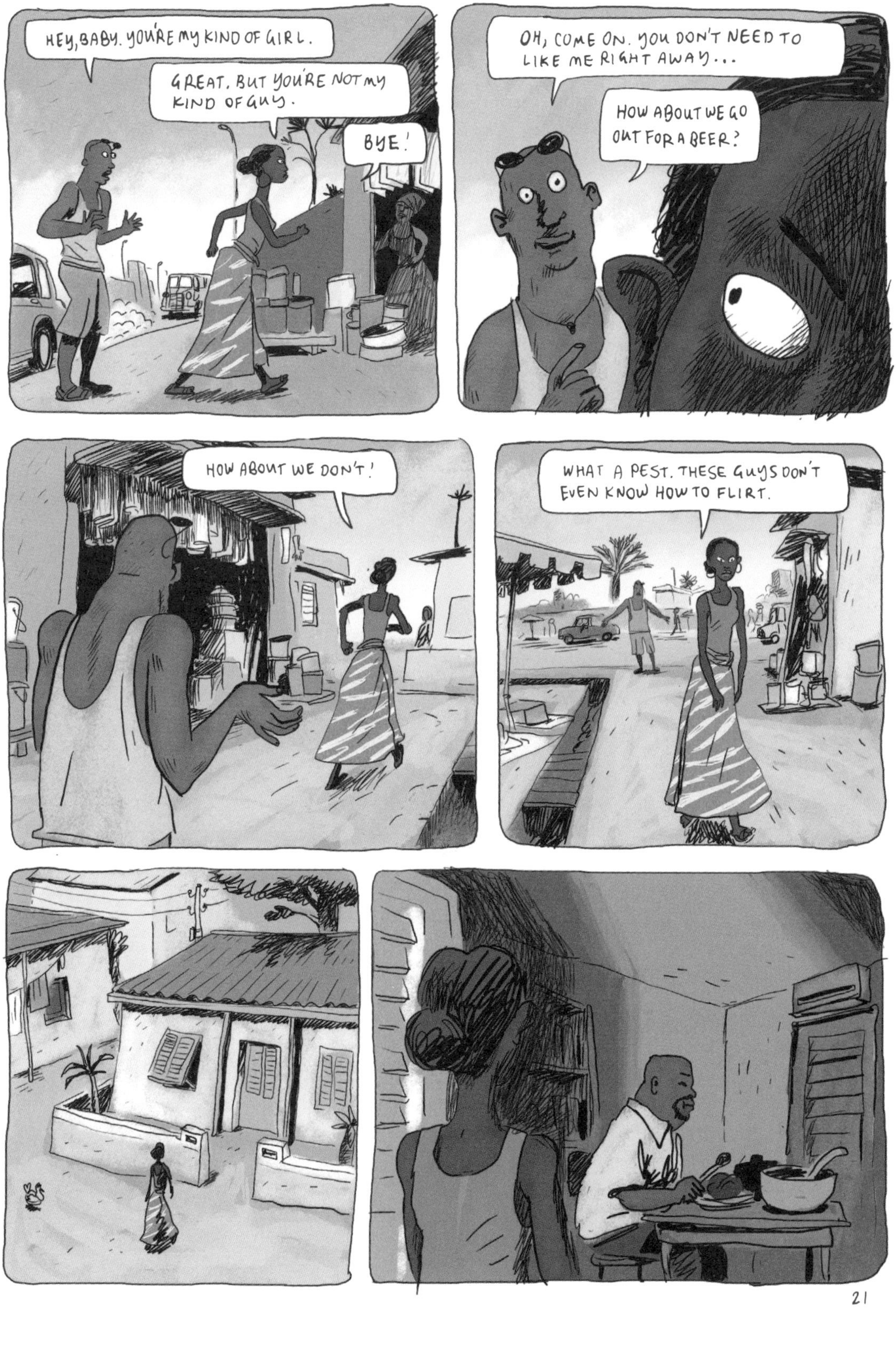
HEY, BABY. YOU'RE MY KIND OF GIRL.
GREAT. BUT YOU'RE NOT MY KIND OF GUY.
BYE!
OH, COME ON. YOU DON'T NEED TO LIKE ME RIGHT AWAY...
HOW ABOUT WE GO OUT FOR A BEER?
HOW ABOUT WE DON'T!
WHAT A PEST. THESE GUYS DON'T EVEN KNOW HOW TO FLIRT.

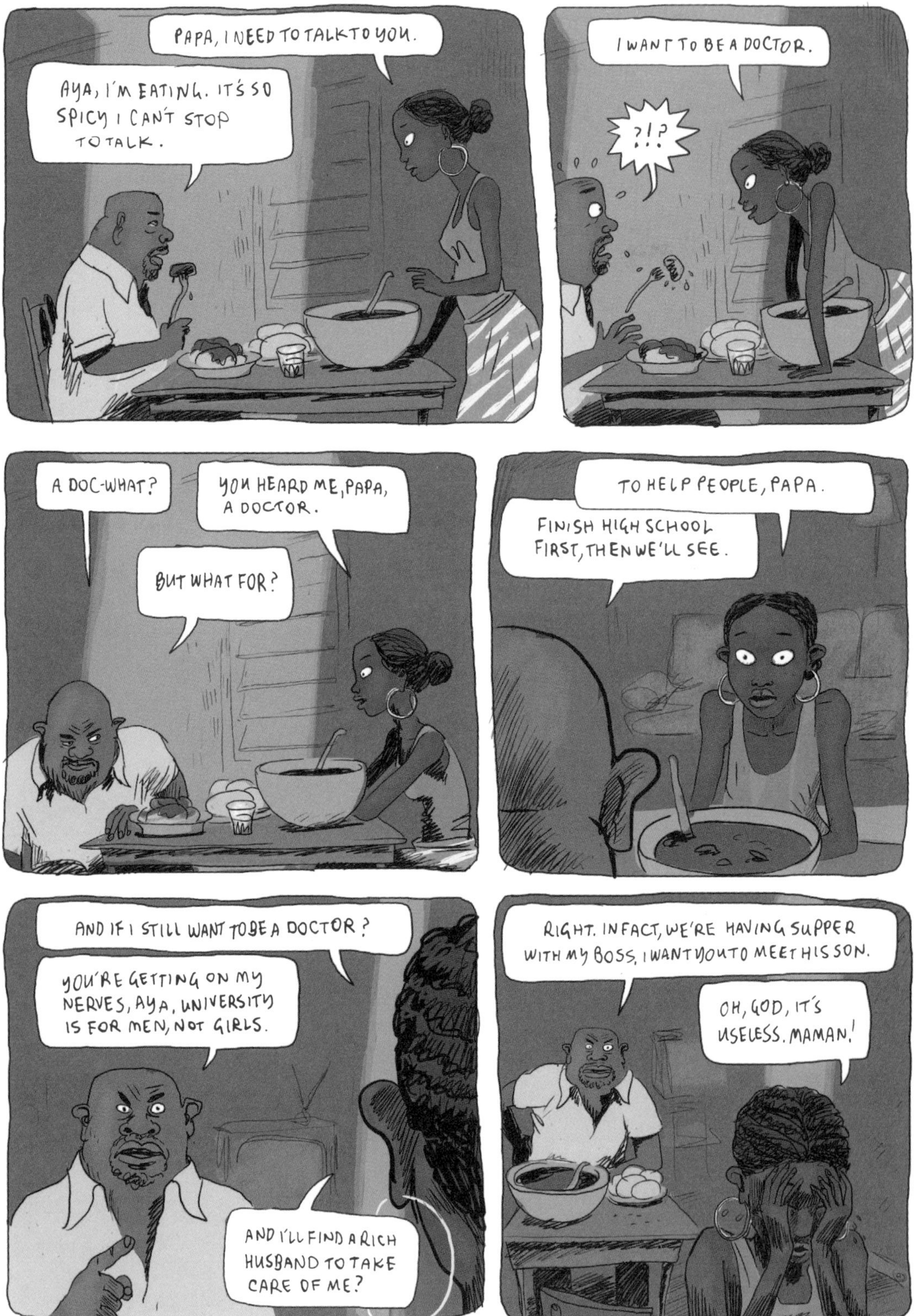
PAPA, I NEED TO TALK TO YOU.
AYA, I'M EATING. IT'S SO SPICY I CAN'T STOP TO TALK.
I WANT TO BE A DOCTOR.
?!?
A DOC-WHAT?
YOU HEARD ME, PAPA, A DOCTOR.
BUT WHAT FOR?
TO HELP PEOPLE, PAPA.
FINISH HIGH SCHOOL FIRST, THEN WE'LL SEE.
AND IF I STILL WANT TO BE A DOCTOR?
YOU'RE GETTING ON MY NERVES, AYA. UNIVERSITY IS FOR MEN, NOT GIRLS.
AND I'LL FIND A RICH HUSBAND TO TAKE CARE OF ME?
RIGHT. IN FACT, WE'RE HAVING SUPPER WITH MY BOSS. I WANT YOU TO MEET HIS SON.
OH, GOD, IT'S USELESS. MAMAN!

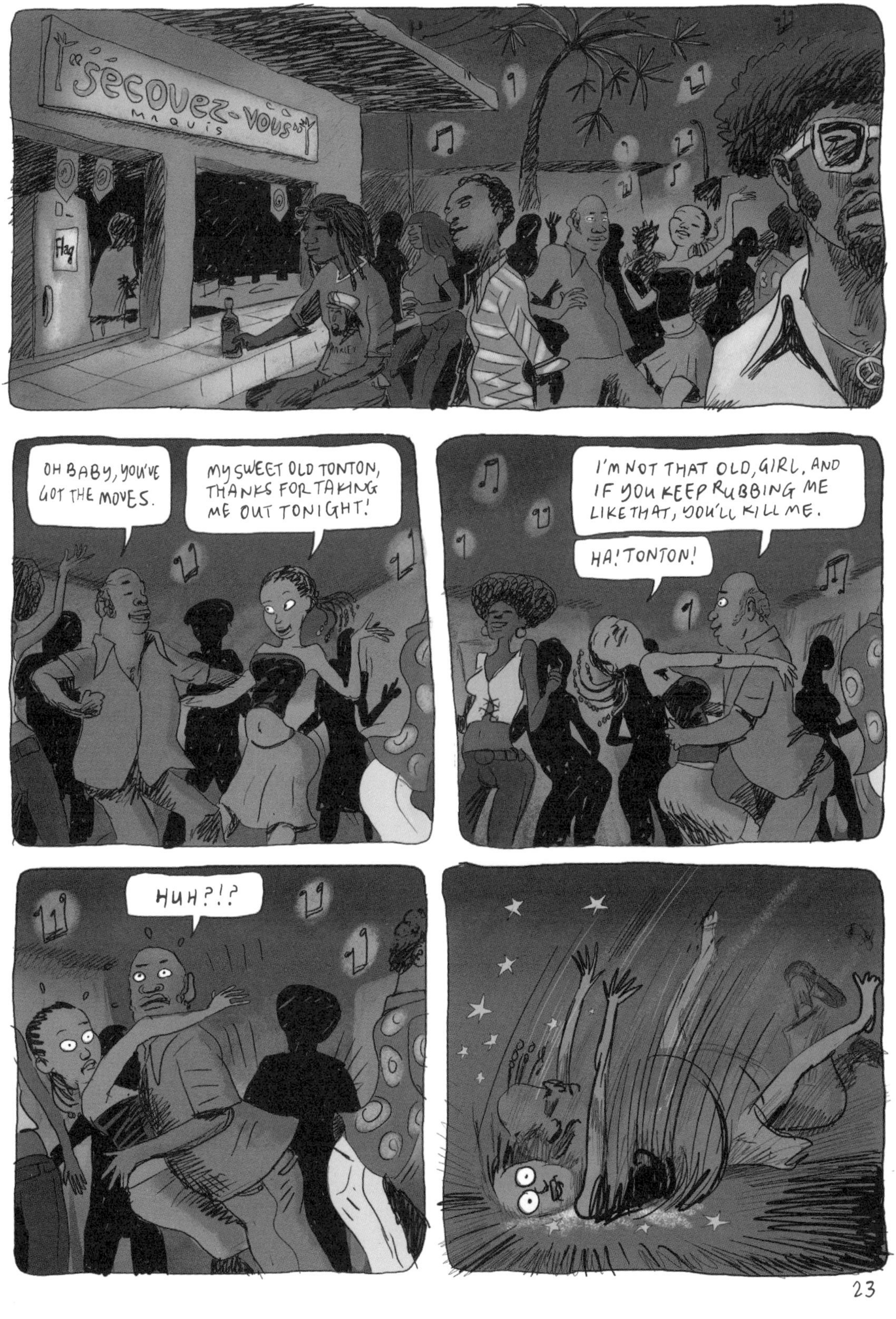
Sécouez-vous
MAQUIS
Flag
OH BABY, YOU'VE GOT THE MOVES.
MY SWEET OLD TONTON, THANKS FOR TAKING ME OUT TONIGHT!
I'M NOT THAT OLD, GIRL, AND IF YOU KEEP RUBBING ME LIKE THAT, YOU'LL KILL ME.
HA! TONTON!
HUH?!?

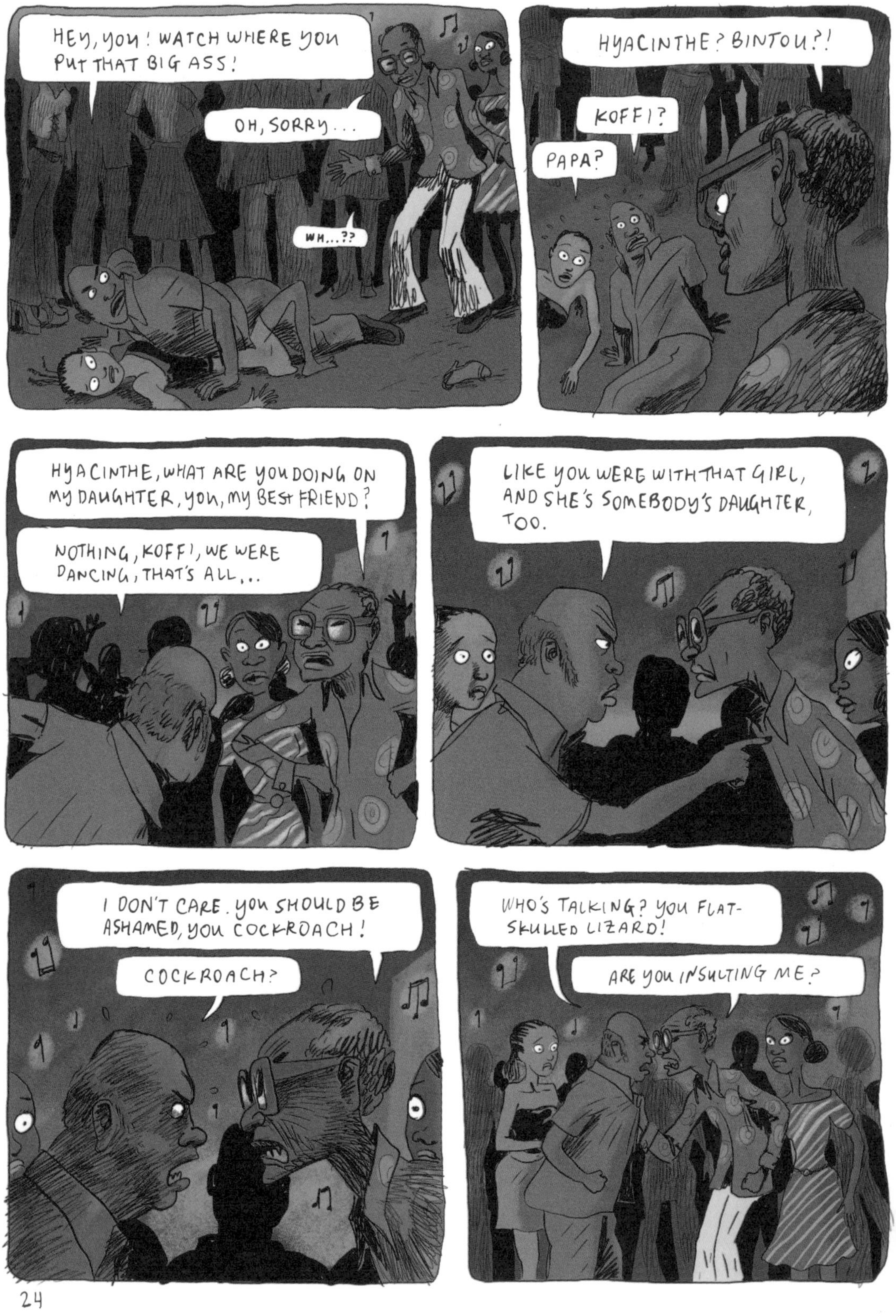
HEY, YOU! WATCH WHERE YOU PUT THAT BIG ASS!
OH, SORRY...
WH...??
HYACINTHE? BINTOU?!
KOFFI?
PAPA?
HYACINTHE, WHAT ARE YOU DOING ON MY DAUGHTER, YOU, MY BEST FRIEND?
NOTHING, KOFFI, WE WERE DANCING, THAT'S ALL...
LIKE YOU WERE WITH THAT GIRL, AND SHE'S SOMEBODY'S DAUGHTER, TOO.
I DON'T CARE. YOU SHOULD BE ASHAMED, YOU COCKROACH!
COCKROACH?
WHO'S TALKING? YOU FLAT-SKULLED LIZARD!
ARE YOU INSULTING ME?

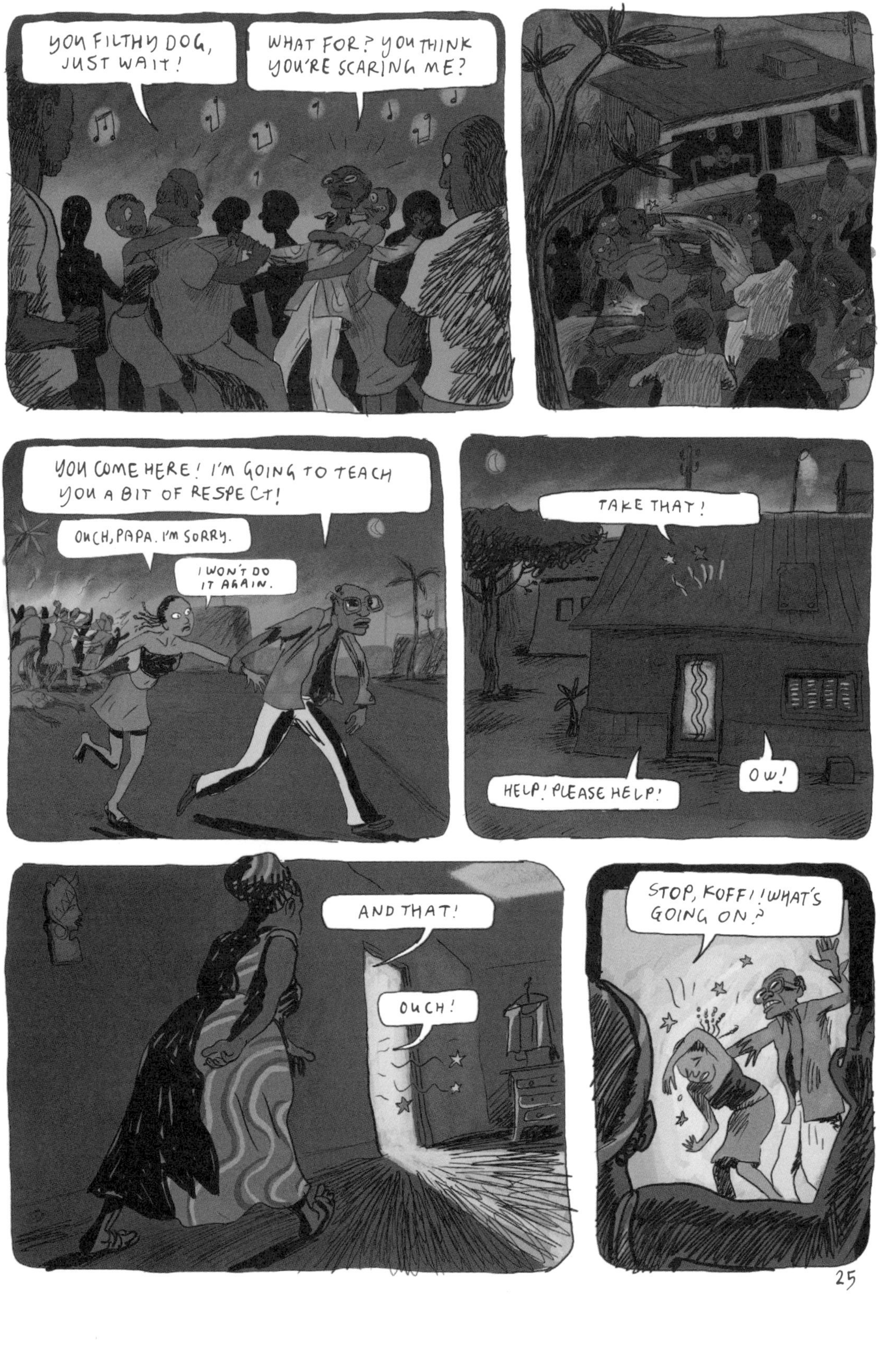
YOU FILTHY DOG, JUST WAIT!
WHAT FOR? YOU THINK YOU'RE SCARING ME?
YOU COME HERE! I'M GOING TO TEACH YOU A BIT OF RESPECT!
OUCH, PAPA. I'M SORRY.
I WON'T DO IT AGAIN.
TAKE THAT!
HELP! PLEASE HELP!
OW!
AND THAT!
OUCH!
STOP, KOFFI! WHAT'S GOING ON?

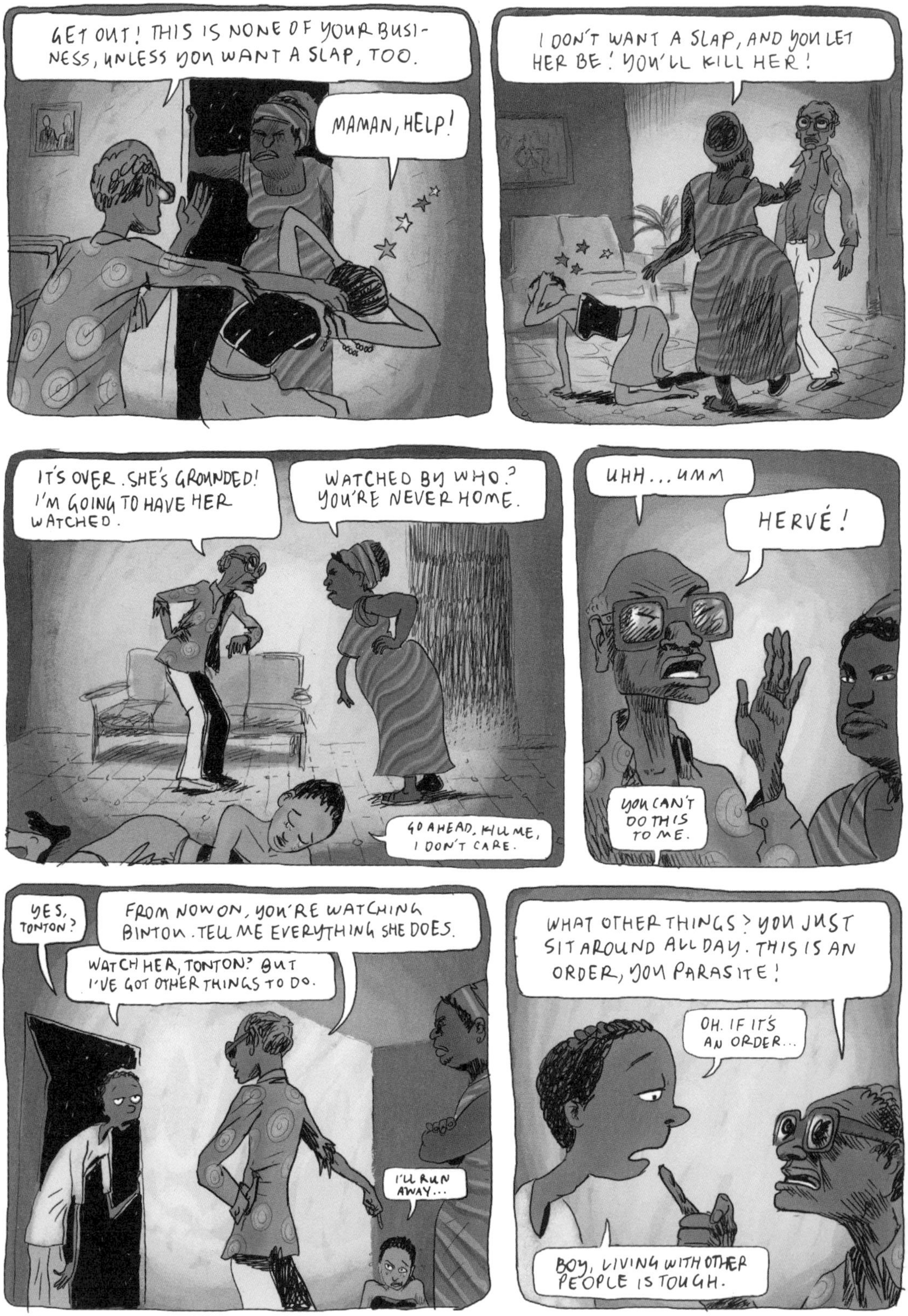
GET OUT! THIS IS NONE OF YOUR BUSINESS, UNLESS YOU WANT A SLAP, TOO.
MAMAN, HELP!
I DON'T WANT A SLAP, AND YOU LET HER BE! YOU'LL KILL HER!
IT'S OVER. SHE'S GROUNDED! I'M GOING TO HAVE HER WATCHED.
WATCHED BY WHO? YOU'RE NEVER HOME.
GO AHEAD. KILL ME, I DON'T CARE.
UHH... UMM
HERVÉ!
YOU CAN'T DO THIS TO ME.
YES, TONTON?
FROM NOW ON, YOU'RE WATCHING BINTOU. TELL ME EVERYTHING SHE DOES.
WATCH HER, TONTON? BUT I'VE GOT OTHER THINGS TO DO.
I'LL RUN AWAY...
WHAT OTHER THINGS? YOU JUST SIT AROUND ALL DAY. THIS IS AN ORDER, YOU PARASITE!
OH. IF IT'S AN ORDER...
BOY, LIVING WITH OTHER PEOPLE IS TOUGH.

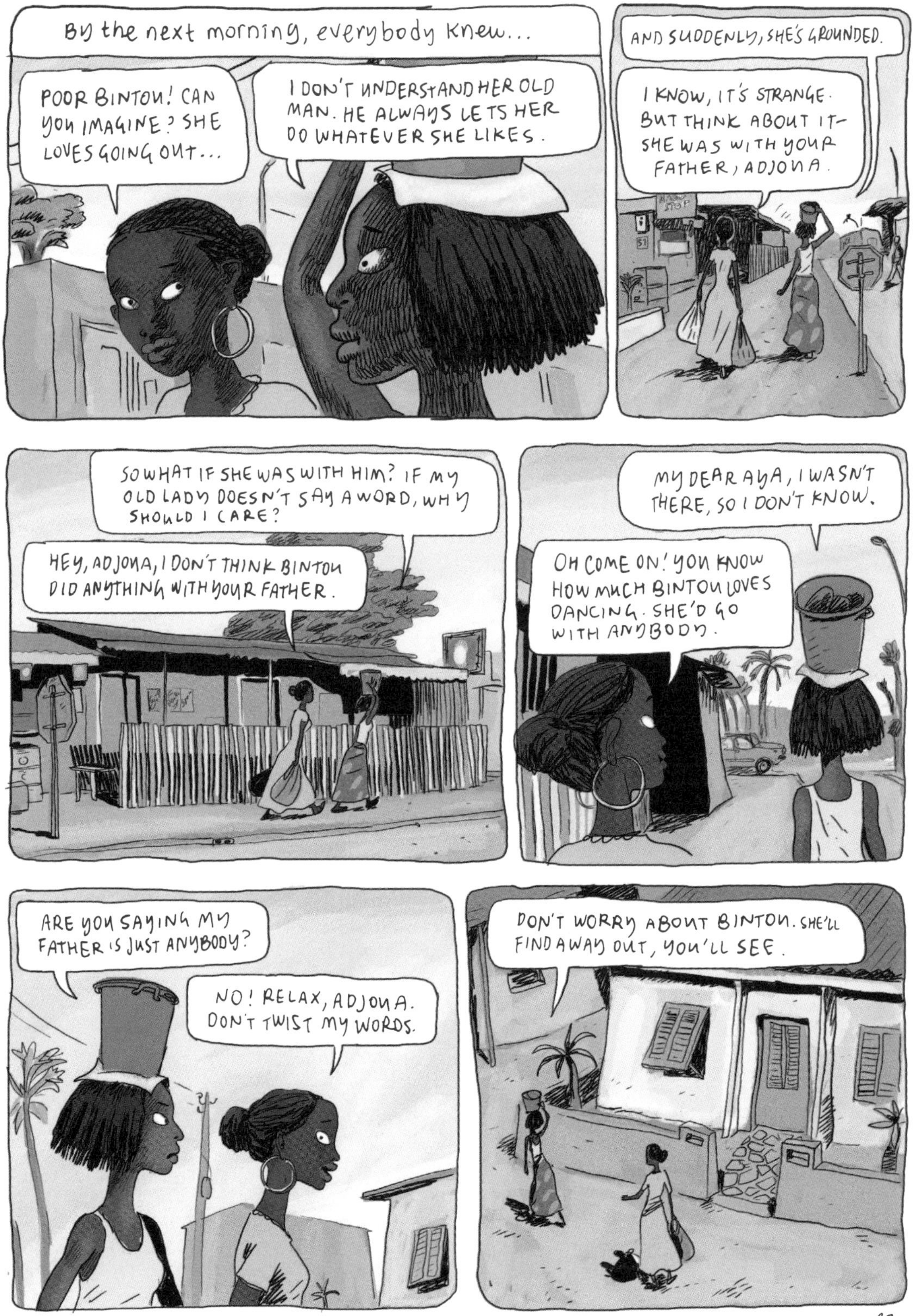
By the next morning, everybody knew...
POOR BINTOU! CAN YOU IMAGINE? SHE LOVES GOING OUT...
I DON'T UNDERSTAND HER OLD MAN. HE ALWAYS LETS HER DO WHATEVER SHE LIKES.
AND SUDDENLY, SHE'S GROUNDED.
I KNOW, IT'S STRANGE. BUT THINK ABOUT IT- SHE WAS WITH YOUR FATHER, ADJOUA.
SO WHAT IF SHE WAS WITH HIM? IF MY OLD LADY DOESN'T SAY A WORD, WHY SHOULD I CARE?
HEY, ADJOUA, I DON'T THINK BINTOU DID ANYTHING WITH YOUR FATHER.
MY DEAR AYA, I WASN'T THERE, SO I DON'T KNOW.
OH COME ON! YOU KNOW HOW MUCH BINTOU LOVES DANCING. SHE'D GO WITH ANYBODY.
ARE YOU SAYING MY FATHER IS JUST ANYBODY?
NO! RELAX, ADJOUA. DON'T TWIST MY WORDS.
DON'T WORRY ABOUT BINTOU. SHE'LL FIND A WAY OUT, YOU'LL SEE.

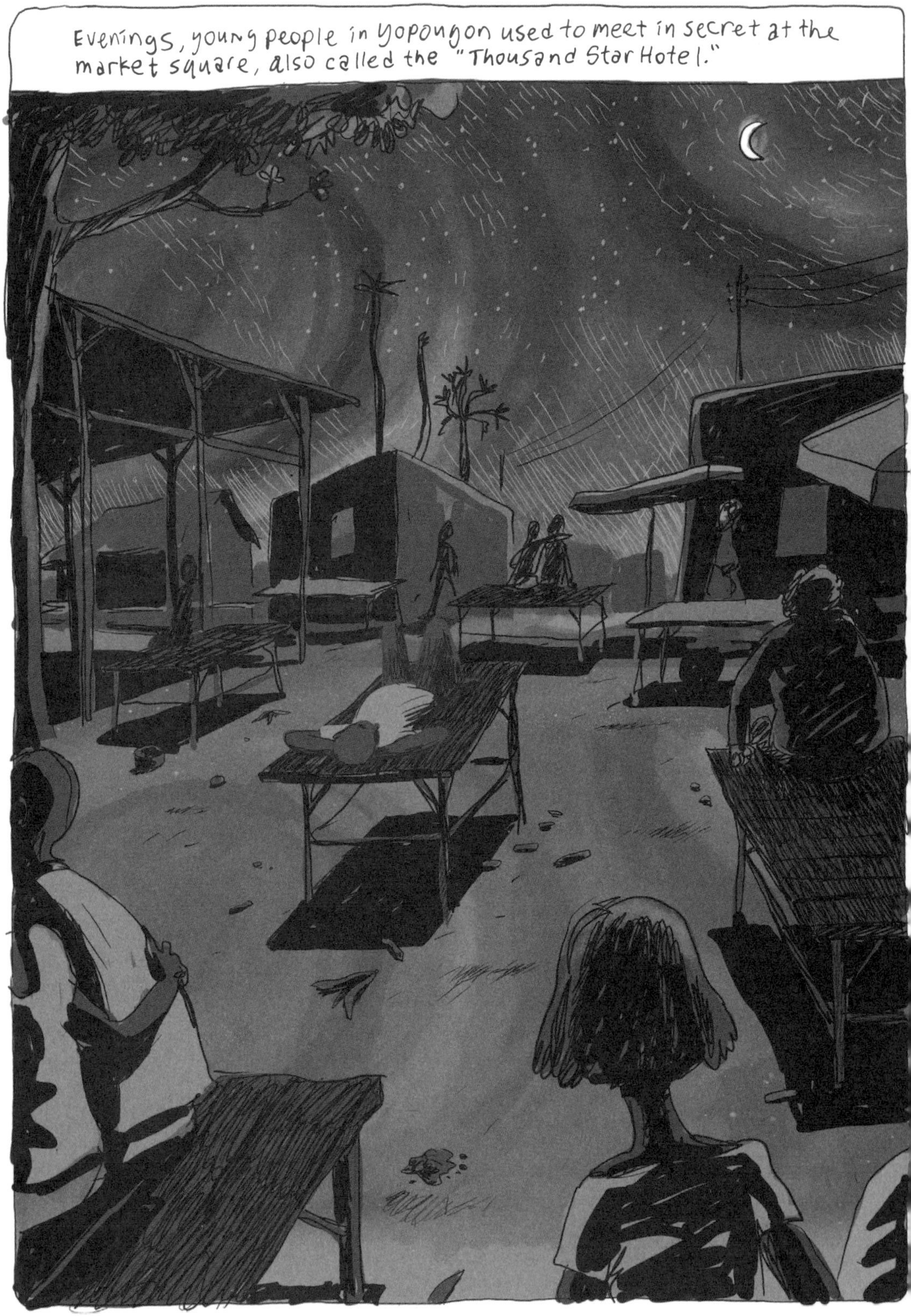
Evenings, young people in Yopougon used to meet in secret at the market square, also called the "Thousand Star Hotel."

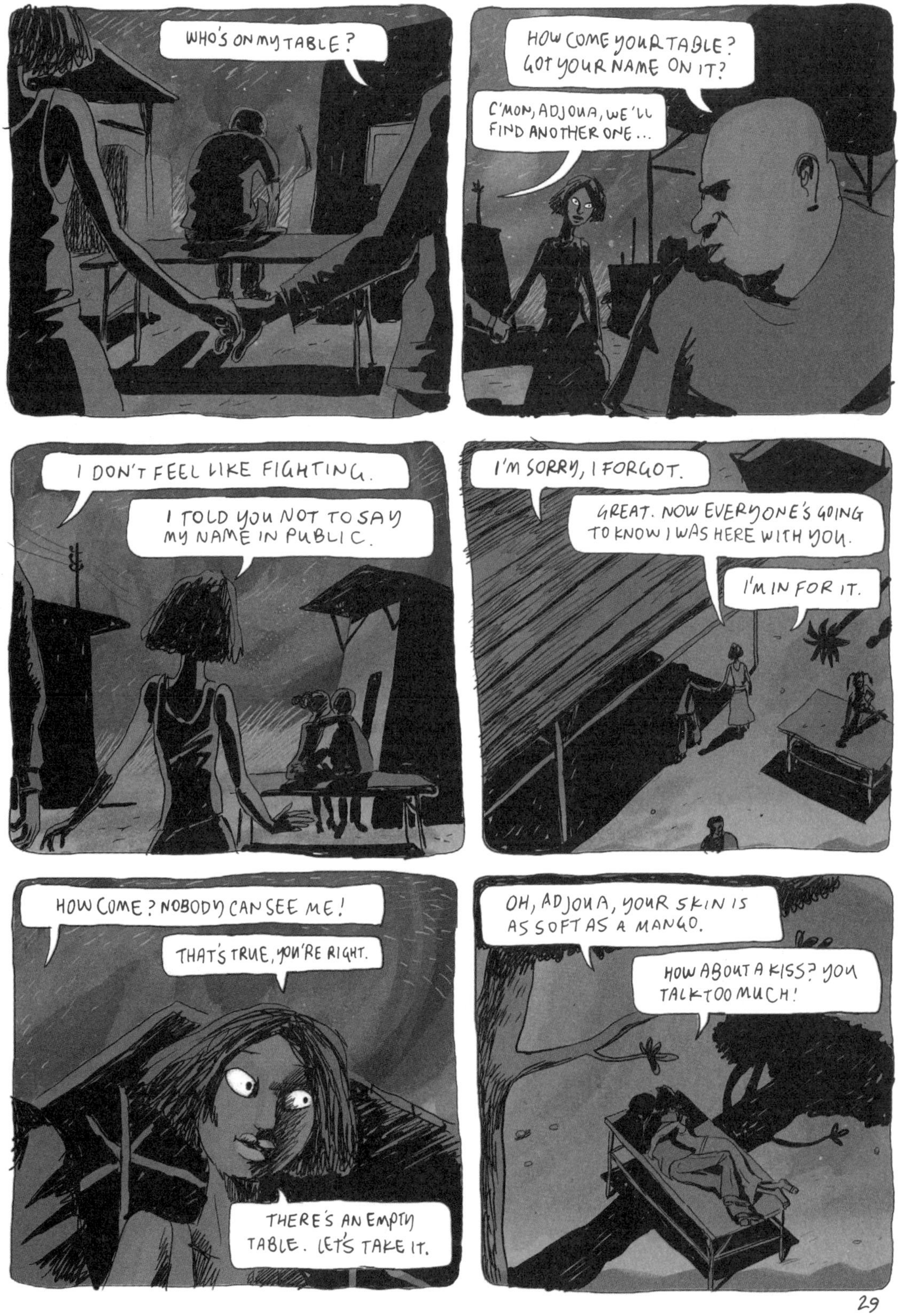
WHO'S ON MY TABLE?
HOW COME YOUR TABLE? GOT YOUR NAME ON IT?
C'MON, ADJOUA, WE'LL FIND ANOTHER ONE...
I DON'T FEEL LIKE FIGHTING.
I TOLD YOU NOT TO SAY MY NAME IN PUBLIC.
I'M SORRY, I FORGOT.
GREAT. NOW EVERYONE'S GOING TO KNOW I WAS HERE WITH YOU.
I'M IN FOR IT.
HOW COME? NOBODY CAN SEE ME!
THAT'S TRUE, YOU'RE RIGHT.
THERE'S AN EMPTY TABLE. LET'S TAKE IT.
OH, ADJOUA, YOUR SKIN IS AS SOFT AS A MANGO.
HOW ABOUT A KISS? YOU TALK TOO MUCH!

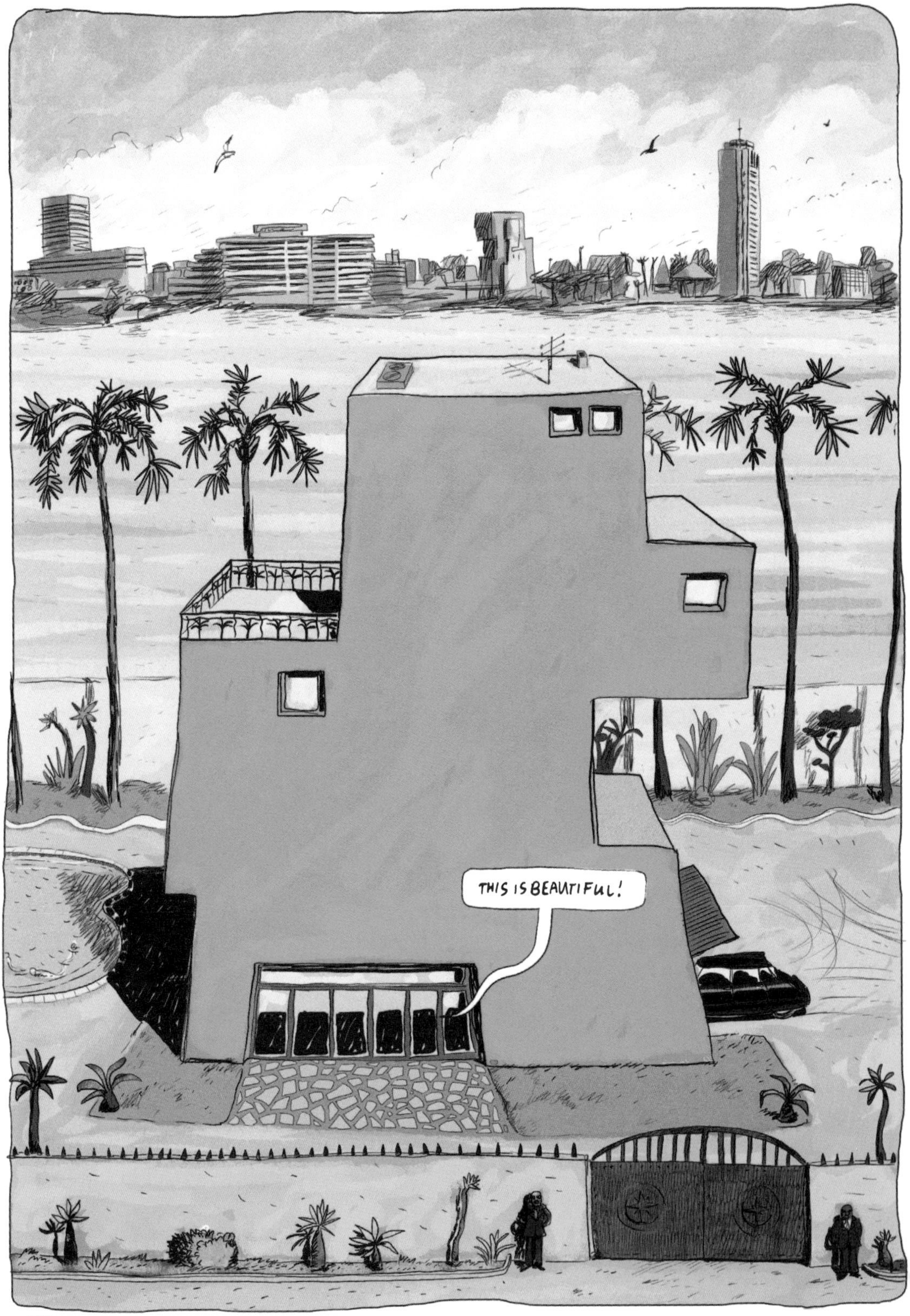
THIS IS BEAUTIFUL!

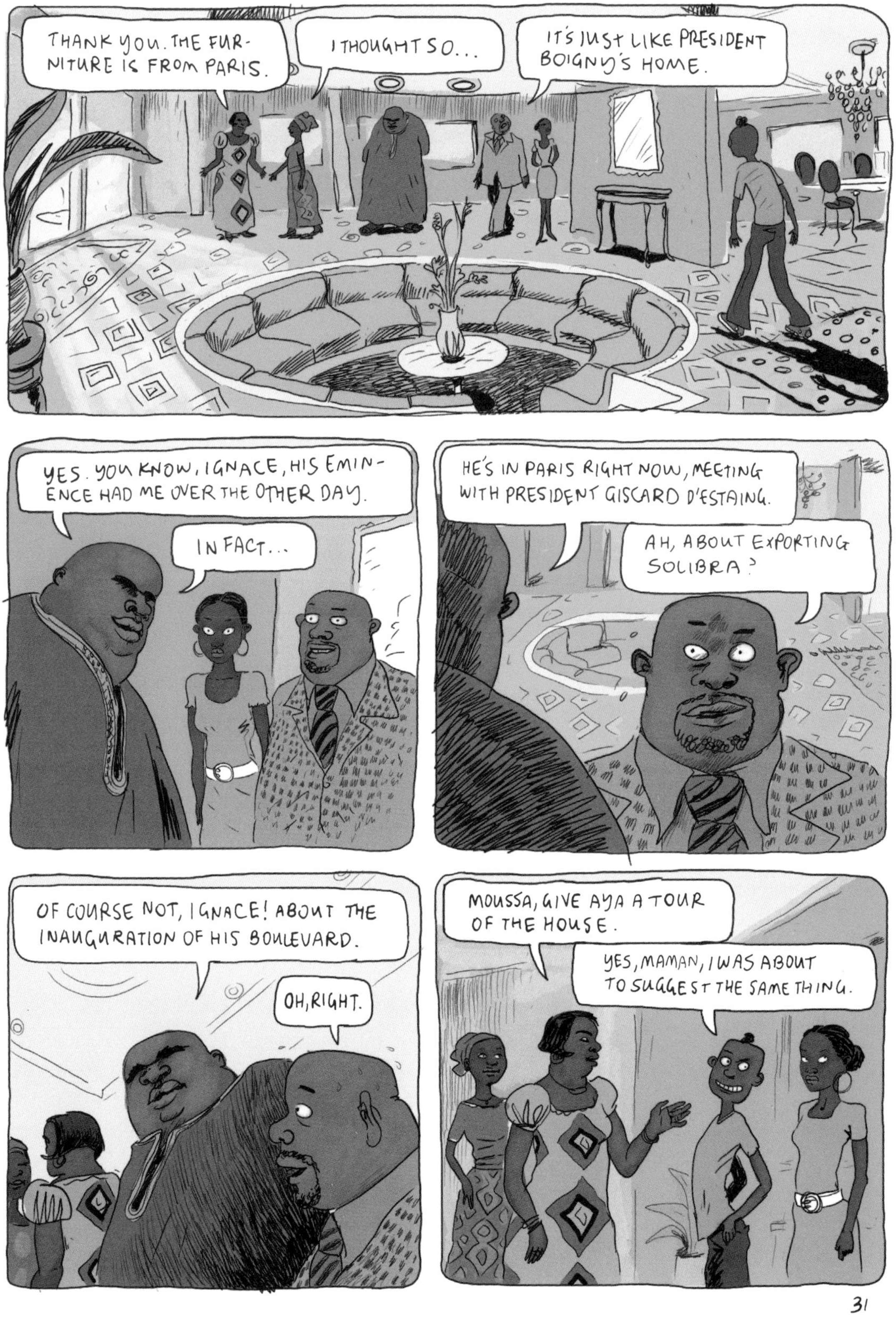
THANK YOU. THE FURNITURE IS FROM PARIS.
I THOUGHT SO...
IT'S JUST LIKE PRESIDENT BOIGNY'S HOME.
YES. YOU KNOW, IGNACE, HIS EMINENCE HAD ME OVER THE OTHER DAY.
IN FACT...
HE'S IN PARIS RIGHT NOW, MEETING WITH PRESIDENT GISCARD D'ESTAING.
AH, ABOUT EXPORTING SOLIBRA?
OF COURSE NOT, IGNACE! ABOUT THE INAUGURATION OF HIS BOULEVARD.
OH, RIGHT.
MOUSSA, GIVE AYA A TOUR OF THE HOUSE.
YES, MAMAN, I WAS ABOUT TO SUGGEST THE SAME THING.

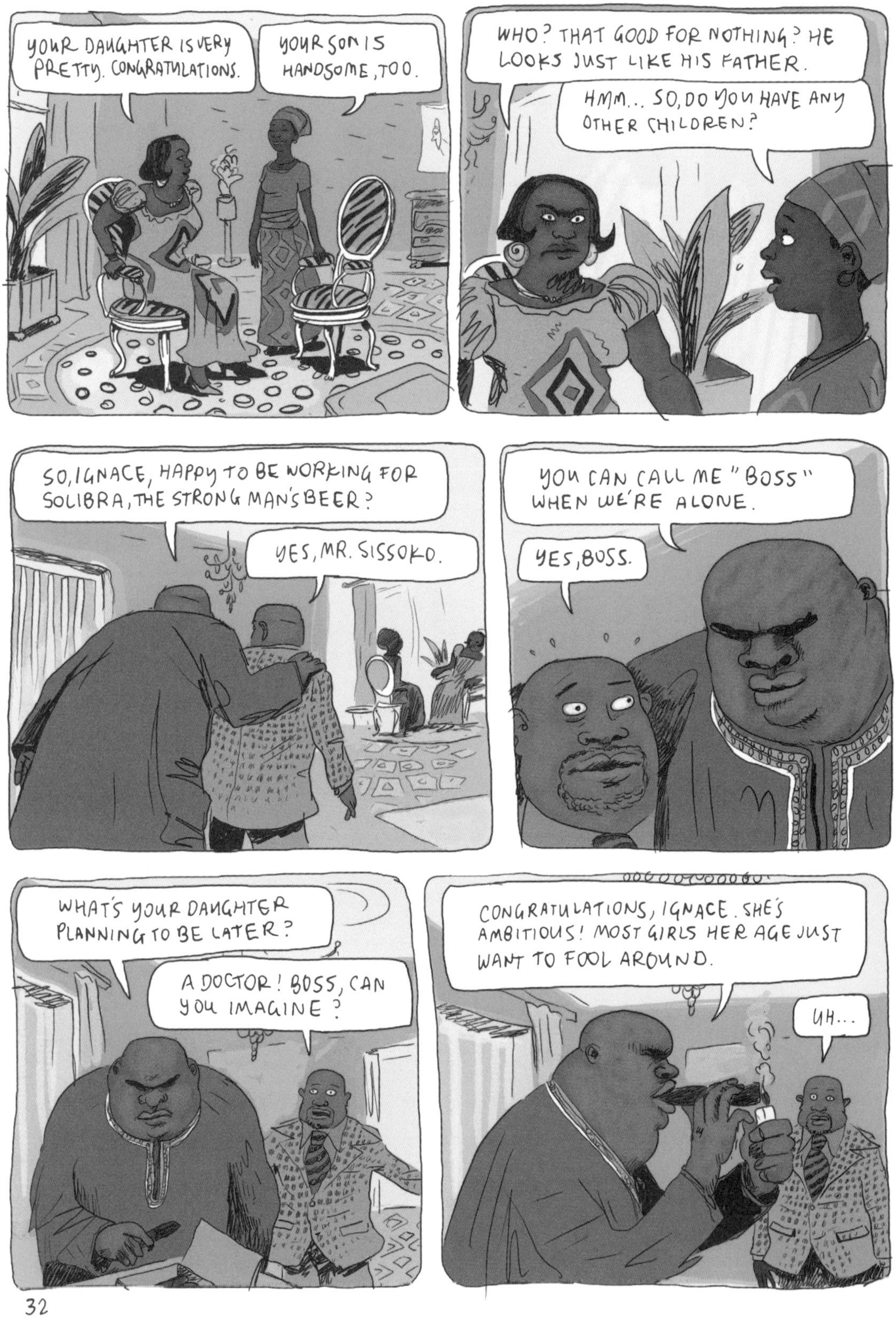
YOUR DAUGHTER IS VERY PRETTY. CONGRATULATIONS.
YOUR SON IS HANDSOME, TOO.
WHO? THAT GOOD FOR NOTHING? HE LOOKS JUST LIKE HIS FATHER.
HMM... SO, DO YOU HAVE ANY OTHER CHILDREN?
SO, IGNACE, HAPPY TO BE WORKING FOR SOLIBRA, THE STRONG MAN'S BEER?
YES, MR. SISSOKO.
YOU CAN CALL ME "BOSS" WHEN WE'RE ALONE.
YES, BOSS.
WHAT'S YOUR DAUGHTER PLANNING TO BE LATER?
A DOCTOR! BOSS, CAN YOU IMAGINE?
CONGRATULATIONS, IGNACE. SHE'S AMBITIOUS! MOST GIRLS HER AGE JUST WANT TO FOOL AROUND.
UH...

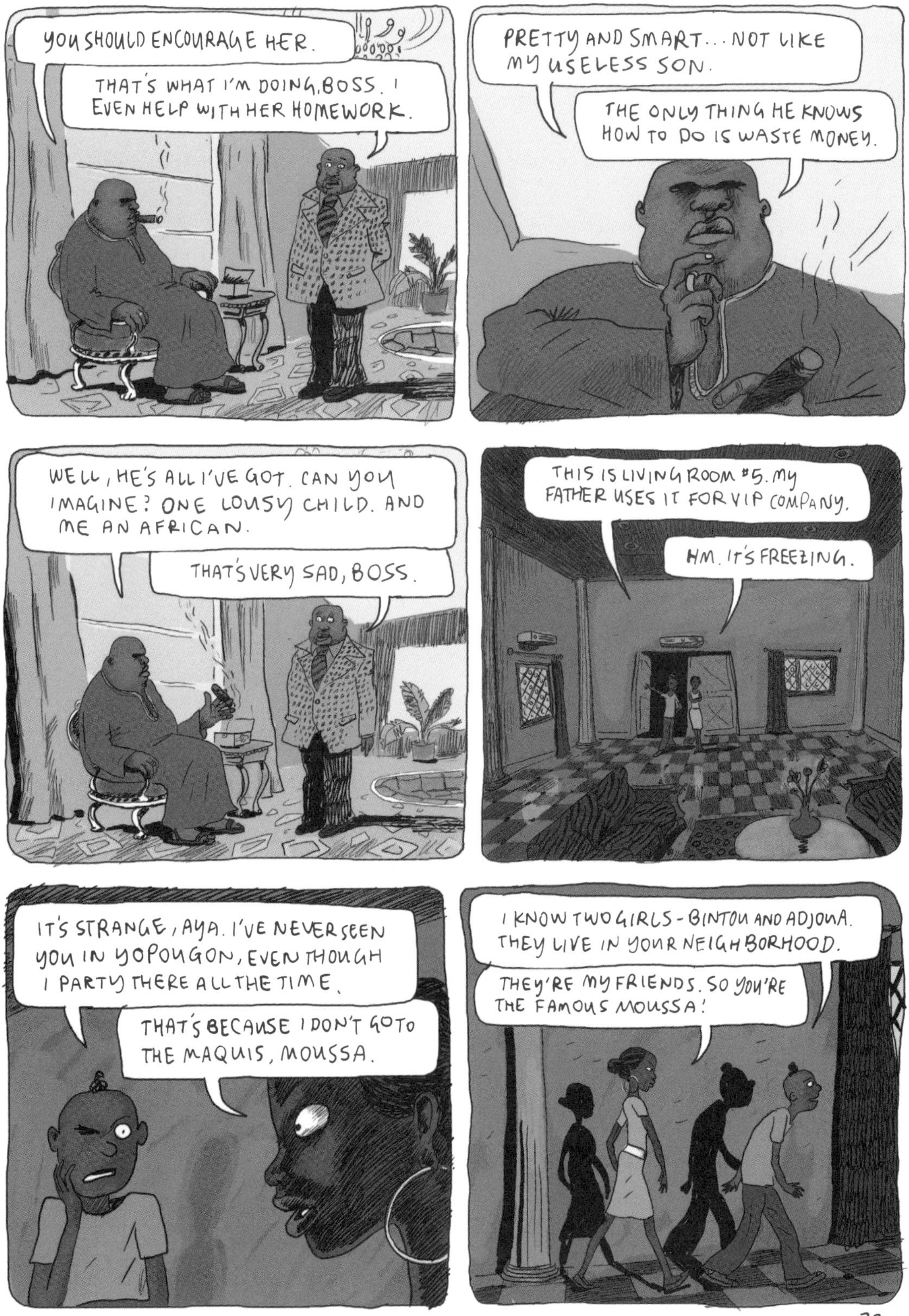
YOU SHOULD ENCOURAGE HER.
THAT'S WHAT I'M DOING, BOSS. I EVEN HELP WITH HER HOMEWORK.
PRETTY AND SMART... NOT LIKE MY USELESS SON.
THE ONLY THING HE KNOWS HOW TO DO IS WASTE MONEY.
WELL, HE'S ALL I'VE GOT. CAN YOU IMAGINE? ONE LOUSY CHILD. AND ME AN AFRICAN.
THAT'S VERY SAD, BOSS.
THIS IS LIVING ROOM #5. MY FATHER USES IT FOR VIP COMPANY.
HM. IT'S FREEZING.
IT'S STRANGE, AYA. I'VE NEVER SEEN YOU IN YOPOUGON, EVEN THOUGH I PARTY THERE ALL THE TIME.
THAT'S BECAUSE I DON'T GO TO THE MAQUIS, MOUSSA.
I KNOW TWO GIRLS - BINTOU AND ADJOUA. THEY LIVE IN YOUR NEIGHBORHOOD.
THEY'RE MY FRIENDS. SO YOU'RE THE FAMOUS MOUSSA!

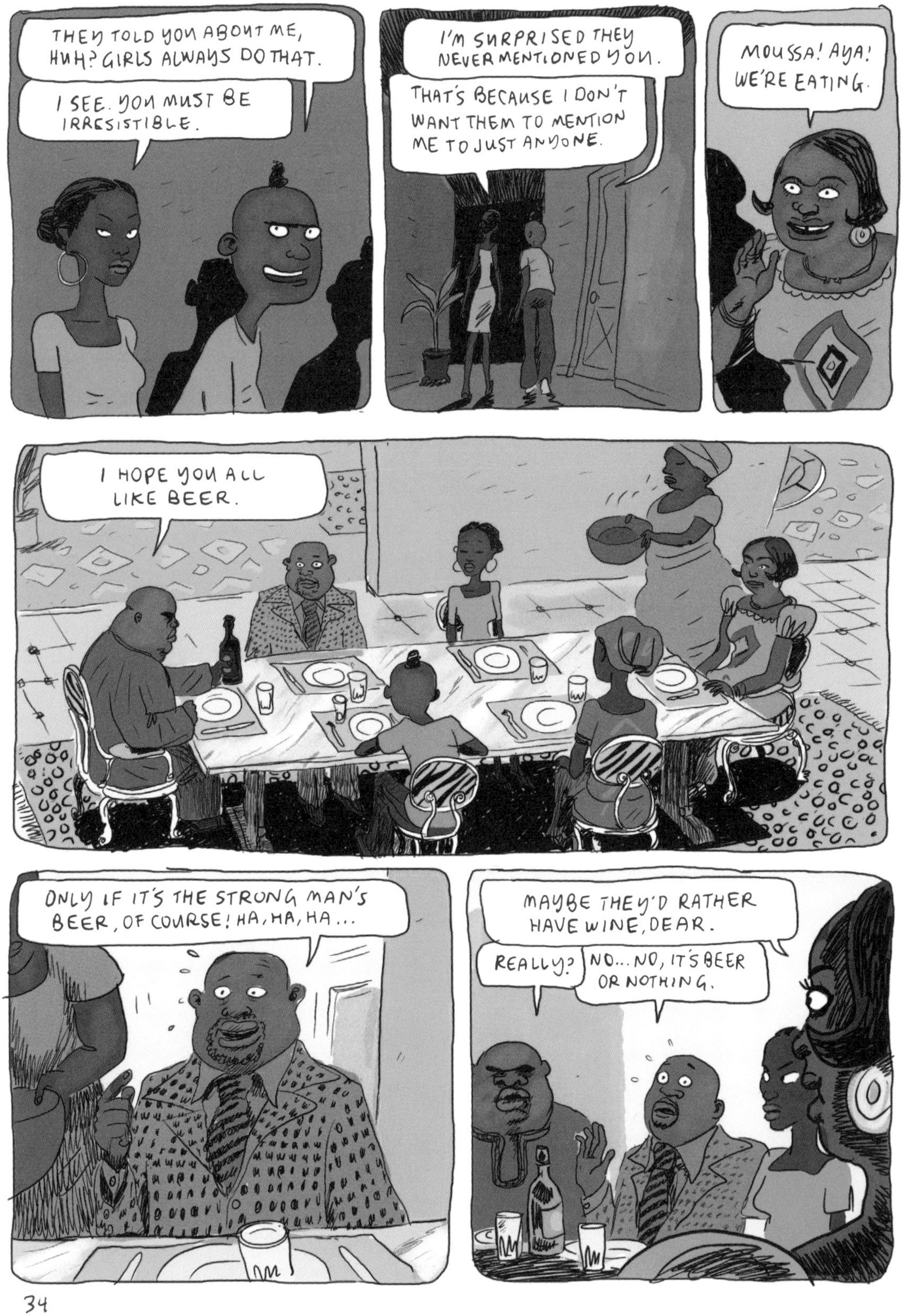
THEY TOLD YOU ABOUT ME, HUH? GIRLS ALWAYS DO THAT.
I SEE. YOU MUST BE IRRESISTIBLE.
I'M SURPRISED THEY NEVER MENTIONED YOU.
THAT'S BECAUSE I DON'T WANT THEM TO MENTION ME TO JUST ANYONE.
MOUSSA! AYA! WE'RE EATING.
I HOPE YOU ALL LIKE BEER.
ONLY IF IT'S THE STRONG MAN'S BEER, OF COURSE! HA, HA, HA...
MAYBE THEY'D RATHER HAVE WINE, DEAR.
REALLY?
NO... NO, IT'S BEER OR NOTHING.

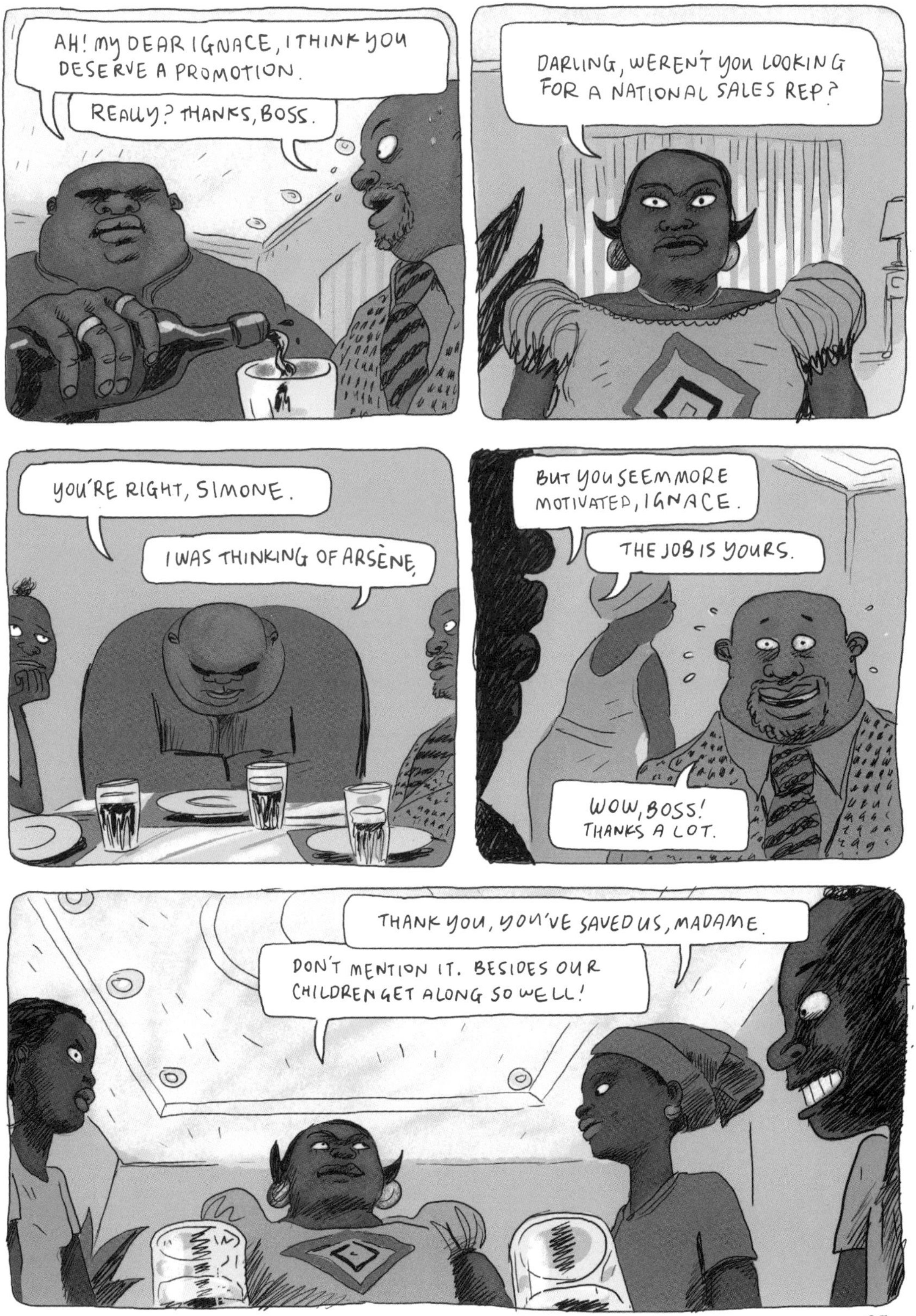
AH! MY DEAR IGNACE, I THINK YOU DESERVE A PROMOTION.
REALLY? THANKS, BOSS.
DARLING, WEREN'T YOU LOOKING FOR A NATIONAL SALES REP?
YOU'RE RIGHT, SIMONE.
I WAS THINKING OF ARSÈNE,
BUT YOU SEEM MORE MOTIVATED, IGNACE.
THE JOB IS YOURS.
WOW, BOSS! THANKS A LOT.
THANK YOU, YOU'VE SAVED US, MADAME.
DON'T MENTION IT. BESIDES OUR CHILDREN GET ALONG SO WELL!

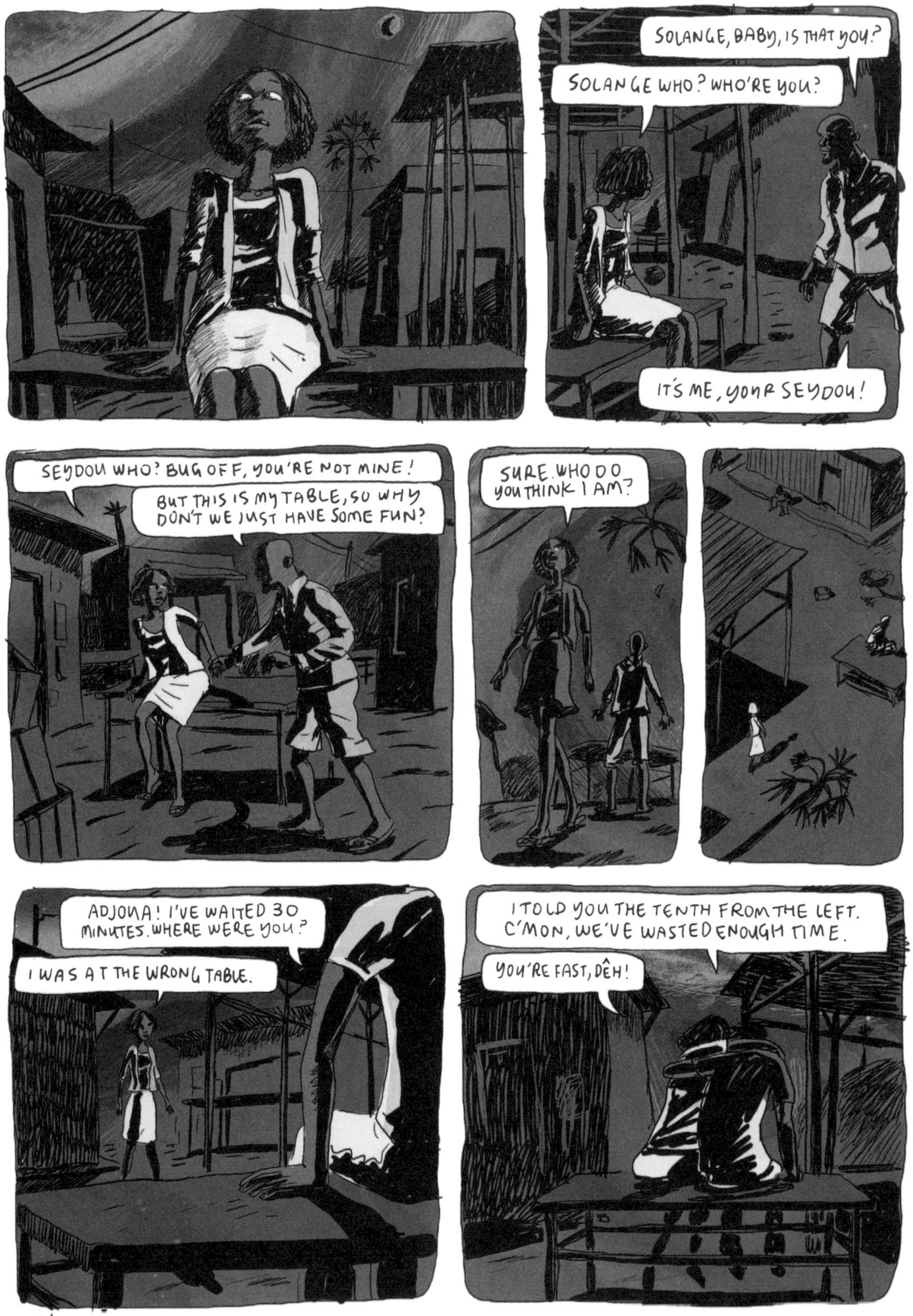
SOLANGE, BABY, IS THAT YOU?
SOLANGE WHO? WHO'RE YOU?
IT'S ME, YOUR SEYDOU!
SEYDOU WHO? BUG OFF, YOU'RE NOT MINE!
BUT THIS IS MY TABLE, SO WHY DON'T WE JUST HAVE SOME FUN?
SURE. WHO DO YOU THINK I AM?
ADJOUA! I'VE WAITED 30 MINUTES. WHERE WERE YOU?
I WAS AT THE WRONG TABLE.
I TOLD YOU THE TENTH FROM THE LEFT. C'MON, WE'VE WASTED ENOUGH TIME.
YOU'RE FAST, DÊH!

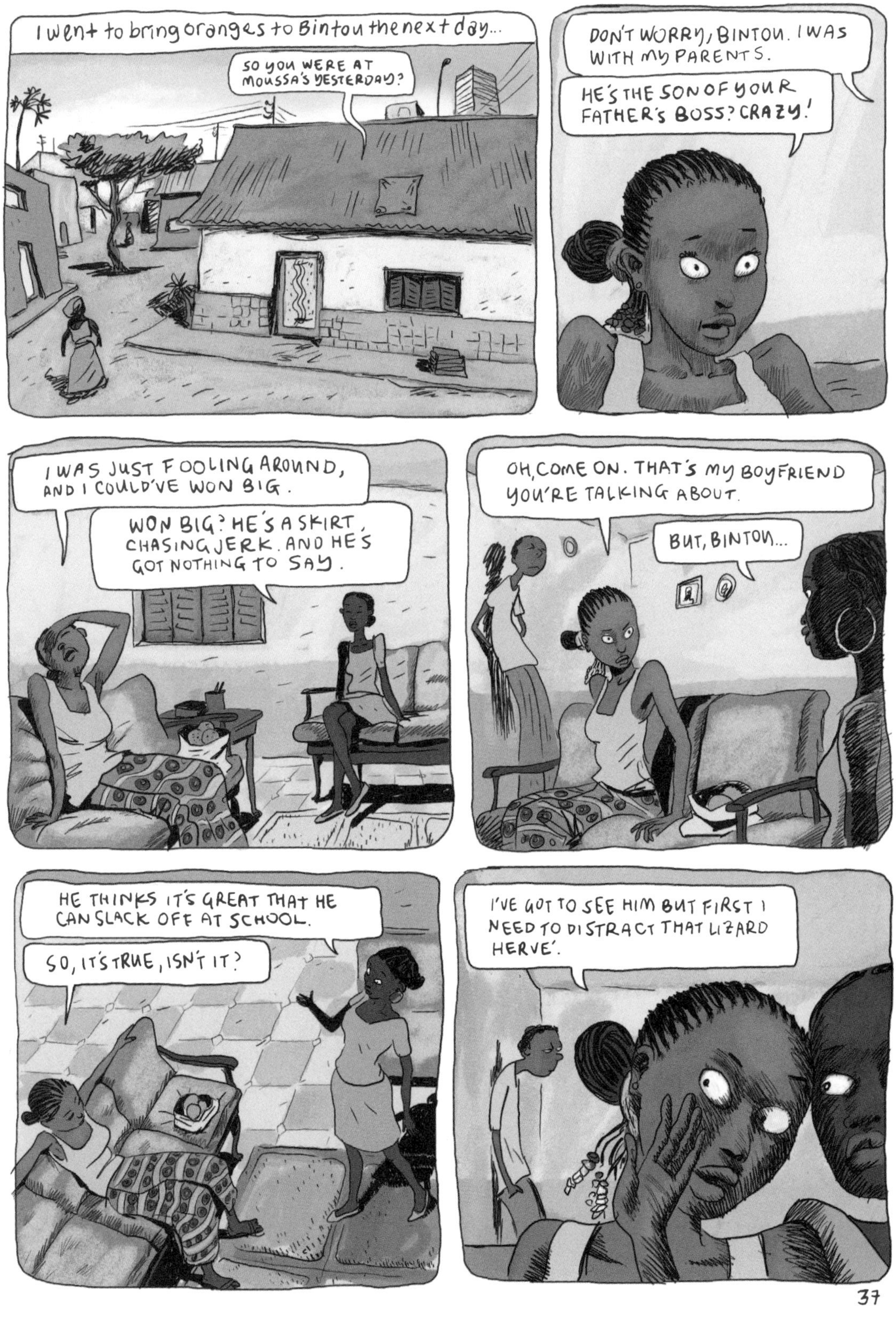

I went to bring oranges to Bintou the next day...
SO YOU WERE AT MOUSSA'S YESTERDAY?
DON'T WORRY, BINTOU. I WAS WITH MY PARENTS.
HE'S THE SON OF YOUR FATHER'S BOSS? CRAZY!
I WAS JUST FOOLING AROUND, AND I COULD'VE WON BIG.
WON BIG? HE'S A SKIRT-CHASING JERK. AND HE'S GOT NOTHING TO SAY.
OH, COME ON. THAT'S MY BOYFRIEND YOU'RE TALKING ABOUT.
BUT, BINTOU...
HE THINKS IT'S GREAT THAT HE CAN SLACK OFF AT SCHOOL.
SO, IT'S TRUE, ISN'T IT?
I'VE GOT TO SEE HIM BUT FIRST I NEED TO DISTRACT THAT LIZARD HERVÉ.

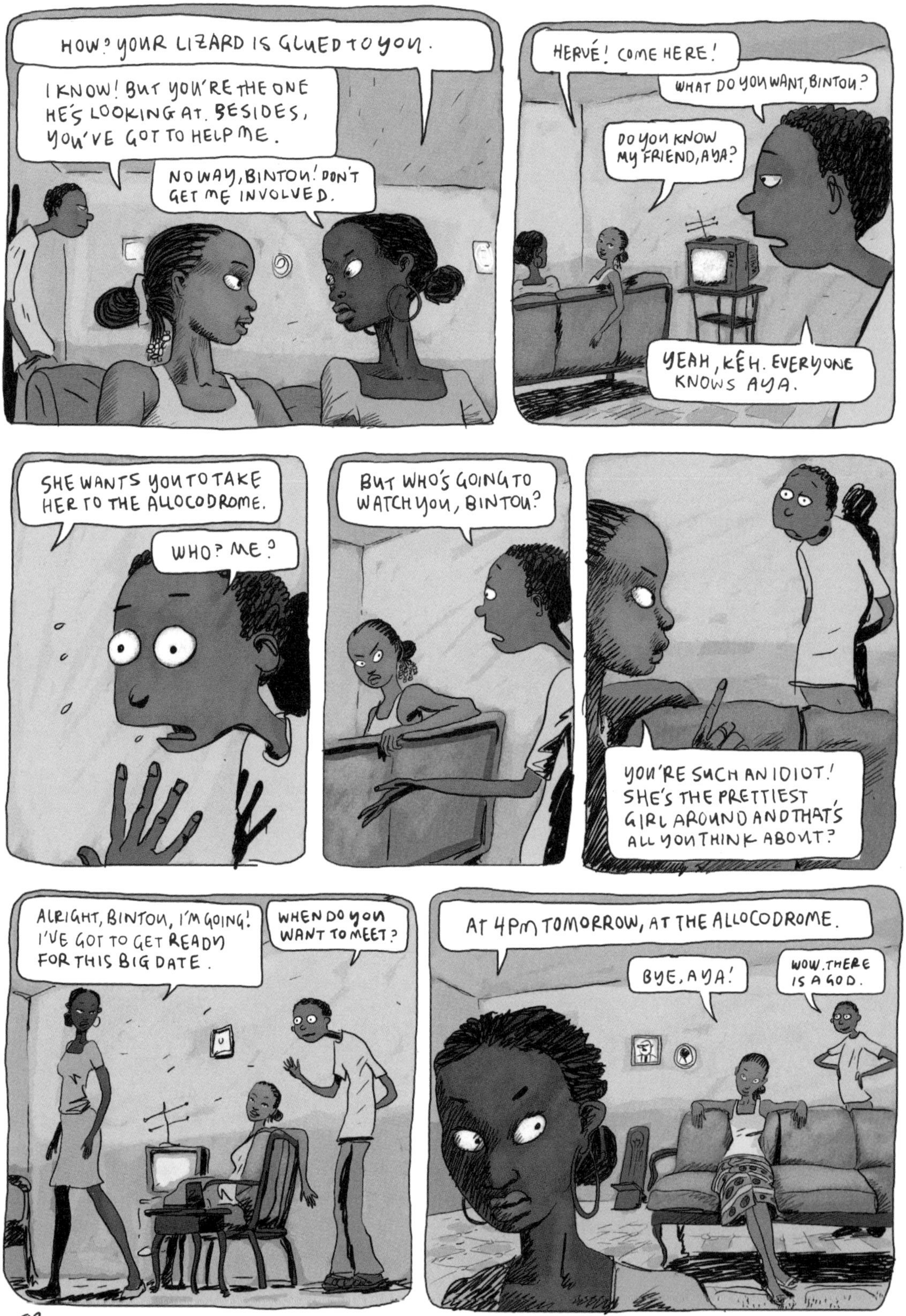
HOW? YOUR LIZARD IS GLUED TO YOU.
I KNOW! BUT YOU'RE THE ONE HE'S LOOKING AT. BESIDES, YOU'VE GOT TO HELP ME.
NO WAY, BINTOU! DON'T GET ME INVOLVED.
HERVÉ! COME HERE!
WHAT DO YOU WANT, BINTOU?
DO YOU KNOW MY FRIEND, AYA?
YEAH, KÊH. EVERYONE KNOWS AYA.
SHE WANTS YOU TO TAKE HER TO THE ALLOCODROME.
WHO? ME?
BUT WHO'S GOING TO WATCH YOU, BINTOU?
YOU'RE SUCH AN IDIOT! SHE'S THE PRETTIEST GIRL AROUND AND THAT'S ALL YOU THINK ABOUT?
ALRIGHT, BINTOU, I'M GOING! I'VE GOT TO GET READY FOR THIS BIG DATE.
WHEN DO YOU WANT TO MEET?
AT 4PM TOMORROW, AT THE ALLOCODROME.
BYE, AYA!
WOW. THERE IS A GOD.

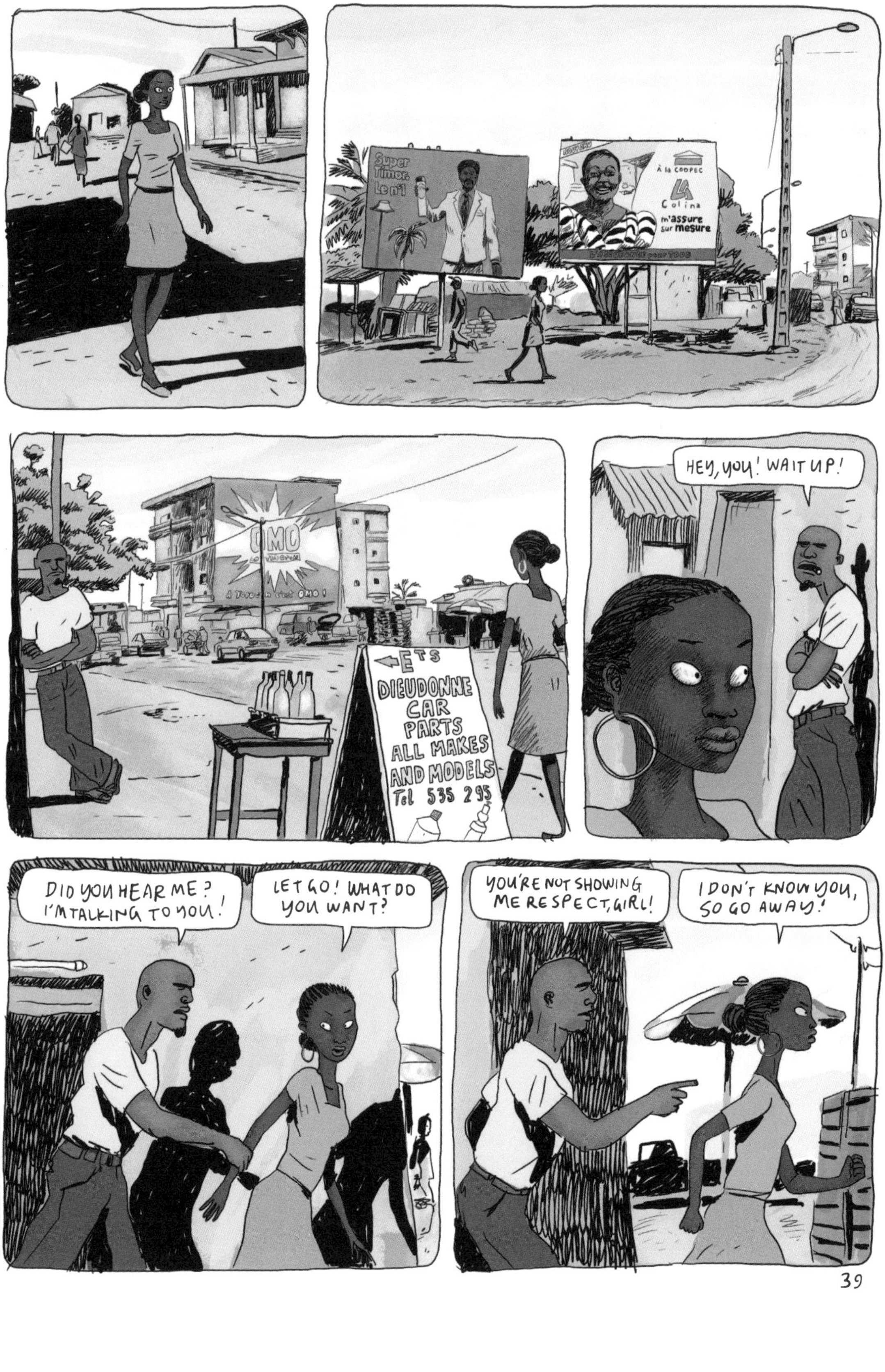
Super Timor Le n°1
À la COOPEC
Colina
m'assure sur mesure
OMO
ETS
DIEUDONNE CAR PARTS ALL MAKES AND MODELS
Tel 535 295
HEY, YOU! WAIT UP!
DID YOU HEAR ME? I'M TALKING TO YOU!
LET GO! WHAT DO YOU WANT?
YOU'RE NOT SHOWING ME RESPECT, GIRL!
I DON'T KNOW YOU, SO GO AWAY!

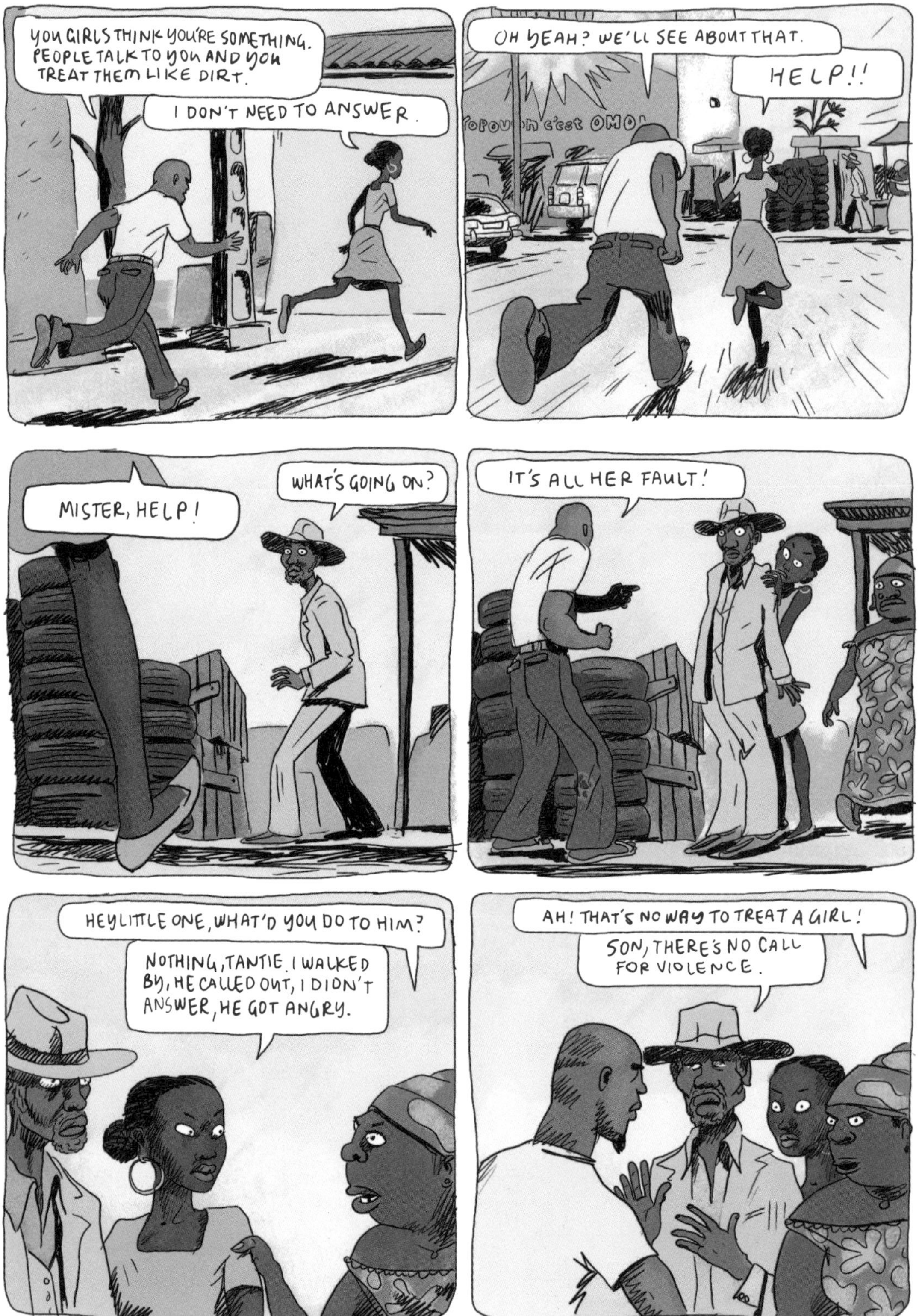
YOU GIRLS THINK YOU'RE SOMETHING. PEOPLE TALK TO YOU AND YOU TREAT THEM LIKE DIRT.
I DON'T NEED TO ANSWER.
OH YEAH? WE'LL SEE ABOUT THAT.
HELP!!
Yopougon c'est OMO
MISTER, HELP!
WHAT'S GOING ON?
IT'S ALL HER FAULT!
HEY LITTLE ONE, WHAT'D YOU DO TO HIM?
NOTHING, TANTIE. I WALKED BY, HE CALLED OUT, I DIDN'T ANSWER, HE GOT ANGRY.
AH! THAT'S NO WAY TO TREAT A GIRL!
SON, THERE'S NO CALL FOR VIOLENCE.

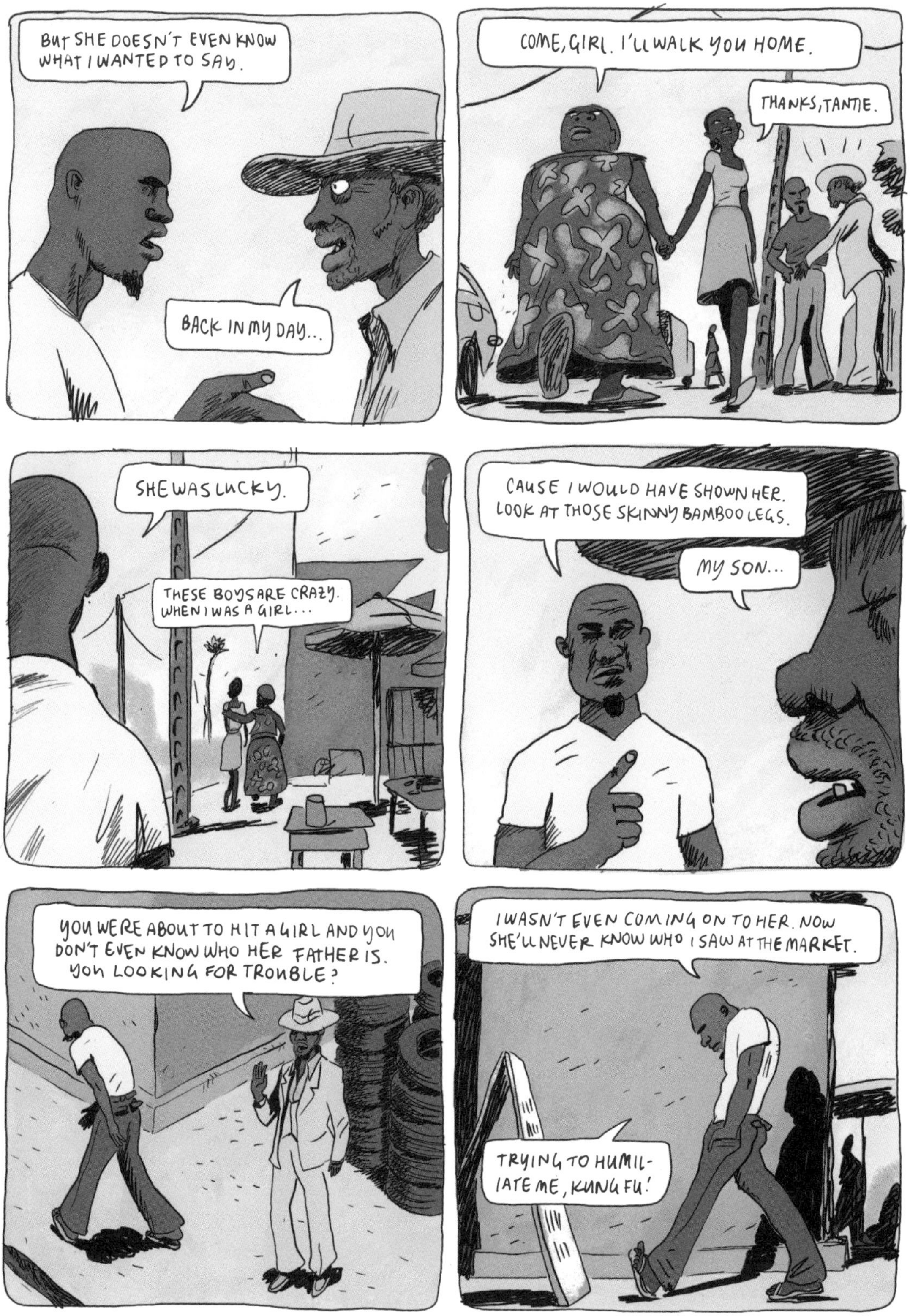
BUT SHE DOESN'T EVEN KNOW WHAT I WANTED TO SAY.
BACK IN MY DAY...
COME, GIRL. I'LL WALK YOU HOME.
THANKS, TANTIE.
SHE WAS LUCKY.
THESE BOYS ARE CRAZY. WHEN I WAS A GIRL...
CAUSE I WOULD HAVE SHOWN HER. LOOK AT THOSE SKINNY BAMBOO LEGS.
MY SON...
YOU WERE ABOUT TO HIT A GIRL AND YOU DON'T EVEN KNOW WHO HER FATHER IS. YOU LOOKING FOR TROUBLE?
I WASN'T EVEN COMING ON TO HER. NOW SHE'LL NEVER KNOW WHO I SAW AT THE MARKET.
TRYING TO HUMILIATE ME, KUNG FU!

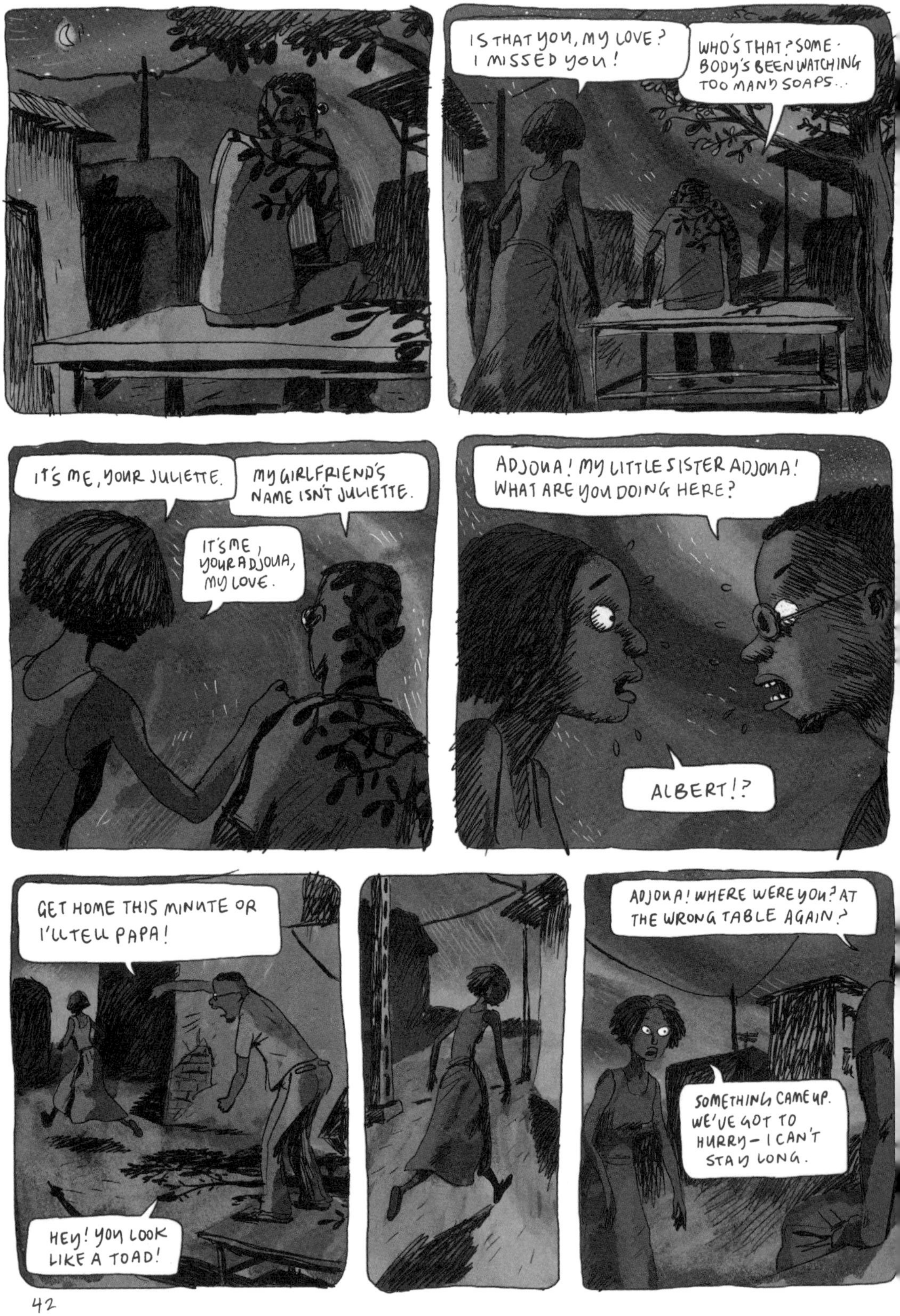
IS THAT YOU, MY LOVE? I MISSED YOU!
WHO'S THAT? SOMEBODY'S BEEN WATCHING TOO MANY SOAPS...
IT'S ME, YOUR JULIETTE.
MY GIRLFRIEND'S NAME ISN'T JULIETTE.
IT'S ME, YOUR ADJOUA, MY LOVE.
ADJOUA! MY LITTLE SISTER ADJOUA! WHAT ARE YOU DOING HERE?
ALBERT!?
GET HOME THIS MINUTE OR I'LL TELL PAPA!
HEY! YOU LOOK LIKE A TOAD!
ADJOUA! WHERE WERE YOU? AT THE WRONG TABLE AGAIN?
SOMETHING CAME UP. WE'VE GOT TO HURRY— I CAN'T STAY LONG.

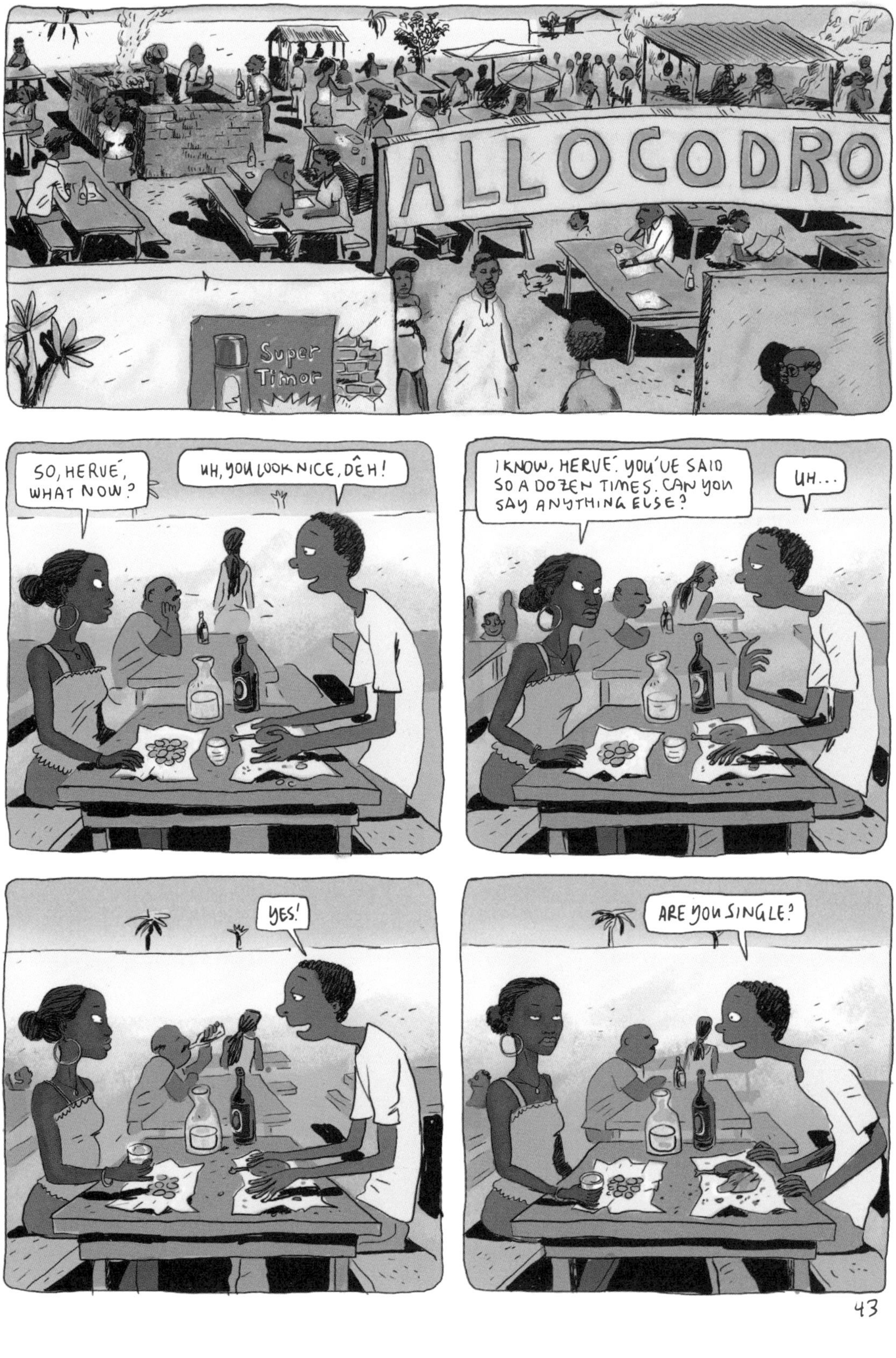
ALLOCODRO
Super Timor
SO, HERVÉ, WHAT NOW?
UH, YOU LOOK NICE, DÊH!
I KNOW, HERVÉ. YOU'VE SAID SO A DOZEN TIMES. CAN YOU SAY ANYTHING ELSE?
UH...
YES!
ARE YOU SINGLE?

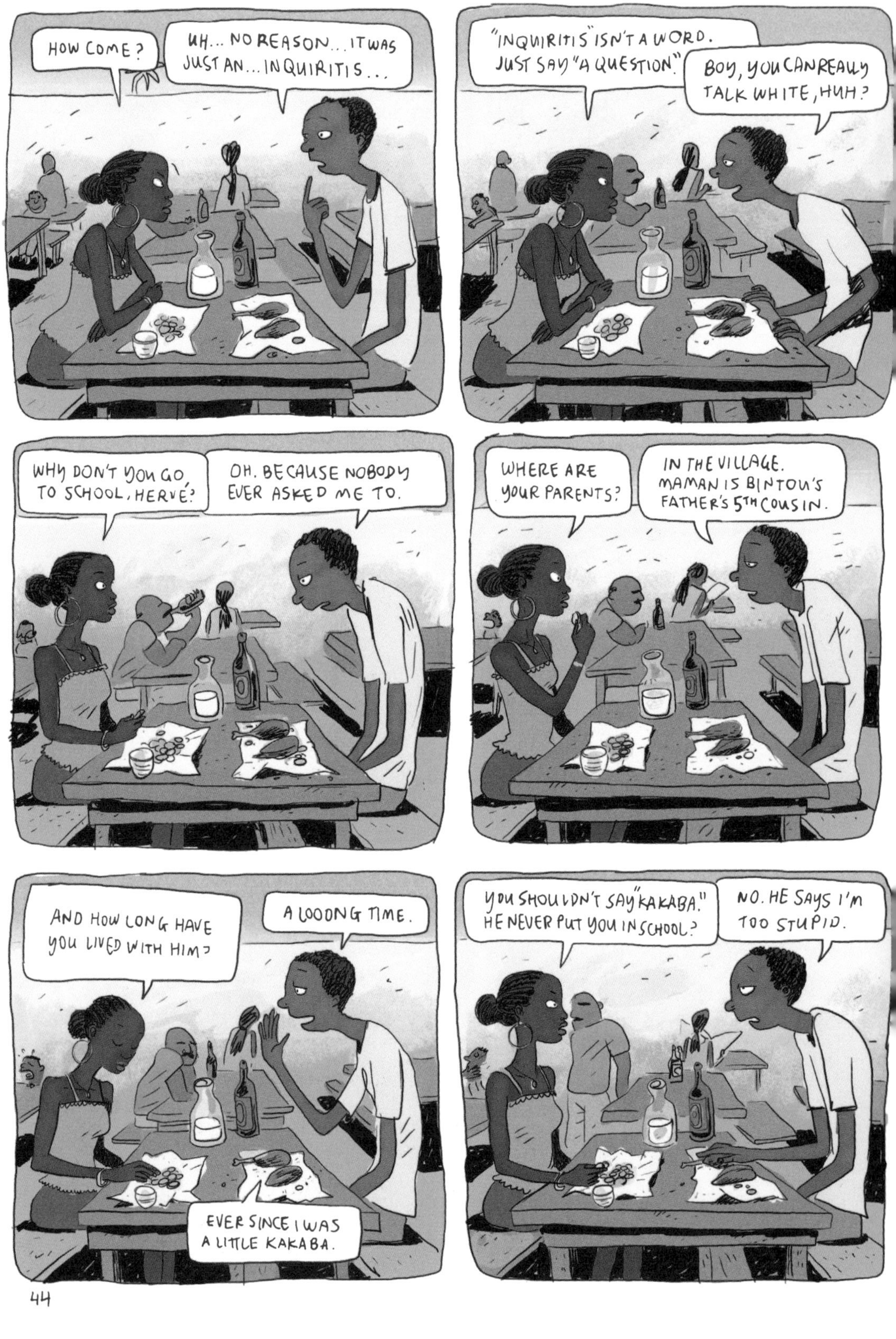
HOW COME?
UH... NO REASON... IT WAS JUST AN... INQUIRITIS...
"INQUIRITIS" ISN'T A WORD. JUST SAY "A QUESTION."
BOY, YOU CAN REALLY TALK WHITE, HUH?
WHY DON'T YOU GO TO SCHOOL, HERVÉ?
OH. BECAUSE NOBODY EVER ASKED ME TO.
WHERE ARE YOUR PARENTS?
IN THE VILLAGE. MAMAN IS BINTOU'S FATHER'S 5TH COUSIN.
AND HOW LONG HAVE YOU LIVED WITH HIM?
A LOOONG TIME.
EVER SINCE I WAS A LITTLE KAKABA.
YOU SHOULDN'T SAY "KAKABA." HE NEVER PUT YOU IN SCHOOL?
NO. HE SAYS I'M TOO STUPID.

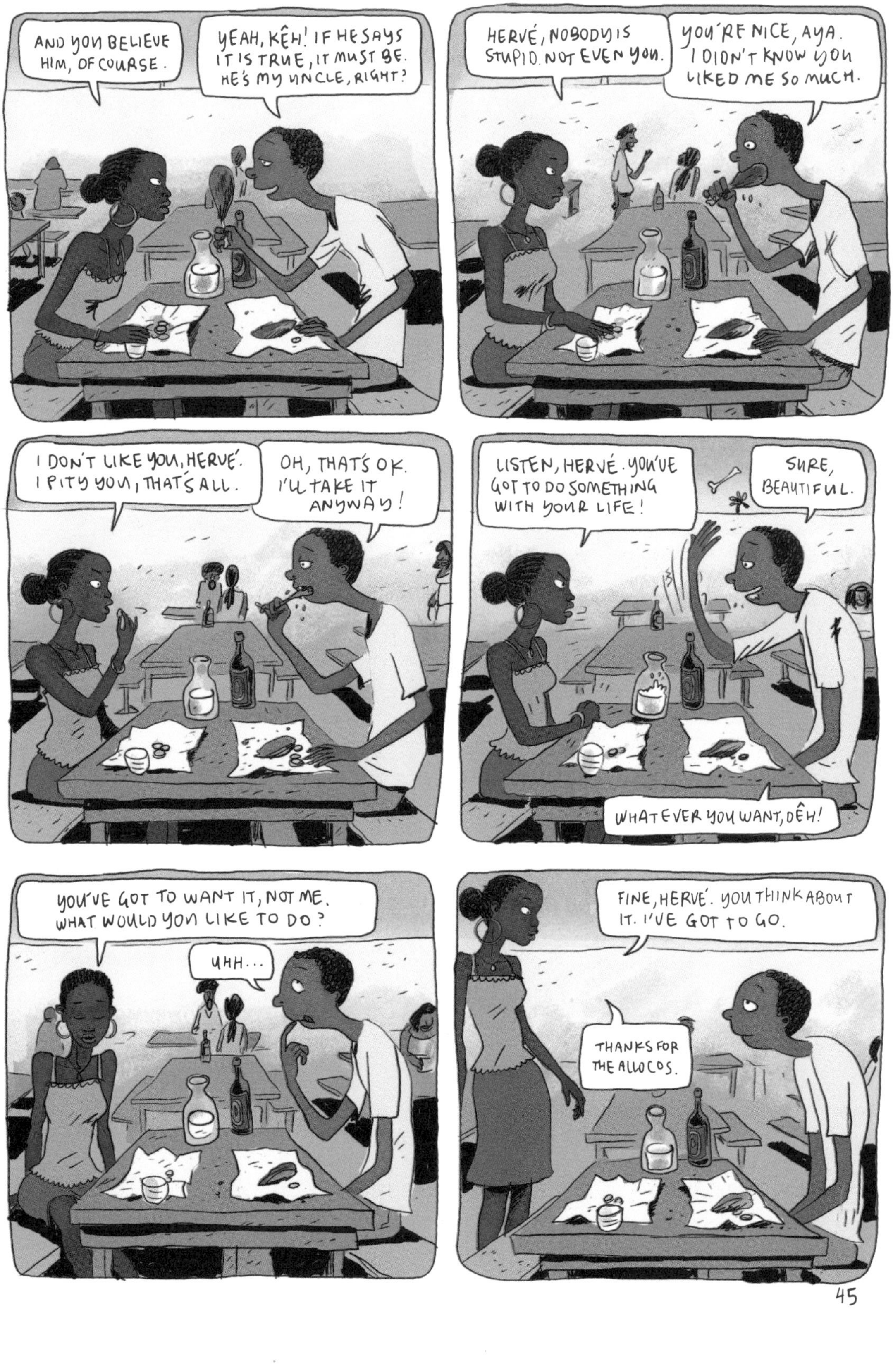
AND YOU BELIEVE HIM, OF COURSE.
YEAH, KÊH! IF HE SAYS IT IS TRUE, IT MUST BE. HE'S MY UNCLE, RIGHT?
HERVÉ, NOBODY IS STUPID. NOT EVEN YOU.
YOU'RE NICE, AYA. I DIDN'T KNOW YOU LIKED ME SO MUCH.
I DON'T LIKE YOU, HERVÉ. I PITY YOU, THAT'S ALL.
OH, THAT'S OK. I'LL TAKE IT ANYWAY!
LISTEN, HERVÉ. YOU'VE GOT TO DO SOMETHING WITH YOUR LIFE!
SURE, BEAUTIFUL.
WHATEVER YOU WANT, DÊH!
YOU'VE GOT TO WANT IT, NOT ME. WHAT WOULD YOU LIKE TO DO?
UHH...
FINE, HERVÉ. YOU THINK ABOUT IT. I'VE GOT TO GO.
THANKS FOR THE ALLOCOS.

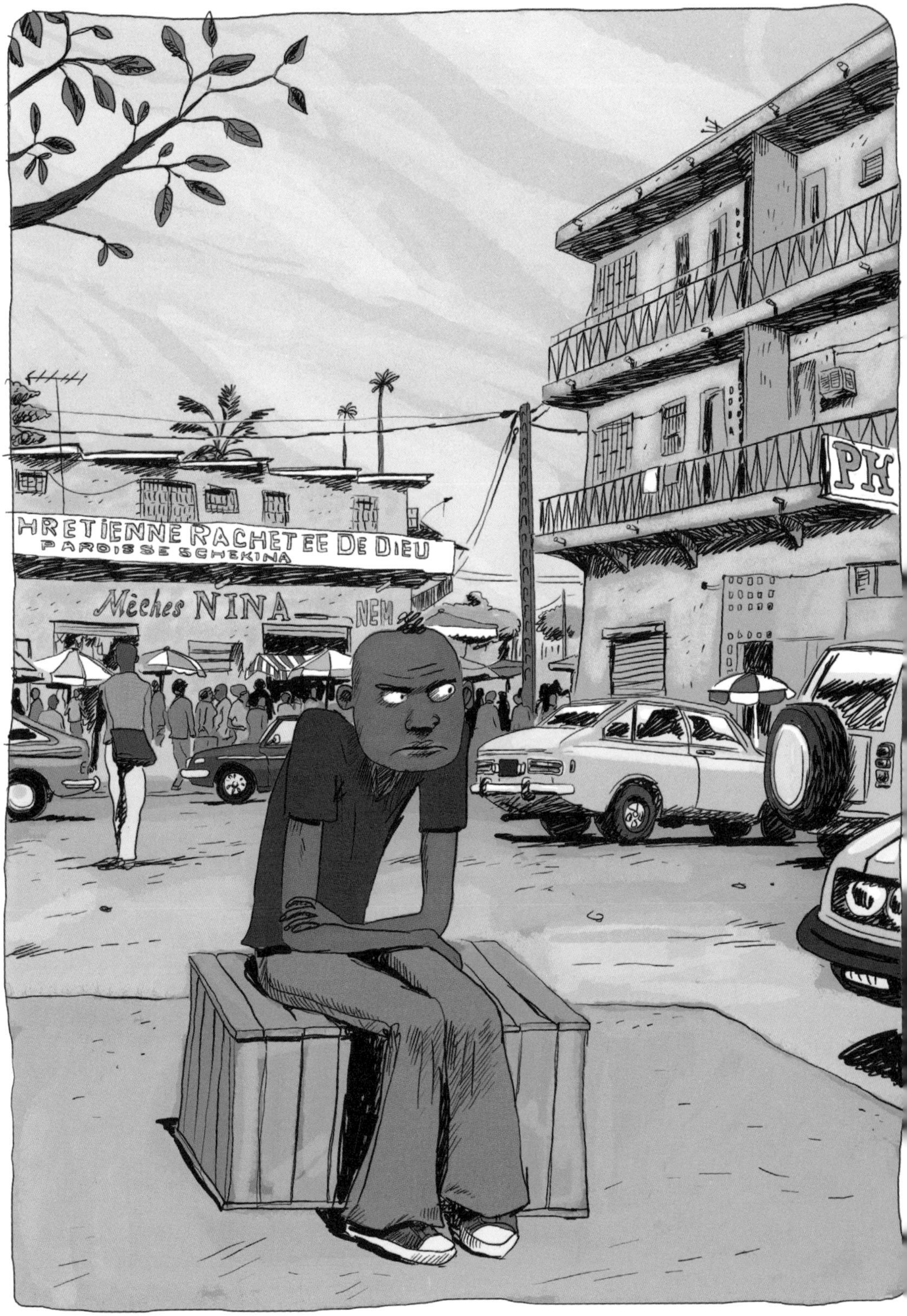
HRETIENNE RACHETEE DE DIEU
PAROISSE SCHEKINA
Mèches NINA
NEM
PH

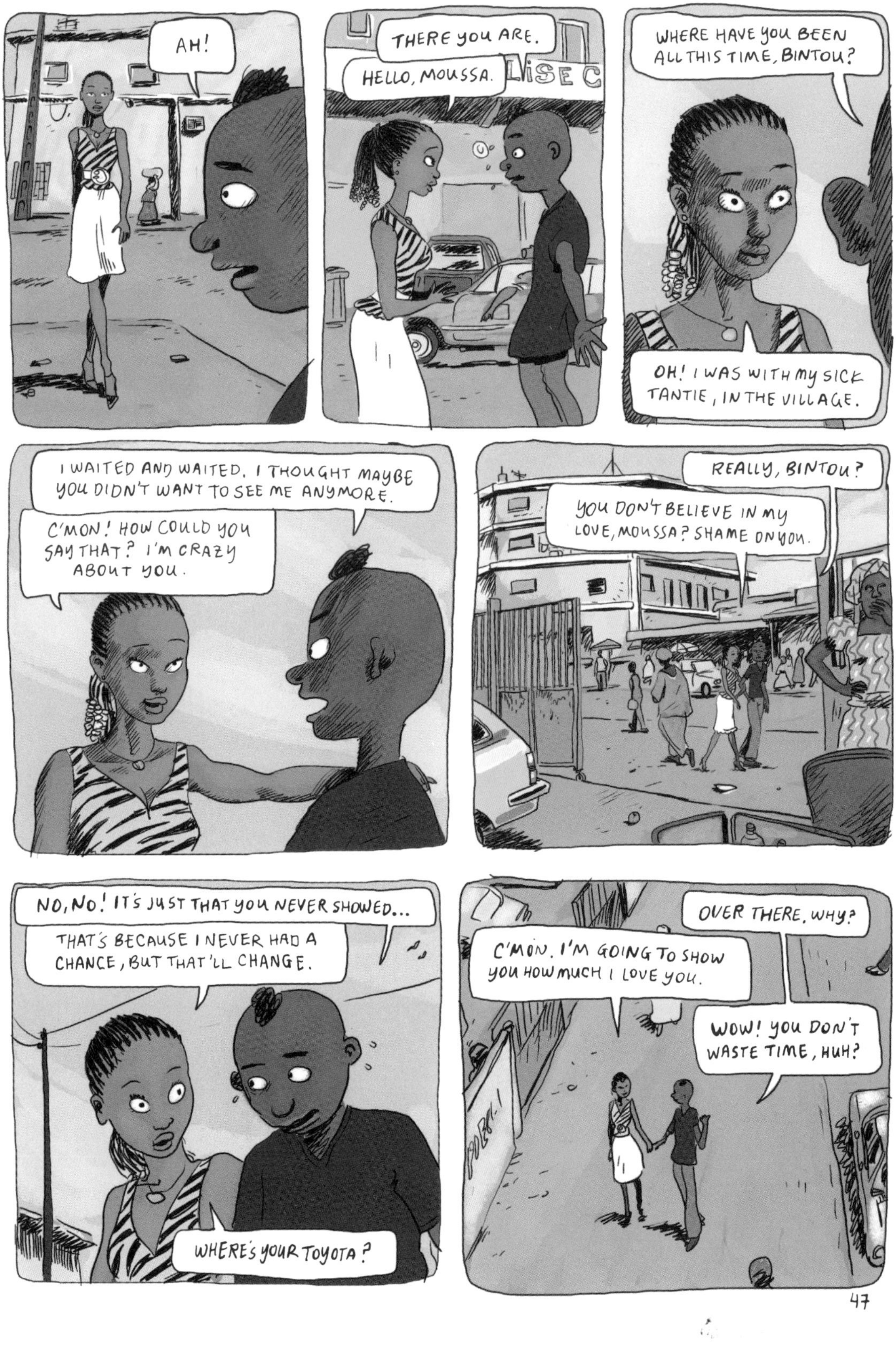
AH!
THERE YOU ARE.
HELLO, MOUSSA.
LISE C
WHERE HAVE YOU BEEN ALL THIS TIME, BINTOU?
OH! I WAS WITH MY SICK TANTIE, IN THE VILLAGE.
I WAITED AND WAITED. I THOUGHT MAYBE YOU DIDN'T WANT TO SEE ME ANYMORE.
C'MON! HOW COULD YOU SAY THAT? I'M CRAZY ABOUT YOU.
REALLY, BINTOU?
YOU DON'T BELIEVE IN MY LOVE, MOUSSA? SHAME ON YOU.
NO, NO! IT'S JUST THAT YOU NEVER SHOWED...
THAT'S BECAUSE I NEVER HAD A CHANCE, BUT THAT'LL CHANGE.
WHERE'S YOUR TOYOTA?
OVER THERE, WHY?
C'MON. I'M GOING TO SHOW YOU HOW MUCH I LOVE YOU.
WOW! YOU DON'T WASTE TIME, HUH?

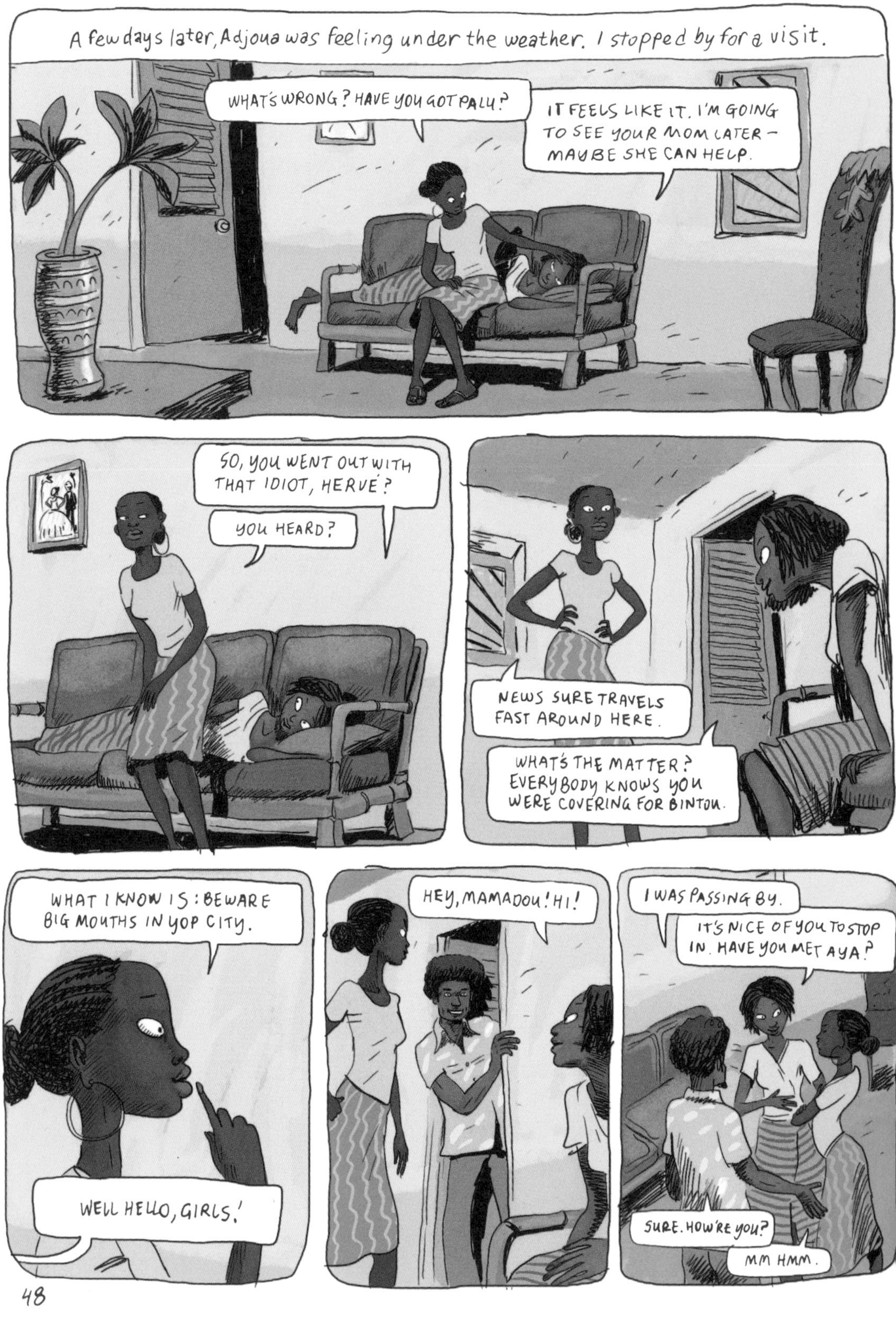
A few days later, Adjoua was feeling under the weather. I stopped by for a visit.
WHAT'S WRONG? HAVE YOU GOT PALU?
IT FEELS LIKE IT. I'M GOING TO SEE YOUR MOM LATER - MAYBE SHE CAN HELP.
SO, YOU WENT OUT WITH THAT IDIOT, HERVÉ?
YOU HEARD?
NEWS SURE TRAVELS FAST AROUND HERE.
WHAT'S THE MATTER? EVERYBODY KNOWS YOU WERE COVERING FOR BINTOU.
WHAT I KNOW IS: BEWARE BIG MOUTHS IN YOP CITY.
WELL HELLO, GIRLS!
HEY, MAMADOU! HI!
I WAS PASSING BY.
IT'S NICE OF YOU TO STOP IN. HAVE YOU MET AYA?
SURE. HOW'RE YOU?
MM HMM.

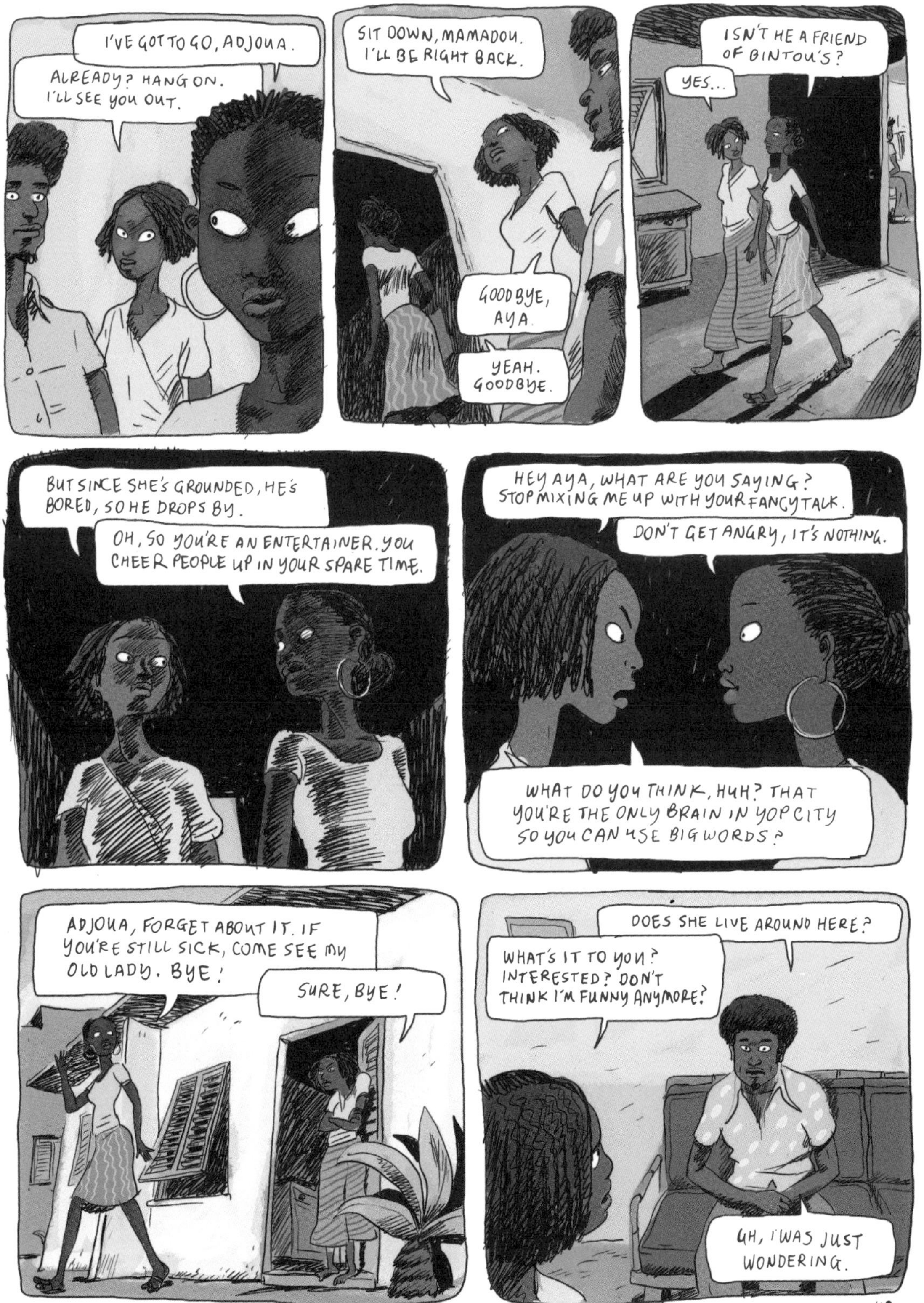
I'VE GOT TO GO, ADJOUA.
ALREADY? HANG ON. I'LL SEE YOU OUT.
SIT DOWN, MAMADOU. I'LL BE RIGHT BACK.
GOODBYE, AYA.
YEAH. GOODBYE.
ISN'T HE A FRIEND OF BINTOU'S?
YES...
BUT SINCE SHE'S GROUNDED, HE'S BORED, SO HE DROPS BY.
OH, SO YOU'RE AN ENTERTAINER. YOU CHEER PEOPLE UP IN YOUR SPARE TIME.
HEY AYA, WHAT ARE YOU SAYING? STOP MIXING ME UP WITH YOUR FANCY TALK.
DON'T GET ANGRY, IT'S NOTHING.
WHAT DO YOU THINK, HUH? THAT YOU'RE THE ONLY BRAIN IN YOP CITY SO YOU CAN USE BIG WORDS?
ADJOUA, FORGET ABOUT IT. IF YOU'RE STILL SICK, COME SEE MY OLD LADY. BYE!
SURE, BYE!
DOES SHE LIVE AROUND HERE?
WHAT'S IT TO YOU? INTERESTED? DON'T THINK I'M FUNNY ANYMORE?
UH, I WAS JUST WONDERING.

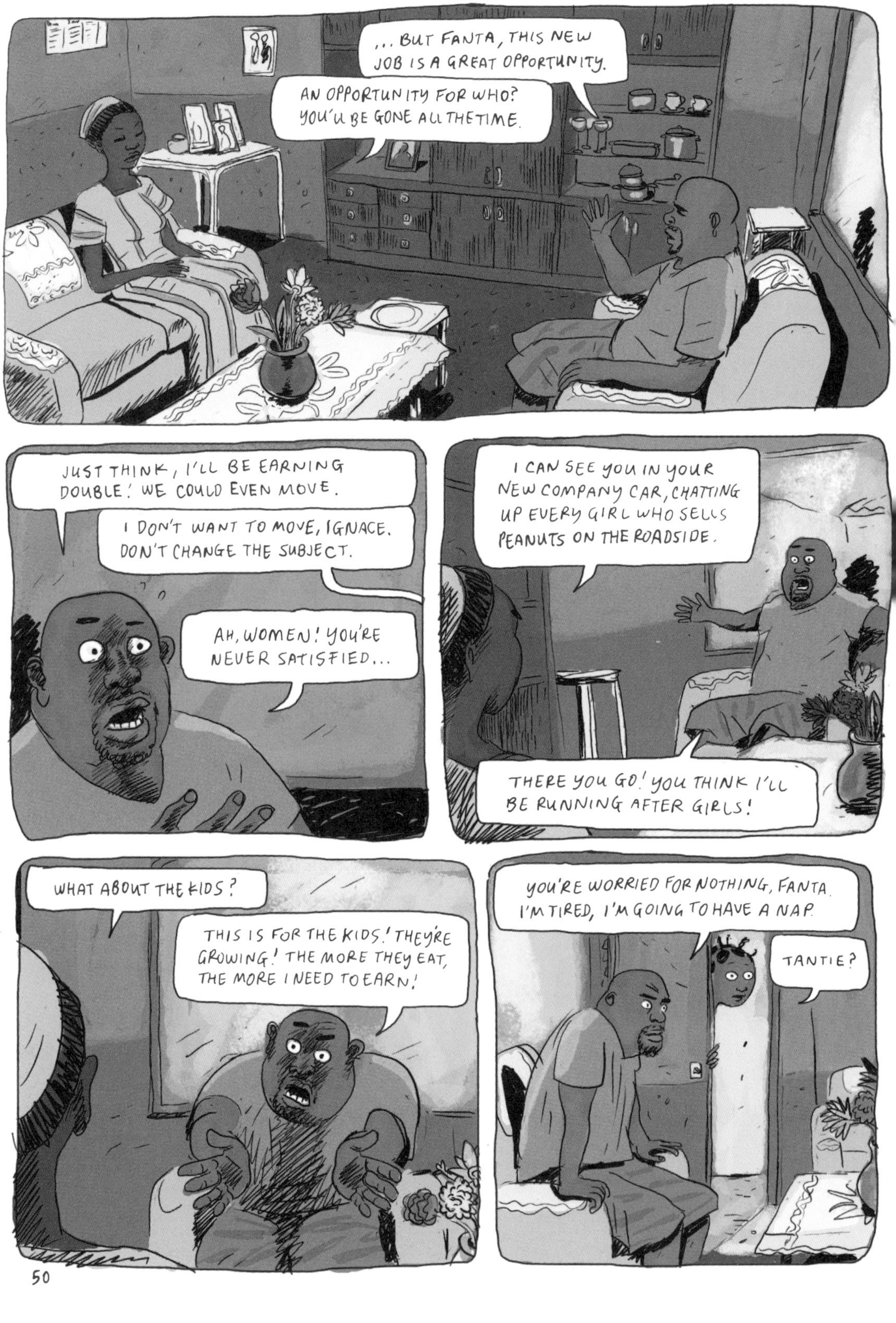
... BUT FANTA, THIS NEW JOB IS A GREAT OPPORTUNITY.
AN OPPORTUNITY FOR WHO? YOU'LL BE GONE ALL THE TIME.
JUST THINK, I'LL BE EARNING DOUBLE! WE COULD EVEN MOVE.
I DON'T WANT TO MOVE, IGNACE. DON'T CHANGE THE SUBJECT.
AH, WOMEN! YOU'RE NEVER SATISFIED...
I CAN SEE YOU IN YOUR NEW COMPANY CAR, CHATTING UP EVERY GIRL WHO SELLS PEANUTS ON THE ROADSIDE.
THERE YOU GO! YOU THINK I'LL BE RUNNING AFTER GIRLS!
WHAT ABOUT THE KIDS?
THIS IS FOR THE KIDS! THEY'RE GROWING! THE MORE THEY EAT, THE MORE I NEED TO EARN!
YOU'RE WORRIED FOR NOTHING, FANTA. I'M TIRED, I'M GOING TO HAVE A NAP.
TANTIE?

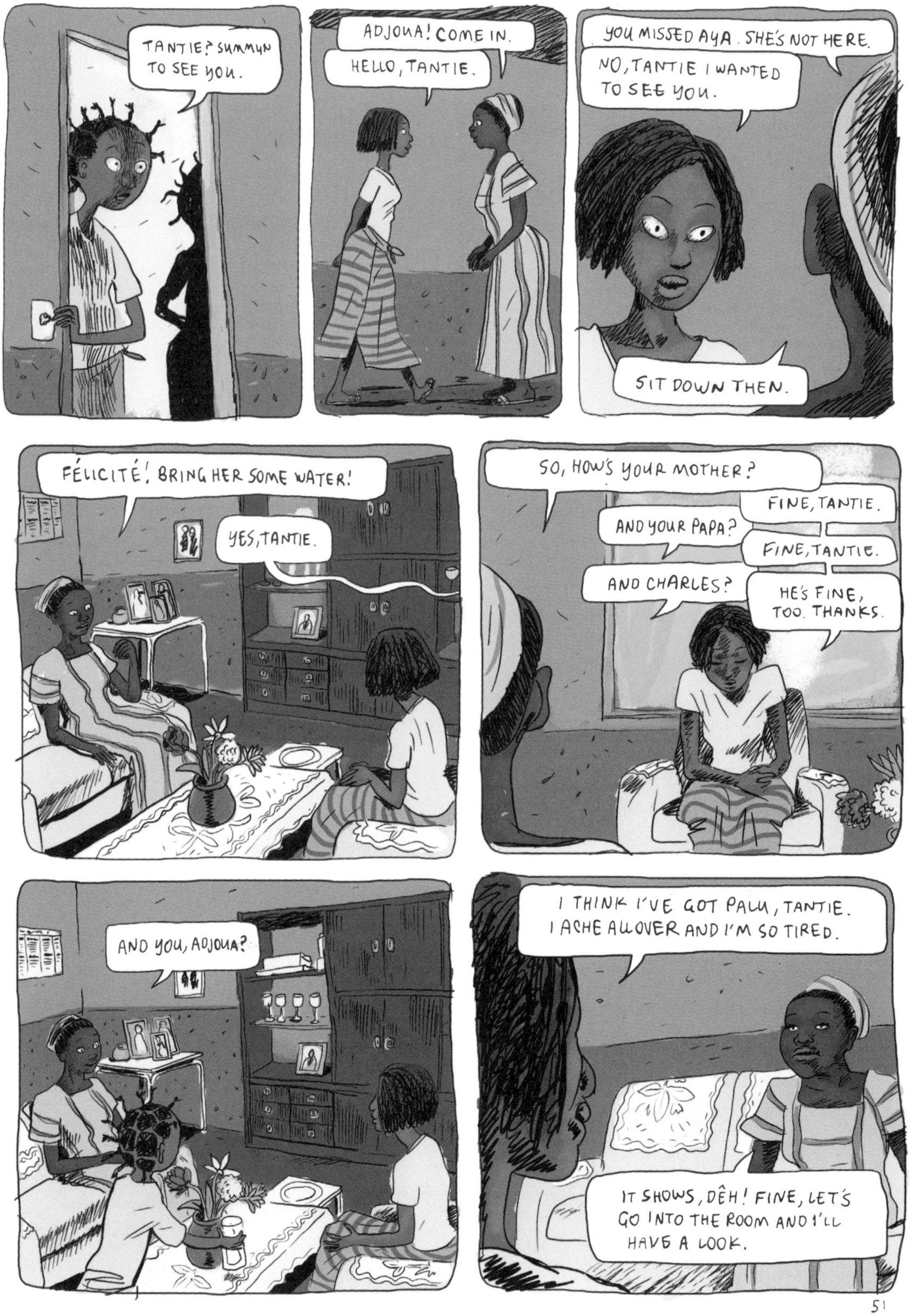
TANTIE? SUMMUN TO SEE YOU.
ADJOUA! COME IN.
HELLO, TANTIE.
YOU MISSED AYA. SHE'S NOT HERE.
NO, TANTIE I WANTED TO SEE YOU.
SIT DOWN THEN.
FÉLICITÉ! BRING HER SOME WATER!
YES, TANTIE.
SO, HOW'S YOUR MOTHER?
FINE, TANTIE.
AND YOUR PAPA?
FINE, TANTIE.
AND CHARLES?
HE'S FINE, TOO. THANKS.
AND YOU, ADJOUA?
I THINK I'VE GOT PALU, TANTIE. I ACHE ALL OVER AND I'M SO TIRED.
IT SHOWS, DÊH! FINE, LET'S GO INTO THE ROOM AND I'LL HAVE A LOOK.

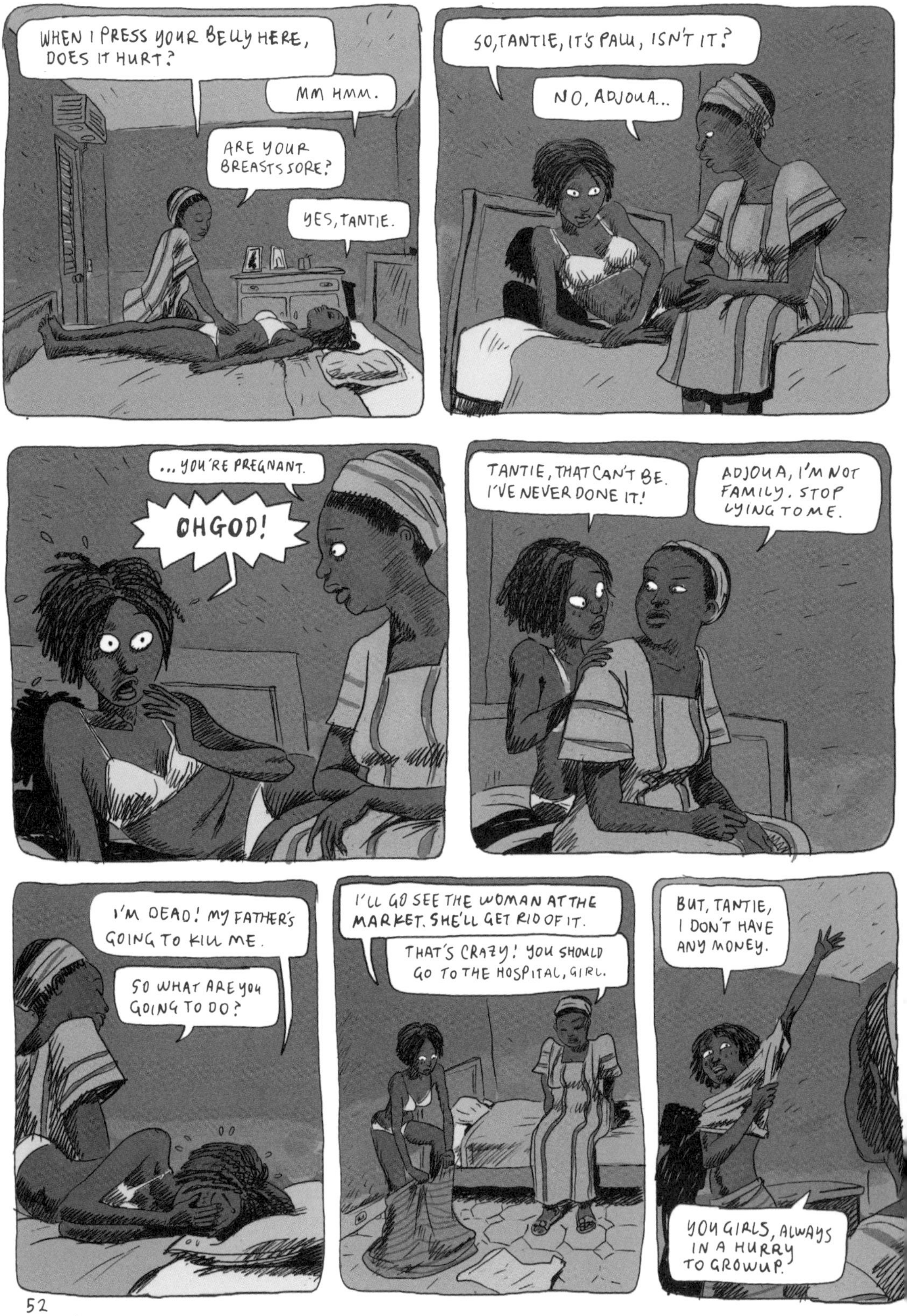
WHEN I PRESS YOUR BELLY HERE, DOES IT HURT?
MM HMM.
ARE YOUR BREASTS SORE?
YES, TANTIE.
SO, TANTIE, IT'S PALU, ISN'T IT?
NO, ADJOUA...
...YOU'RE PREGNANT.
OHGOD!
TANTIE, THAT CAN'T BE. I'VE NEVER DONE IT!
ADJOUA, I'M NOT FAMILY. STOP LYING TO ME.
I'M DEAD! MY FATHER'S GOING TO KILL ME.
SO WHAT ARE YOU GOING TO DO?
I'LL GO SEE THE WOMAN AT THE MARKET. SHE'LL GET RID OF IT.
THAT'S CRAZY! YOU SHOULD GO TO THE HOSPITAL, GIRL.
BUT, TANTIE, I DON'T HAVE ANY MONEY.
YOU GIRLS, ALWAYS IN A HURRY TO GROW UP.

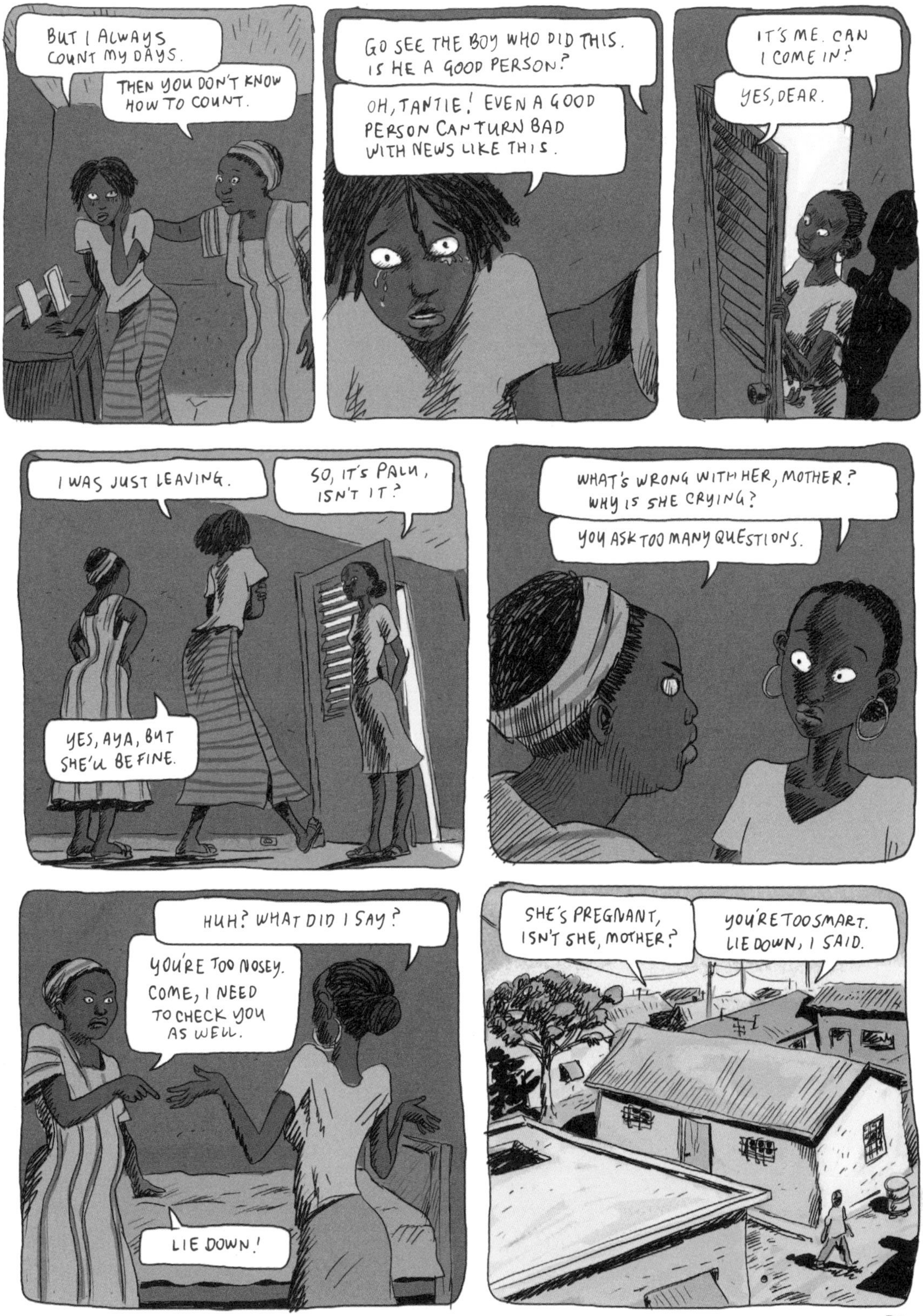

BUT I ALWAYS COUNT MY DAYS.
THEN YOU DON'T KNOW HOW TO COUNT.
GO SEE THE BOY WHO DID THIS. IS HE A GOOD PERSON?
OH, TANTIE! EVEN A GOOD PERSON CAN TURN BAD WITH NEWS LIKE THIS.
IT'S ME. CAN I COME IN?
YES, DEAR.
I WAS JUST LEAVING.
SO, IT'S PALU, ISN'T IT?
YES, AYA, BUT SHE'LL BE FINE.
WHAT'S WRONG WITH HER, MOTHER? WHY IS SHE CRYING?
YOU ASK TOO MANY QUESTIONS.
HUH? WHAT DID I SAY?
YOU'RE TOO NOSEY. COME, I NEED TO CHECK YOU AS WELL.
LIE DOWN!
SHE'S PREGNANT, ISN'T SHE, MOTHER?
YOU'RE TOO SMART. LIE DOWN, I SAID.

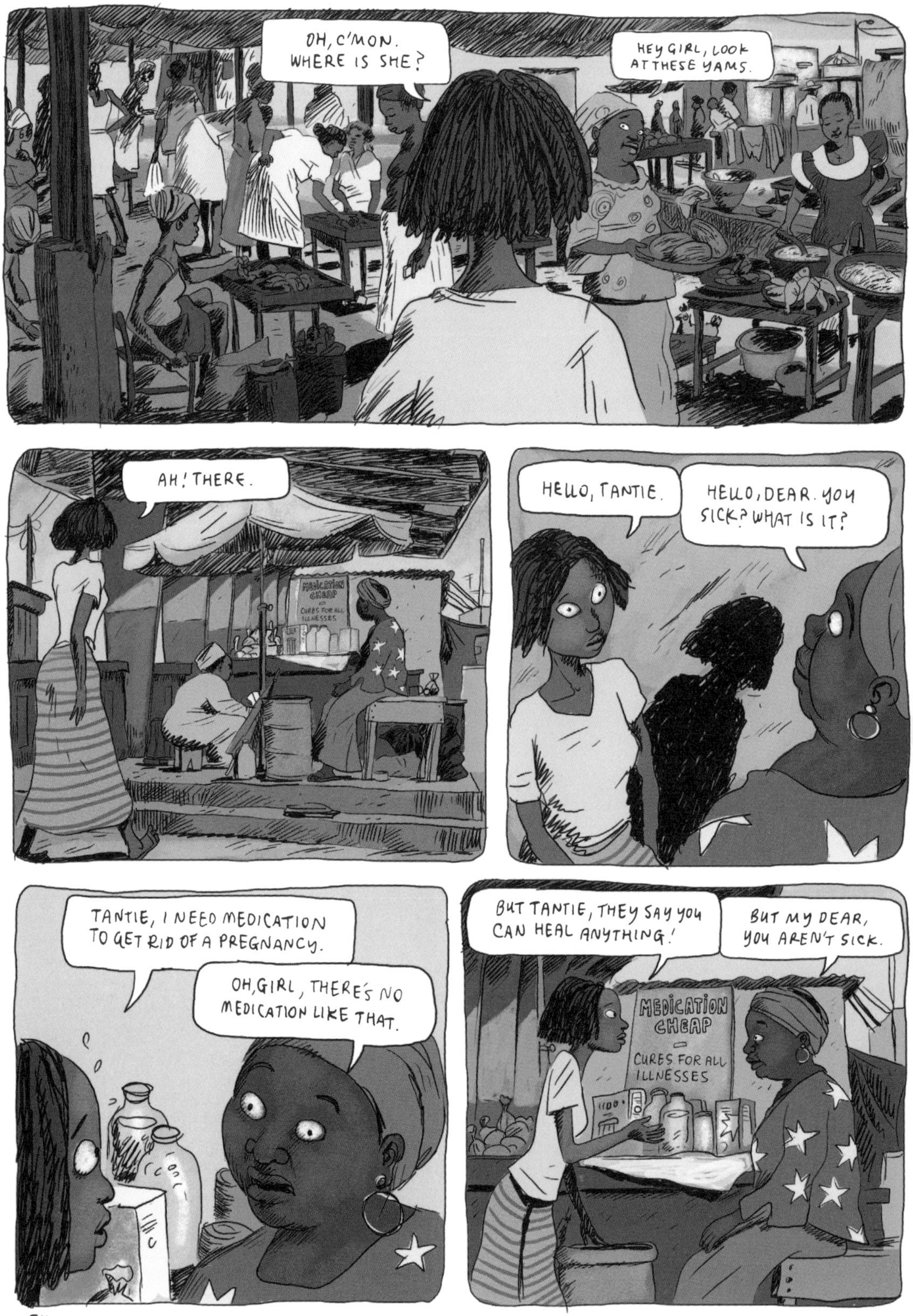
OH, C'MON. WHERE IS SHE?
HEY GIRL, LOOK AT THESE YAMS.
AH! THERE.
MEDICATION CHEAP — CURES FOR ALL ILLNESSES
HELLO, TANTIE.
HELLO, DEAR. YOU SICK? WHAT IS IT?
TANTIE, I NEED MEDICATION TO GET RID OF A PREGNANCY.
OH, GIRL, THERE'S NO MEDICATION LIKE THAT.
BUT TANTIE, THEY SAY YOU CAN HEAL ANYTHING!
BUT MY DEAR, YOU AREN'T SICK.
MEDICATION CHEAP — CURES FOR ALL ILLNESSES

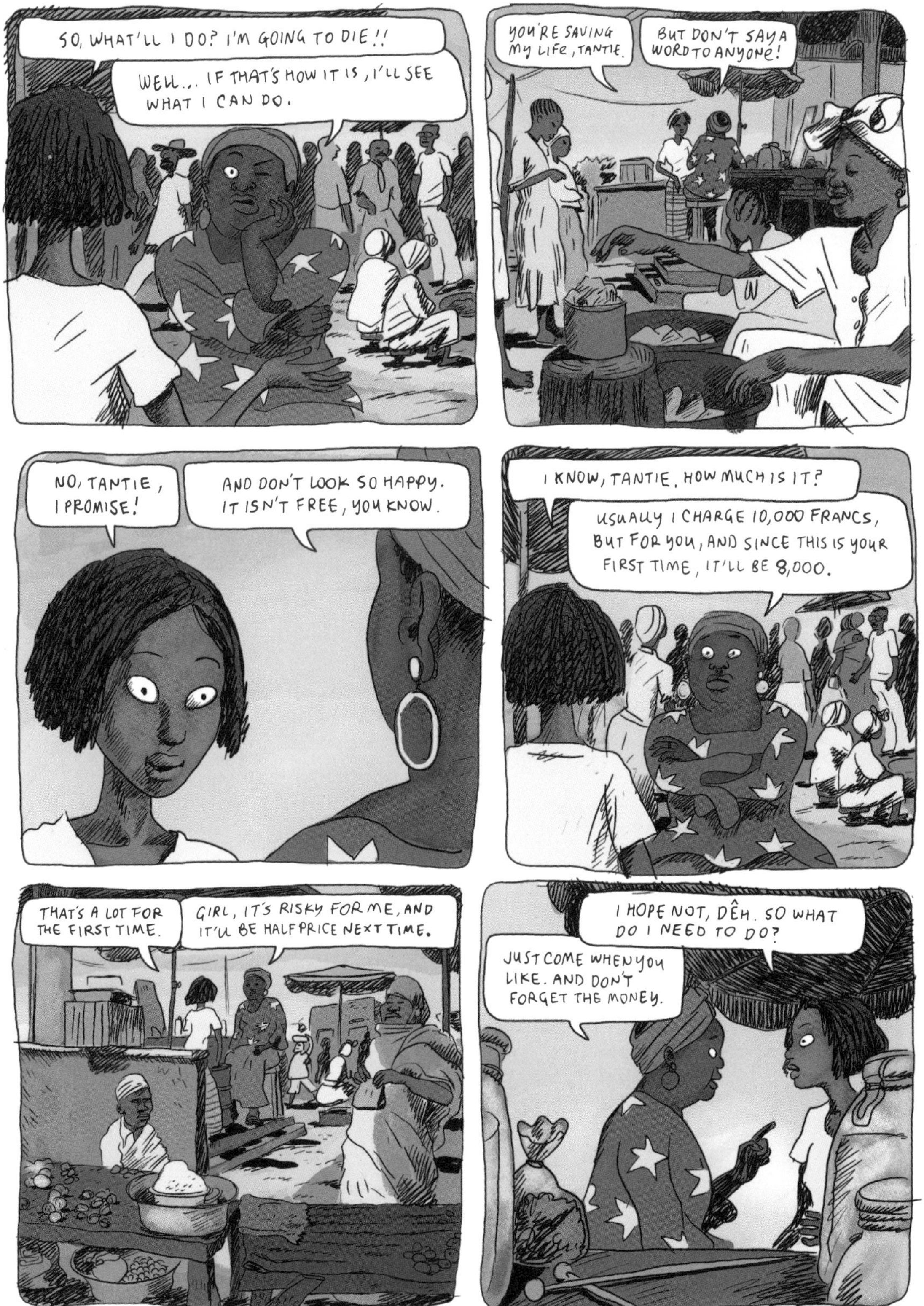

SO, WHAT'LL I DO? I'M GOING TO DIE!!
WELL... IF THAT'S HOW IT IS, I'LL SEE WHAT I CAN DO.
YOU'RE SAVING MY LIFE, TANTIE.
BUT DON'T SAY A WORD TO ANYONE!
NO, TANTIE, I PROMISE!
AND DON'T LOOK SO HAPPY. IT ISN'T FREE, YOU KNOW.
I KNOW, TANTIE. HOW MUCH IS IT?
USUALLY I CHARGE 10,000 FRANCS, BUT FOR YOU, AND SINCE THIS IS YOUR FIRST TIME, IT'LL BE 8,000.
THAT'S A LOT FOR THE FIRST TIME.
GIRL, IT'S RISKY FOR ME, AND IT'LL BE HALF PRICE NEXT TIME.
I HOPE NOT, DÊH. SO WHAT DO I NEED TO DO?
JUST COME WHEN YOU LIKE. AND DON'T FORGET THE MONEY.

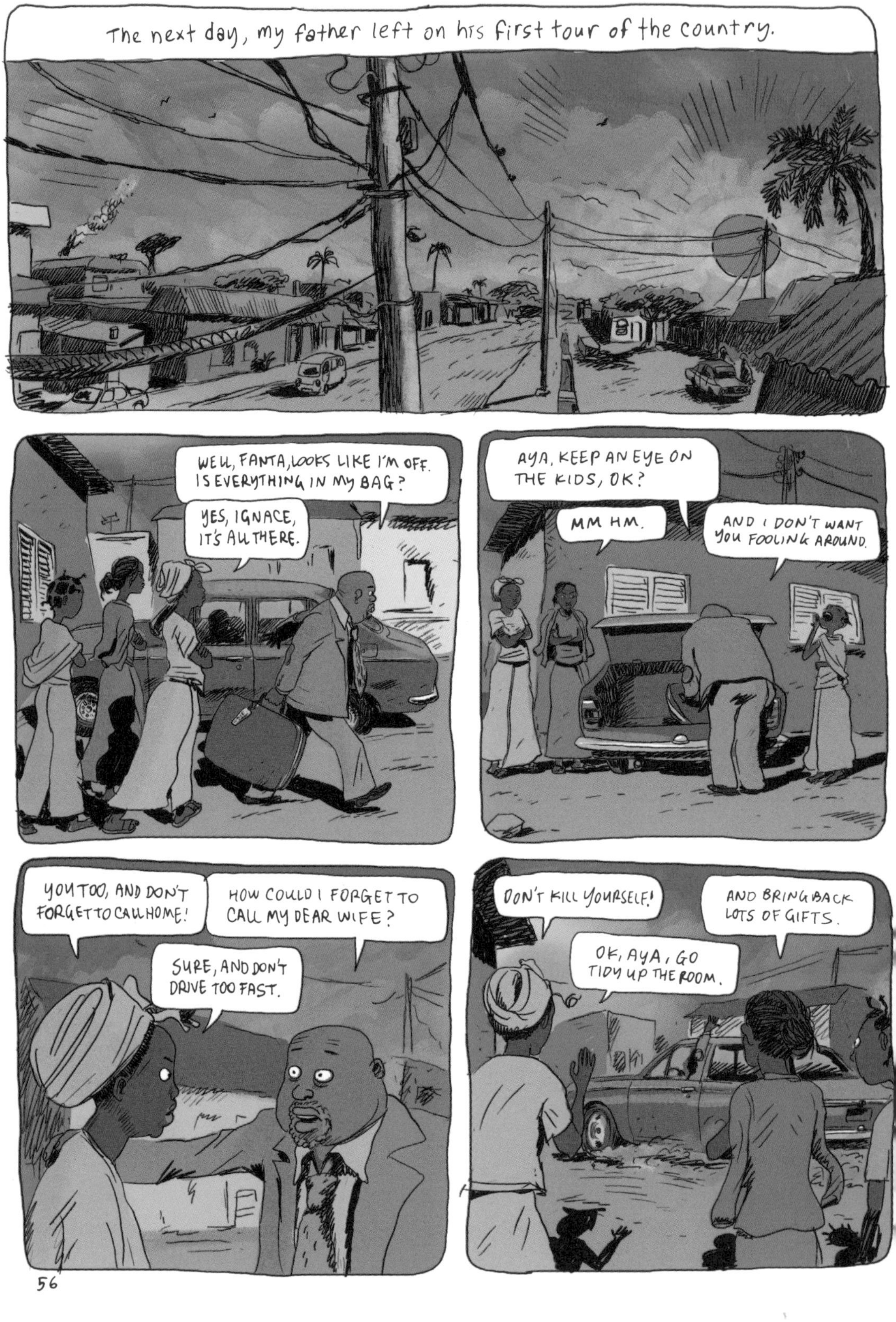
The next day, my father left on his first tour of the country.
WELL, FANTA, LOOKS LIKE I'M OFF. IS EVERYTHING IN MY BAG?
YES, IGNACE, IT'S ALL THERE.
AYA, KEEP AN EYE ON THE KIDS, OK?
MM HM.
AND I DON'T WANT YOU FOOLING AROUND.
YOU TOO, AND DON'T FORGET TO CALL HOME!
HOW COULD I FORGET TO CALL MY DEAR WIFE?
SURE, AND DON'T DRIVE TOO FAST.
DON'T KILL YOURSELF!
AND BRING BACK LOTS OF GIFTS.
OK, AYA, GO TIDY UP THE ROOM.

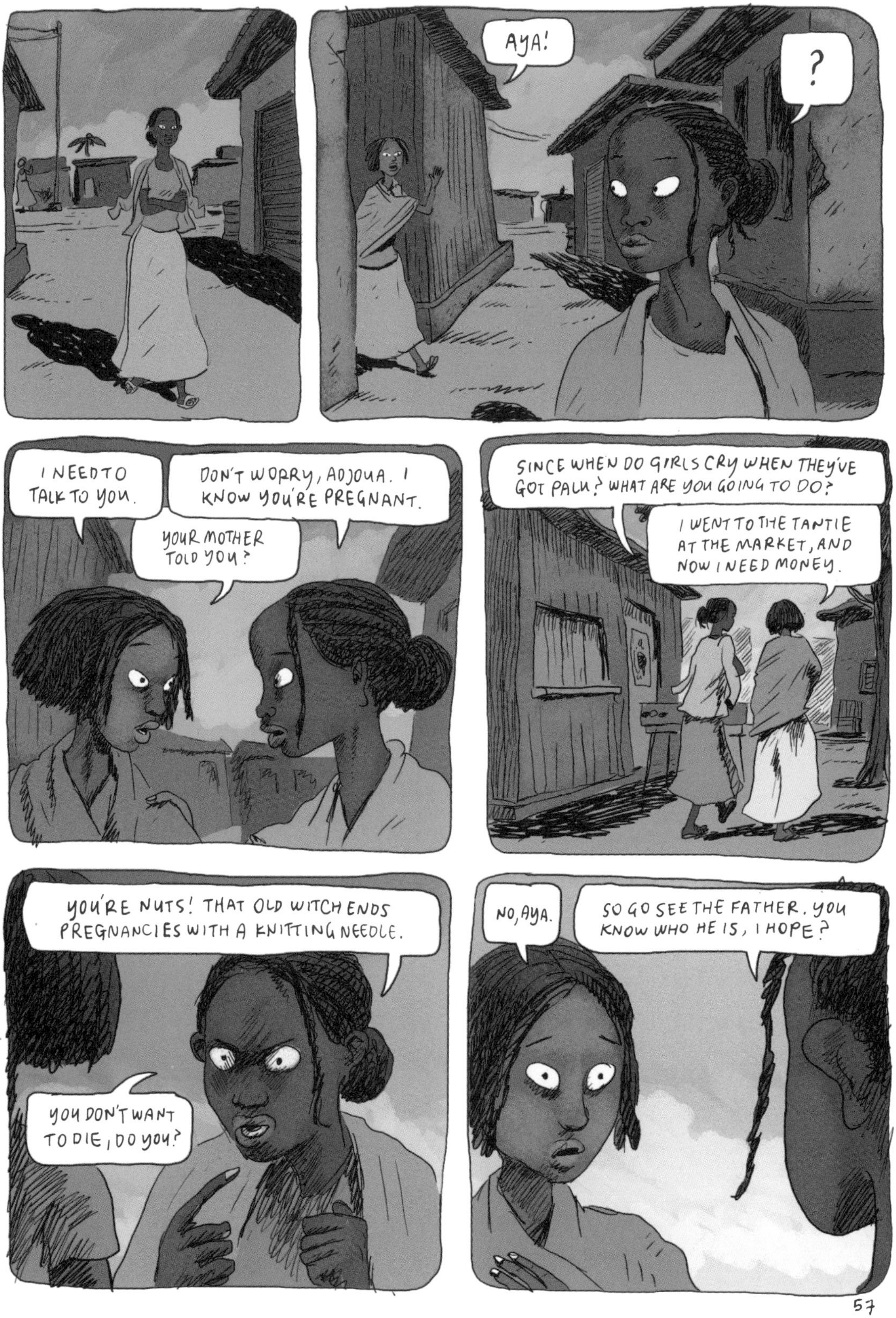
AYA!
?
I NEED TO TALK TO YOU.
DON'T WORRY, ADJOUA. I KNOW YOU'RE PREGNANT.
YOUR MOTHER TOLD YOU?
SINCE WHEN DO GIRLS CRY WHEN THEY'VE GOT PAIN? WHAT ARE YOU GOING TO DO?
I WENT TO THE TANTIE AT THE MARKET, AND NOW I NEED MONEY.
YOU'RE NUTS! THAT OLD WITCH ENDS PREGNANCIES WITH A KNITTING NEEDLE.
YOU DON'T WANT TO DIE, DO YOU?
NO, AYA.
SO GO SEE THE FATHER. YOU KNOW WHO HE IS, I HOPE?

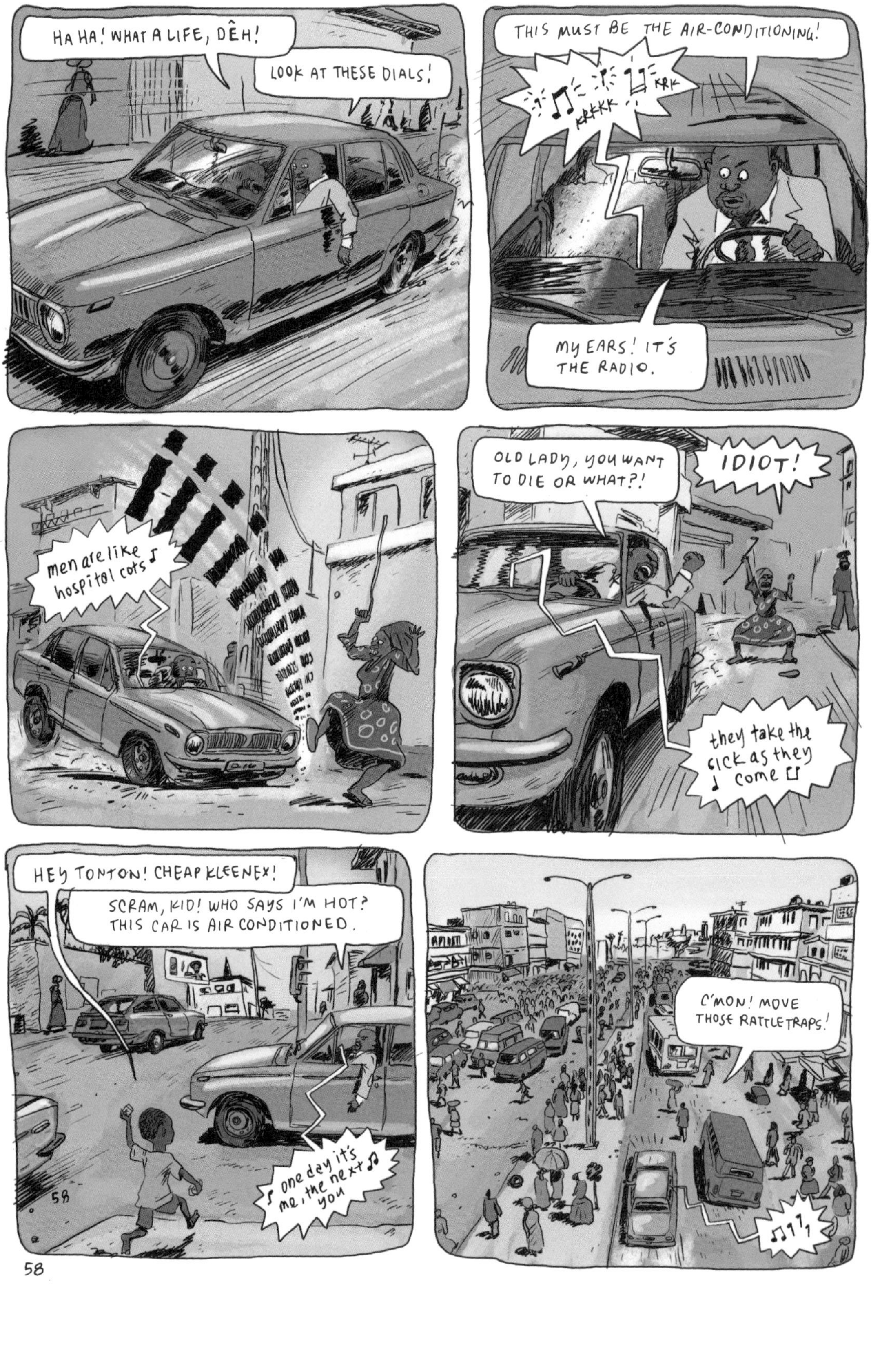
HA HA! WHAT A LIFE, DÊH!
LOOK AT THESE DIALS!
THIS MUST BE THE AIR-CONDITIONING!
KRKKK
KRK
MY EARS! IT'S THE RADIO.
men are like hospitol cots
OLD LADY, YOU WANT TO DIE OR WHAT?!
IDIOT!
they take the sick as they come
HEY TONTON! CHEAP KLEENEX!
SCRAM, KID! WHO SAYS I'M HOT? THIS CAR IS AIR CONDITIONED.
one day it's me, the next you
C'MON! MOVE THOSE RATTLETRAPS!

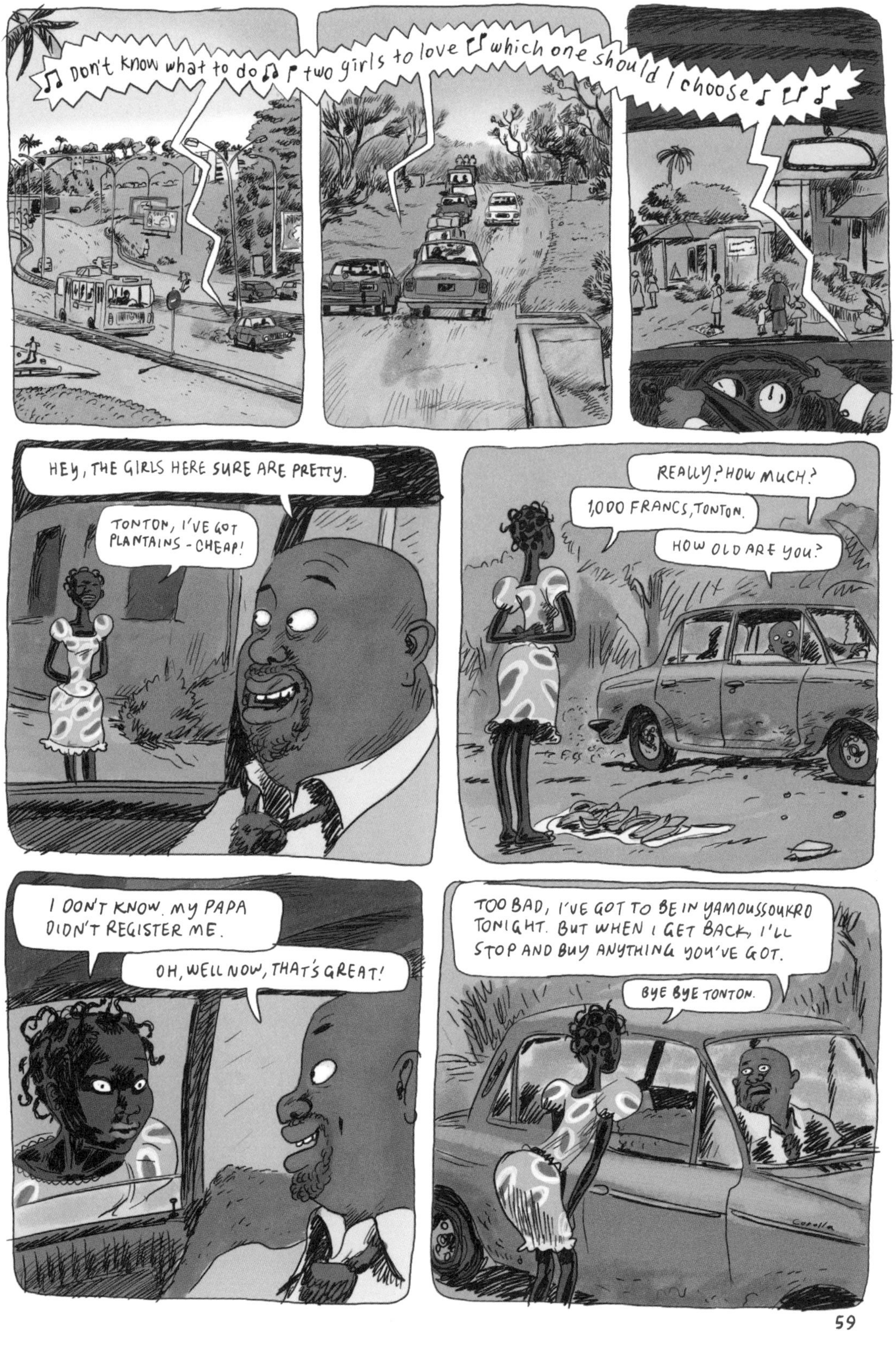
♫ Don't know what to do ♫ ♪ two girls to love ♫ which one should I choose ♪ ♫ ♪
HEY, THE GIRLS HERE SURE ARE PRETTY.
TONTON, I'VE GOT PLANTAINS - CHEAP!
REALLY? HOW MUCH?
1,000 FRANCS, TONTON.
HOW OLD ARE YOU?
I DON'T KNOW. MY PAPA DIDN'T REGISTER ME.
OH, WELL NOW, THAT'S GREAT!
TOO BAD, I'VE GOT TO BE IN YAMOUSSOUKRO TONIGHT. BUT WHEN I GET BACK, I'LL STOP AND BUY ANYTHING YOU'VE GOT.
BYE BYE TONTON.

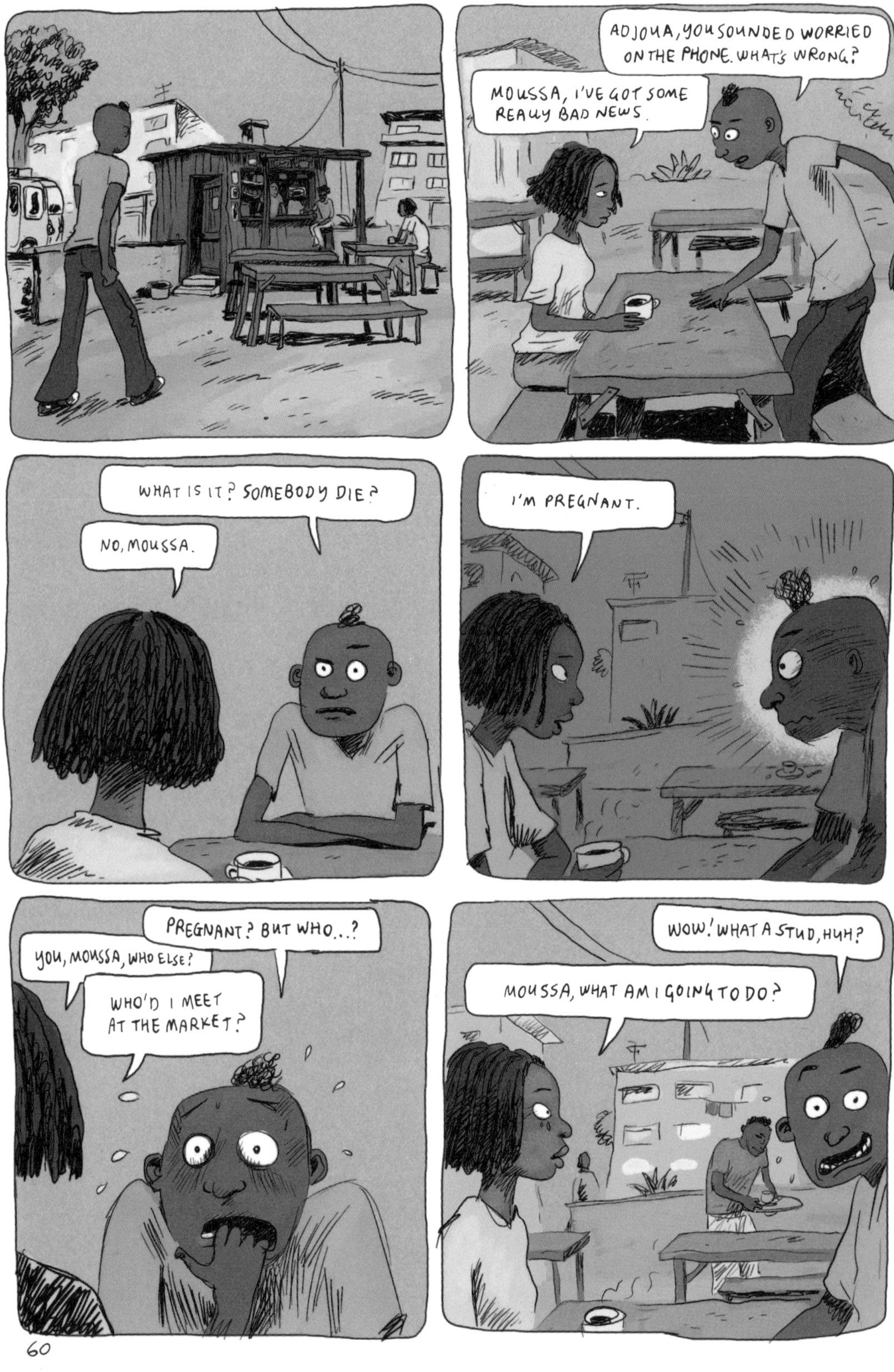
ADJOUA, YOU SOUNDED WORRIED ON THE PHONE. WHAT'S WRONG?
MOUSSA, I'VE GOT SOME REALLY BAD NEWS.
WHAT IS IT? SOMEBODY DIE?
NO, MOUSSA.
I'M PREGNANT.
PREGNANT? BUT WHO...?
YOU, MOUSSA, WHO ELSE?
WHO'D I MEET AT THE MARKET?
WOW! WHAT A STUD, HUH?
MOUSSA, WHAT AM I GOING TO DO?

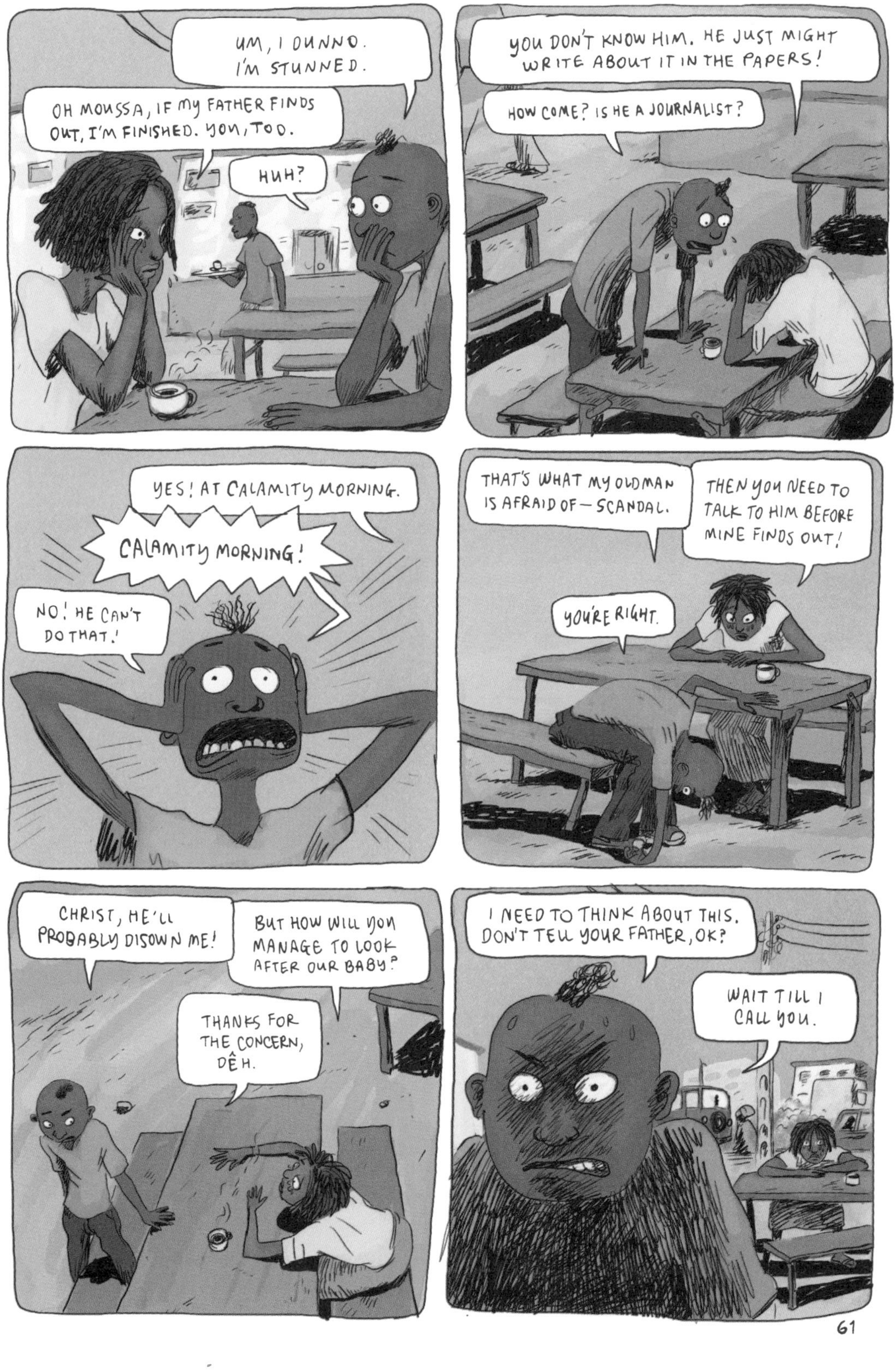
UM, I DUNNO. I'M STUNNED.
OH MOUSSA, IF MY FATHER FINDS OUT, I'M FINISHED. YOU, TOO.
HUH?
YOU DON'T KNOW HIM. HE JUST MIGHT WRITE ABOUT IT IN THE PAPERS!
HOW COME? IS HE A JOURNALIST?
YES! AT CALAMITY MORNING.
CALAMITY MORNING!
NO! HE CAN'T DO THAT!
THAT'S WHAT MY OLDMAN IS AFRAID OF—SCANDAL.
THEN YOU NEED TO TALK TO HIM BEFORE MINE FINDS OUT!
YOU'RE RIGHT.
CHRIST, HE'LL PROBABLY DISOWN ME!
BUT HOW WILL YOU MANAGE TO LOOK AFTER OUR BABY?
THANKS FOR THE CONCERN, DÊH.
I NEED TO THINK ABOUT THIS. DON'T TELL YOUR FATHER, OK?
WAIT TILL I CALL YOU.

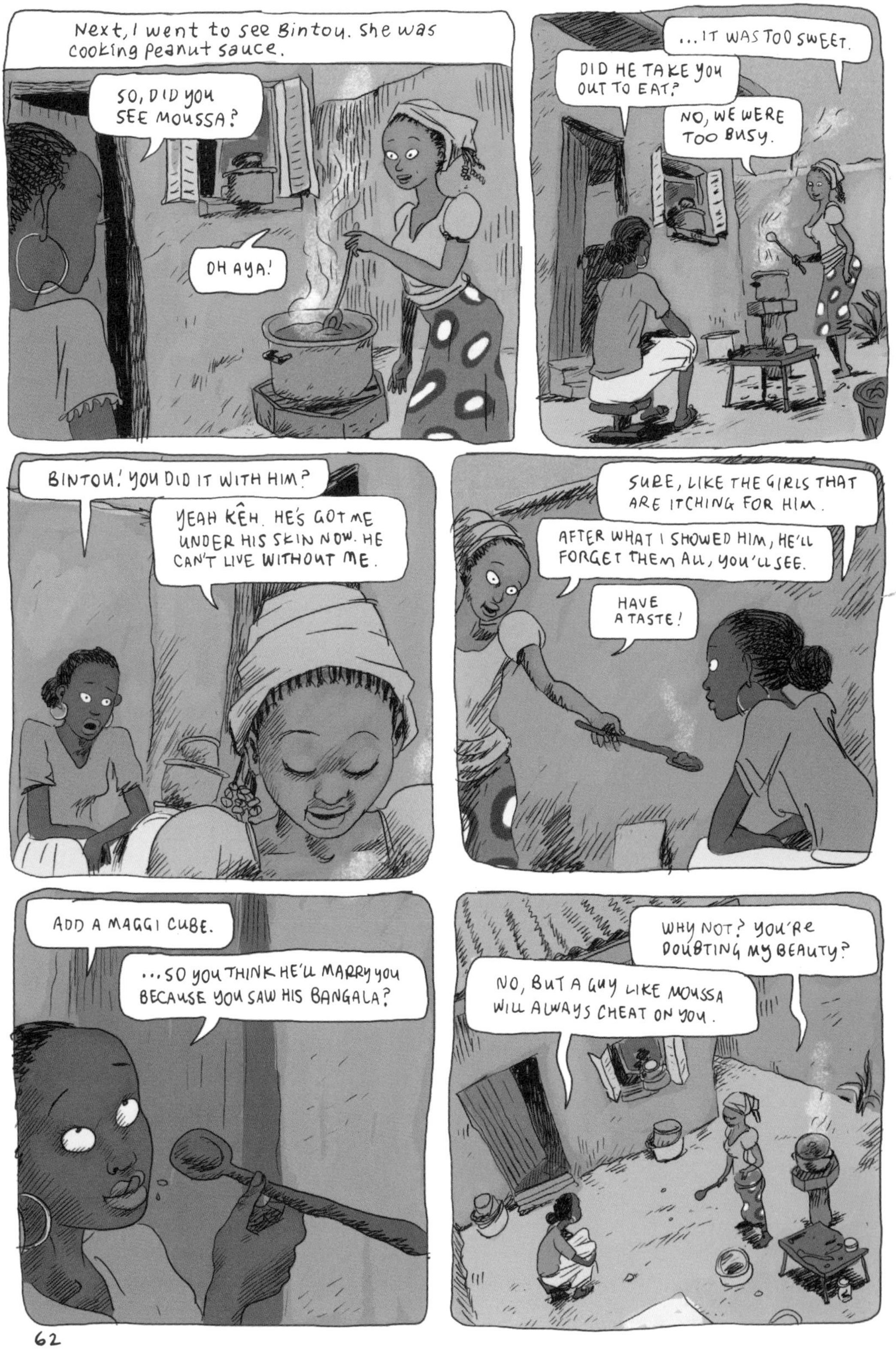
Next, I went to see Bintou. She was cooking peanut sauce.
SO, DID YOU SEE MOUSSA?
OH AYA!
...IT WAS TOO SWEET.
DID HE TAKE YOU OUT TO EAT?
NO, WE WERE TOO BUSY.
BINTOU! YOU DID IT WITH HIM?
YEAH KÊH. HE'S GOT ME UNDER HIS SKIN NOW. HE CAN'T LIVE WITHOUT ME.
SURE, LIKE THE GIRLS THAT ARE ITCHING FOR HIM.
AFTER WHAT I SHOWED HIM, HE'LL FORGET THEM ALL, YOU'LL SEE.
HAVE A TASTE!
ADD A MAGGI CUBE.
...SO YOU THINK HE'LL MARRY YOU BECAUSE YOU SAW HIS BANGALA?
WHY NOT? YOU'RE DOUBTING MY BEAUTY?
NO, BUT A GUY LIKE MOUSSA WILL ALWAYS CHEAT ON YOU.

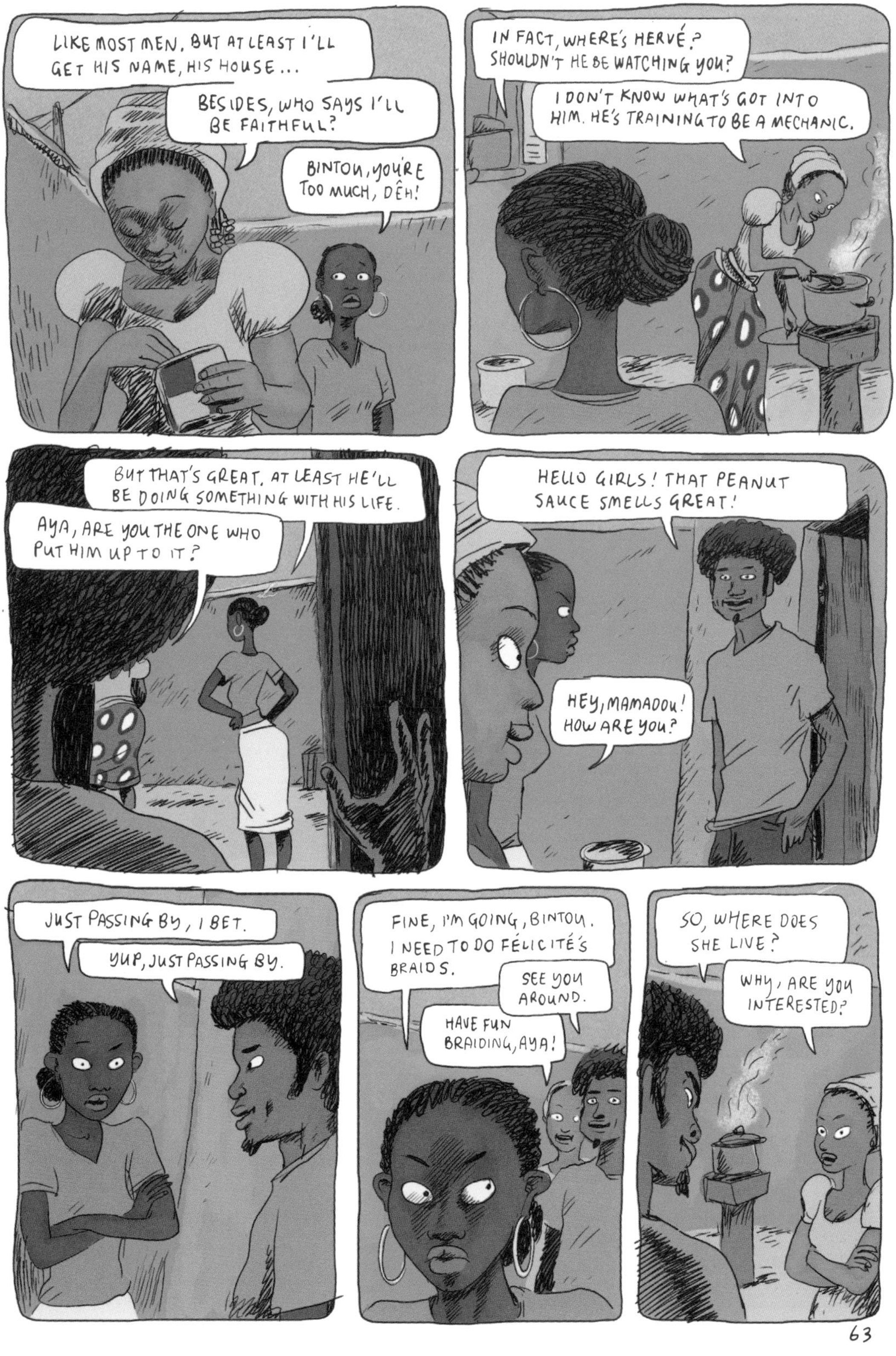
LIKE MOST MEN. BUT AT LEAST I'LL GET HIS NAME, HIS HOUSE...
BESIDES, WHO SAYS I'LL BE FAITHFUL?
BINTOU, YOU'RE TOO MUCH, DÊH!
IN FACT, WHERE'S HERVÉ? SHOULDN'T HE BE WATCHING YOU?
I DON'T KNOW WHAT'S GOT INTO HIM. HE'S TRAINING TO BE A MECHANIC.
BUT THAT'S GREAT. AT LEAST HE'LL BE DOING SOMETHING WITH HIS LIFE.
AYA, ARE YOU THE ONE WHO PUT HIM UP TO IT?
HELLO GIRLS! THAT PEANUT SAUCE SMELLS GREAT!
HEY, MAMADOU! HOW ARE YOU?
JUST PASSING BY, I BET.
YUP, JUST PASSING BY.
FINE, I'M GOING, BINTOU. I NEED TO DO FÉLICITÉ'S BRAIDS.
SEE YOU AROUND.
HAVE FUN BRAIDING, AYA!
SO, WHERE DOES SHE LIVE?
WHY, ARE YOU INTERESTED?

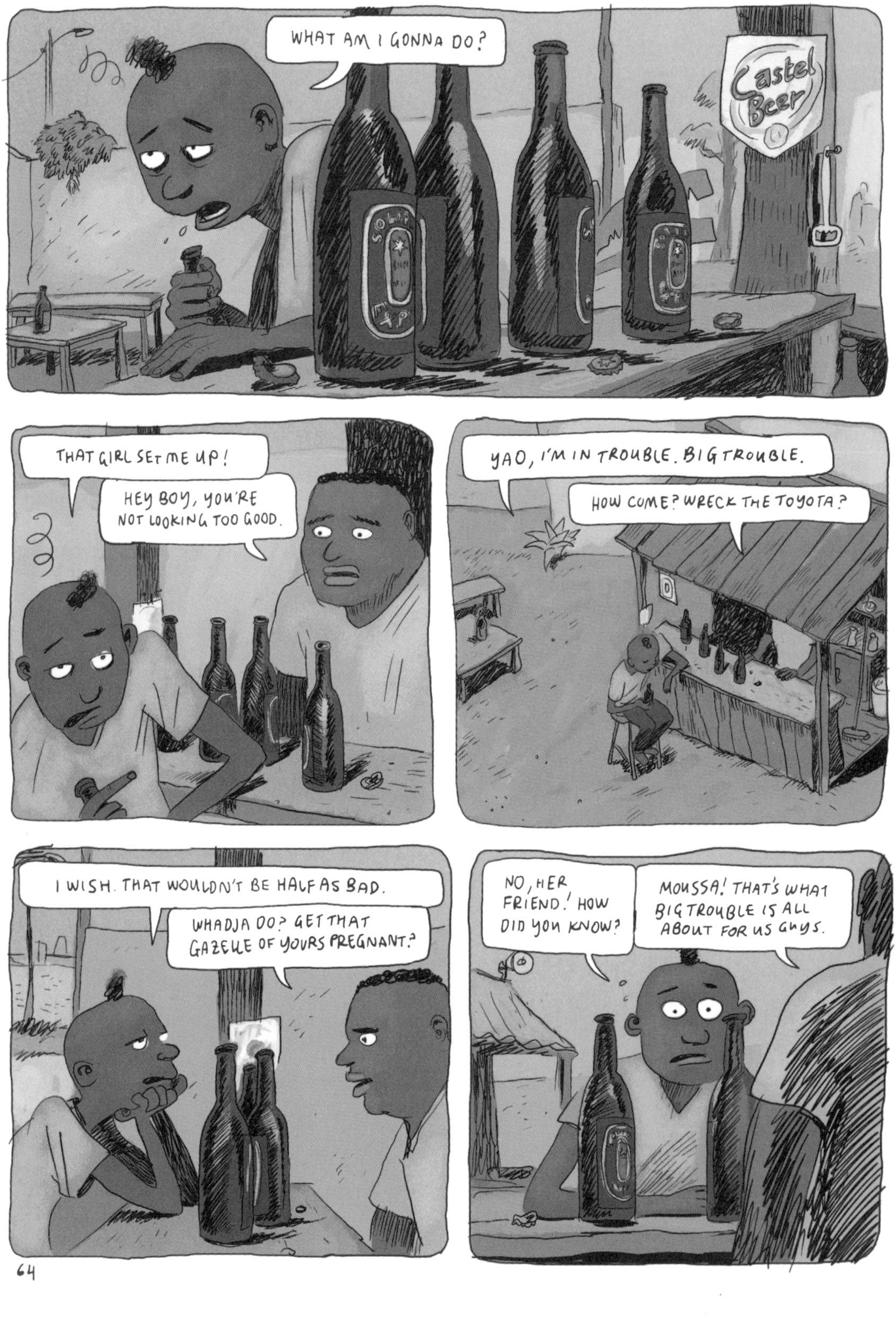
WHAT AM I GONNA DO?
Castel Beer
THAT GIRL SET ME UP!
HEY BOY, YOU'RE NOT LOOKING TOO GOOD.
YAO, I'M IN TROUBLE. BIG TROUBLE.
HOW COME? WRECK THE TOYOTA?
I WISH. THAT WOULDN'T BE HALF AS BAD.
WHADJA DO? GET THAT GAZELLE OF YOURS PREGNANT?
NO, HER FRIEND! HOW DID YOU KNOW?
MOUSSA! THAT'S WHAT BIG TROUBLE IS ALL ABOUT FOR US GUYS.

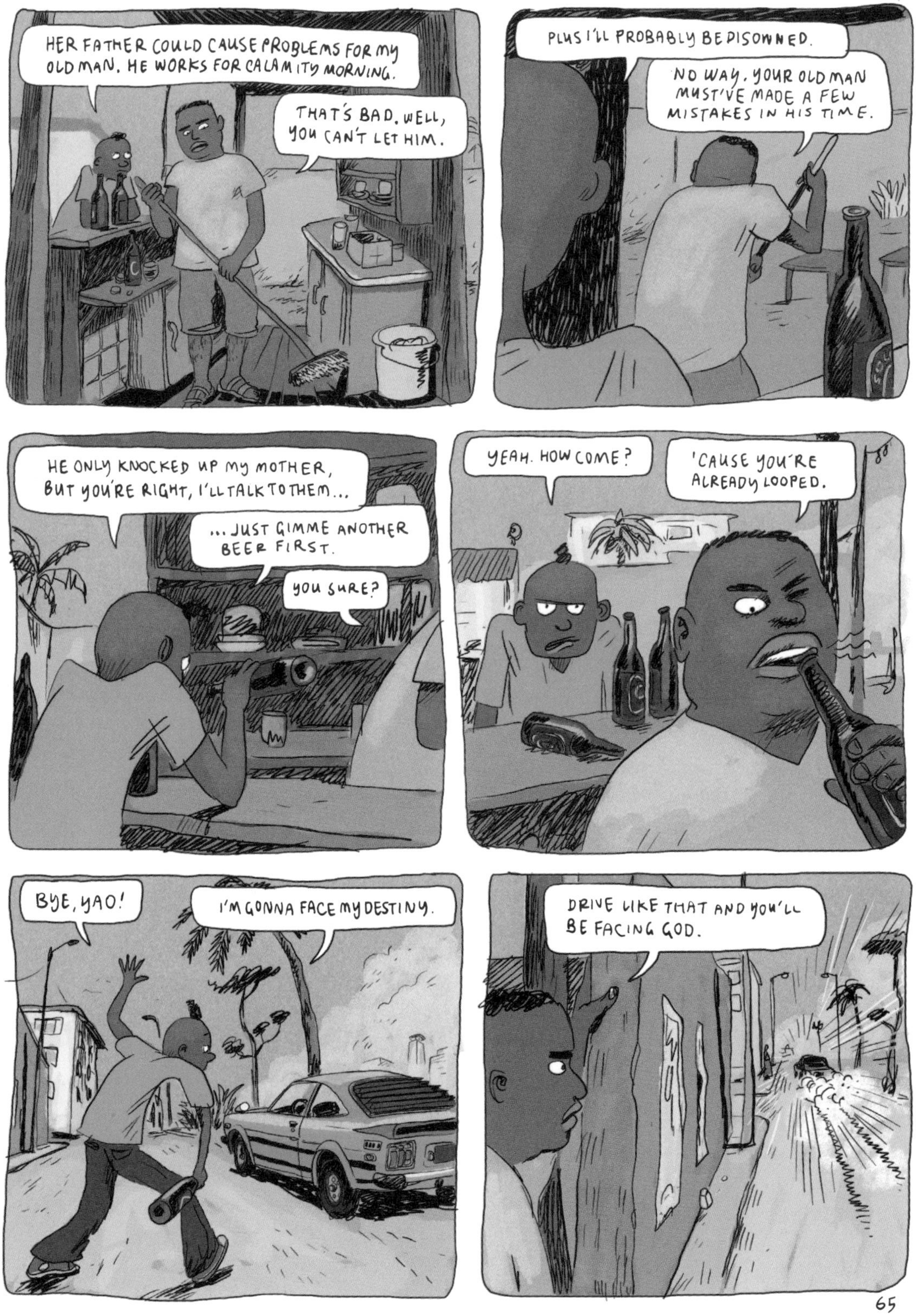
HER FATHER COULD CAUSE PROBLEMS FOR MY OLD MAN. HE WORKS FOR CALAMITY MORNING.
THAT'S BAD. WELL, YOU CAN'T LET HIM.
PLUS I'LL PROBABLY BE DISOWNED.
NO WAY. YOUR OLD MAN MUST'VE MADE A FEW MISTAKES IN HIS TIME.
HE ONLY KNOCKED UP MY MOTHER, BUT YOU'RE RIGHT, I'LL TALK TO THEM...
...JUST GIMME ANOTHER BEER FIRST.
YOU SURE?
YEAH. HOW COME?
'CAUSE YOU'RE ALREADY LOOPED.
BYE, YAO!
I'M GONNA FACE MY DESTINY.
DRIVE LIKE THAT AND YOU'LL BE FACING GOD.

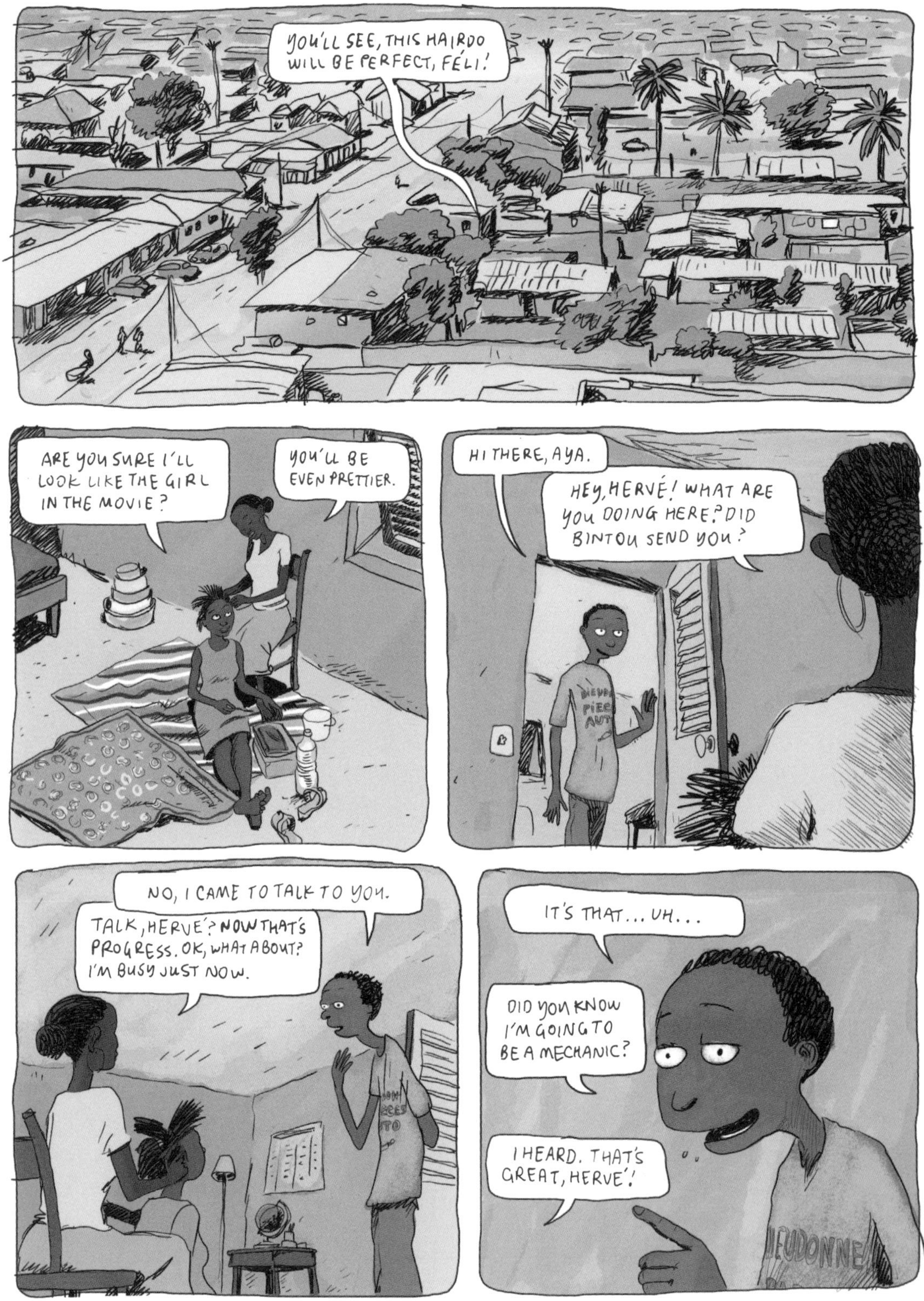
YOU'LL SEE, THIS HAIRDO WILL BE PERFECT, FÉLI!
ARE YOU SURE I'LL LOOK LIKE THE GIRL IN THE MOVIE?
YOU'LL BE EVEN PRETTIER.
HI THERE, AYA.
HEY, HERVÉ! WHAT ARE YOU DOING HERE? DID BINTOU SEND YOU?
NO, I CAME TO TALK TO YOU.
TALK, HERVÉ? NOW THAT'S PROGRESS. OK, WHAT ABOUT? I'M BUSY JUST NOW.
IT'S THAT... UH...
DID YOU KNOW I'M GOING TO BE A MECHANIC?
I HEARD. THAT'S GREAT, HERVÉ!

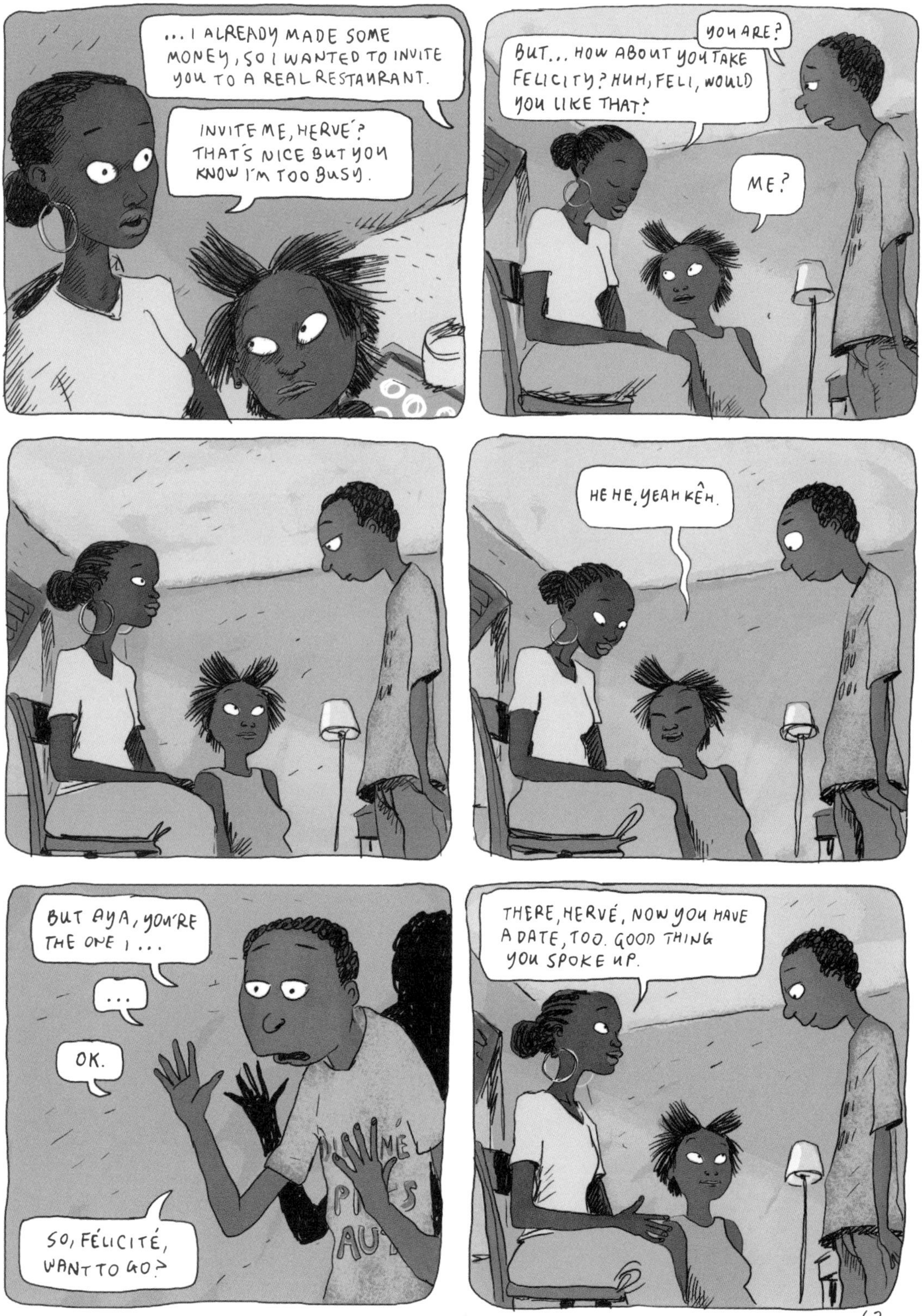
...I ALREADY MADE SOME MONEY, SO I WANTED TO INVITE YOU TO A REAL RESTAURANT.
INVITE ME, HERVÉ? THAT'S NICE BUT YOU KNOW I'M TOO BUSY.
BUT... HOW ABOUT YOU TAKE FELICITY? HUH, FELI, WOULD YOU LIKE THAT?
YOU ARE?
ME?
HE HE, YEAH KÊH.
BUT AYA, YOU'RE THE ONE I...
...
OK.
SO, FÉLICITÉ, WANT TO GO?
THERE, HERVÉ, NOW YOU HAVE A DATE, TOO. GOOD THING YOU SPOKE UP.

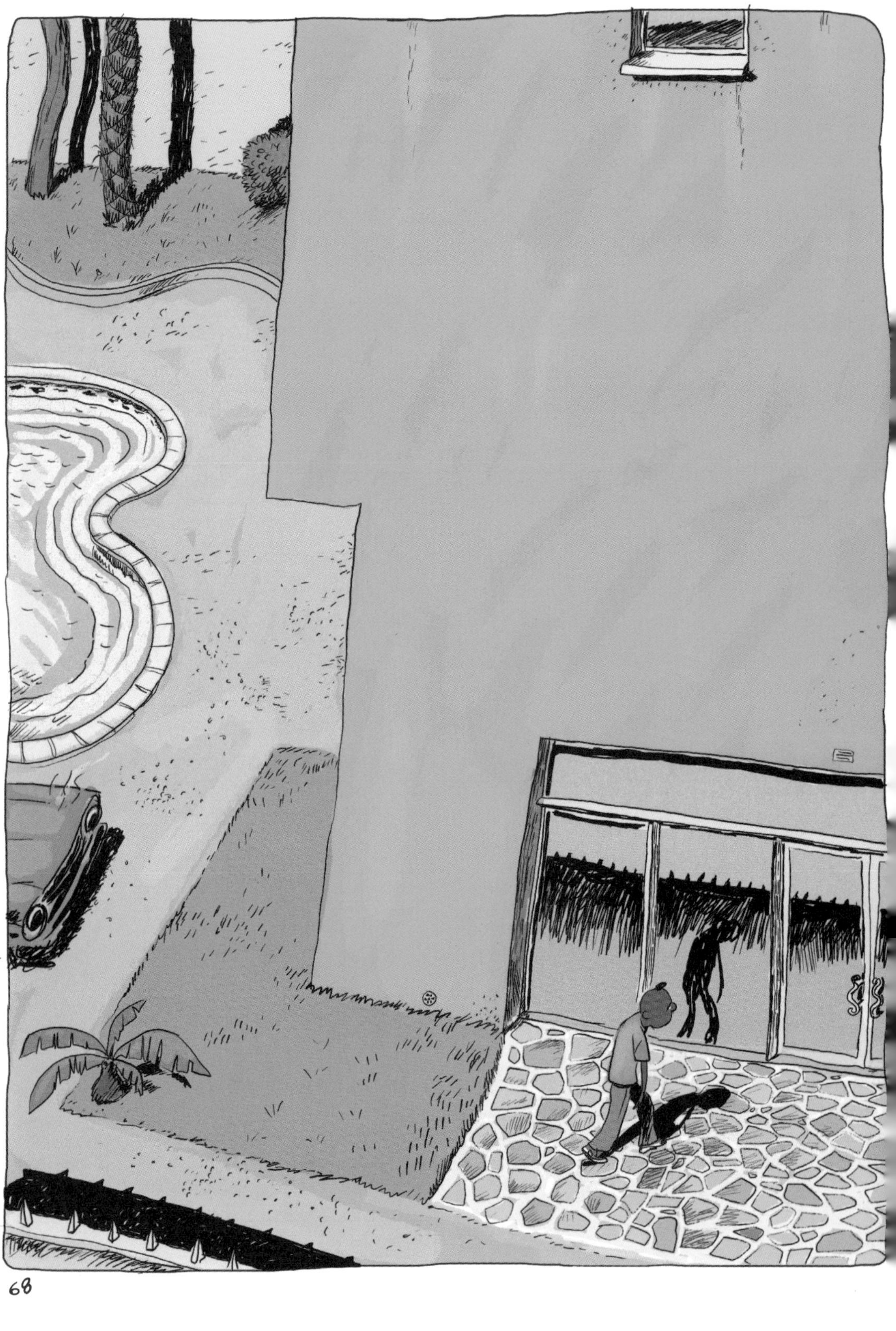

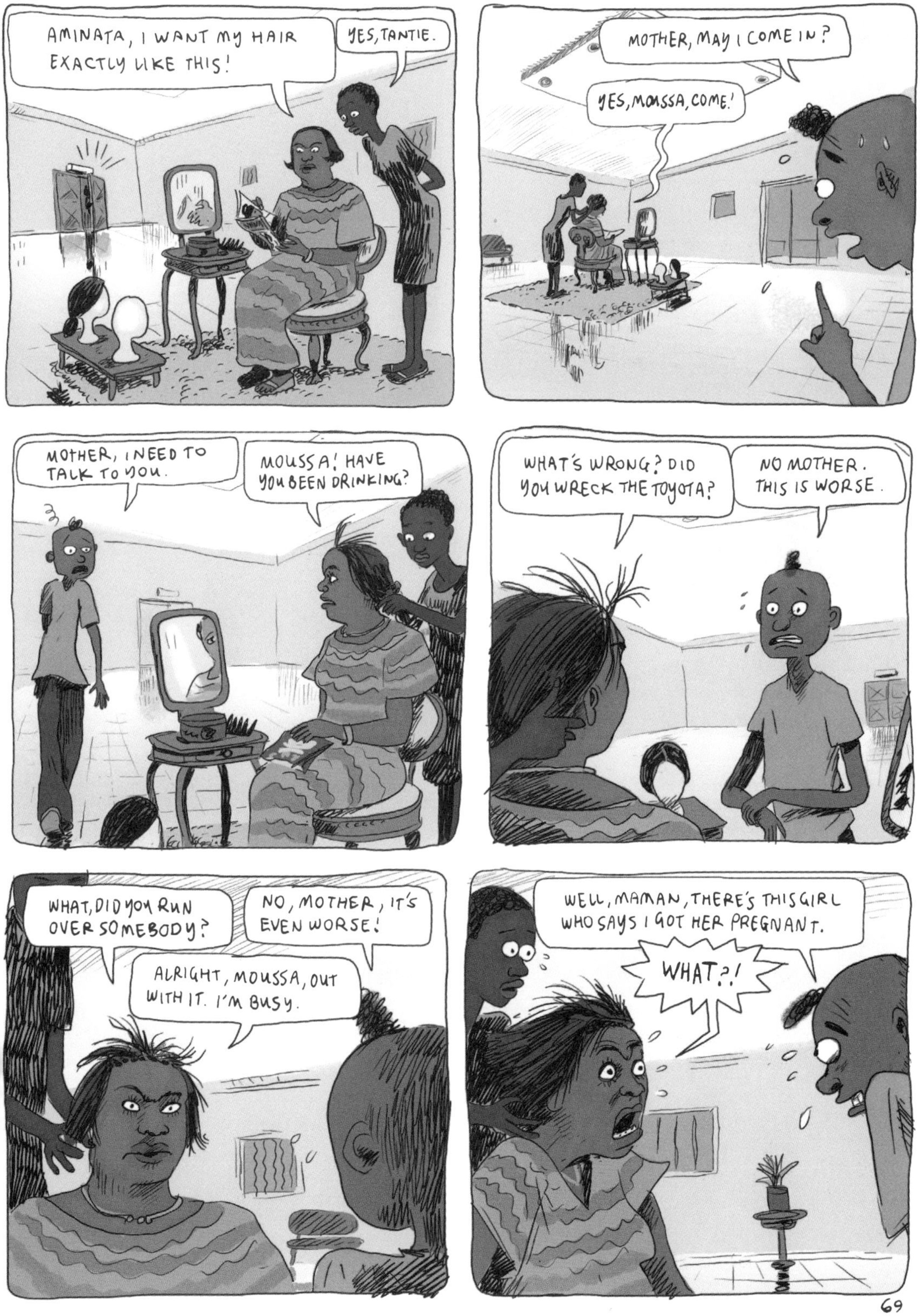
AMINATA, I WANT MY HAIR EXACTLY LIKE THIS!
YES, TANTIE.
MOTHER, MAY I COME IN?
YES, MOUSSA, COME!
MOTHER, I NEED TO TALK TO YOU.
MOUSSA! HAVE YOU BEEN DRINKING?
WHAT'S WRONG? DID YOU WRECK THE TOYOTA?
NO MOTHER. THIS IS WORSE.
WHAT, DID YOU RUN OVER SOMEBODY?
NO, MOTHER, IT'S EVEN WORSE!
ALRIGHT, MOUSSA, OUT WITH IT. I'M BUSY.
WELL, MAMAN, THERE'S THIS GIRL WHO SAYS I GOT HER PREGNANT.
WHAT?!

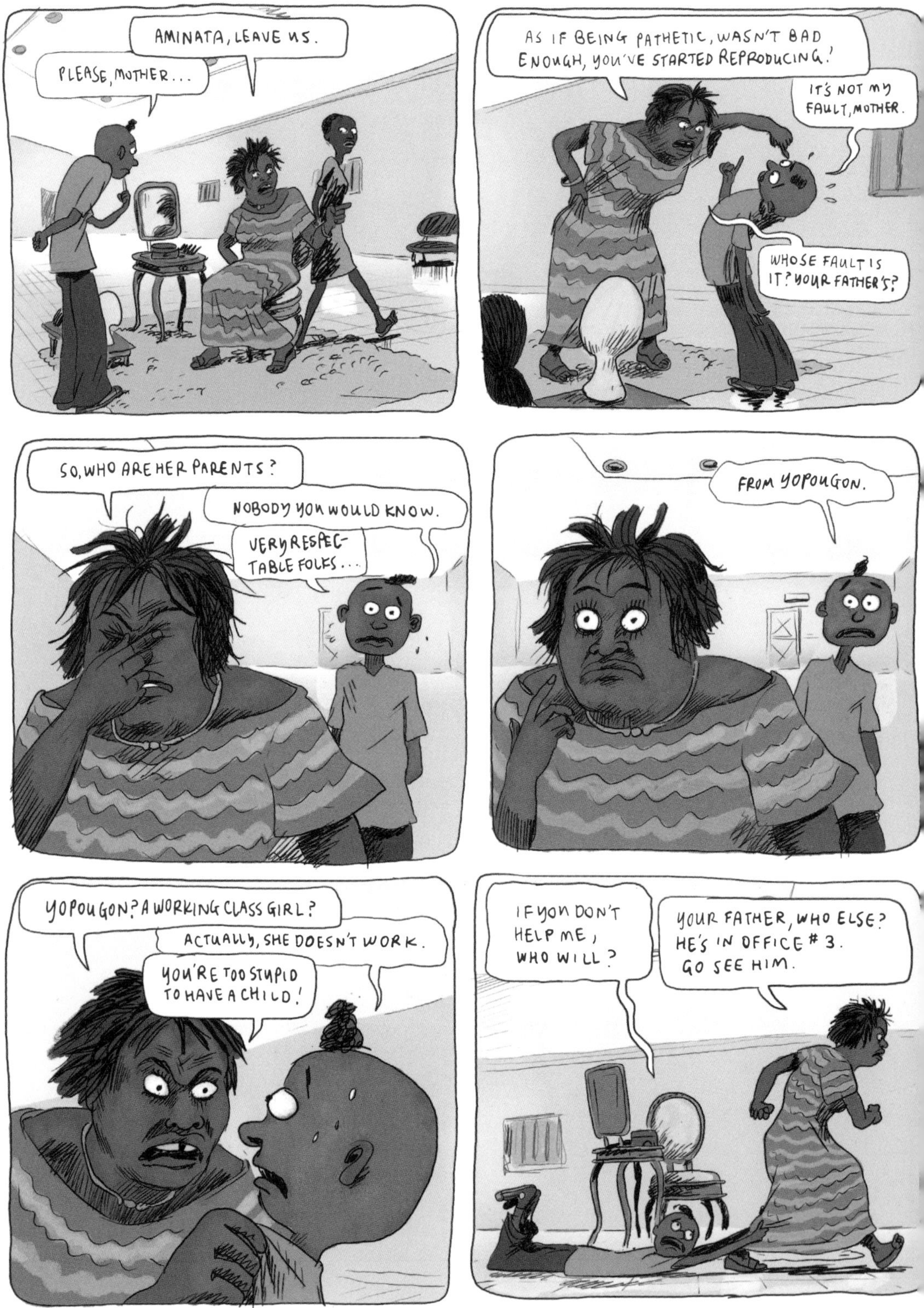
PLEASE, MOTHER...
AMINATA, LEAVE US.
AS IF BEING PATHETIC, WASN'T BAD ENOUGH, YOU'VE STARTED REPRODUCING!
IT'S NOT MY FAULT, MOTHER.
WHOSE FAULT IS IT? YOUR FATHER'S?
SO, WHO ARE HER PARENTS?
NOBODY YOU WOULD KNOW.
VERY RESPECTABLE FOLKS...
FROM YOPOUGON.
YOPOUGON? A WORKING CLASS GIRL?
ACTUALLY, SHE DOESN'T WORK.
YOU'RE TOO STUPID TO HAVE A CHILD!
IF YOU DON'T HELP ME, WHO WILL?
YOUR FATHER, WHO ELSE? HE'S IN OFFICE # 3. GO SEE HIM.

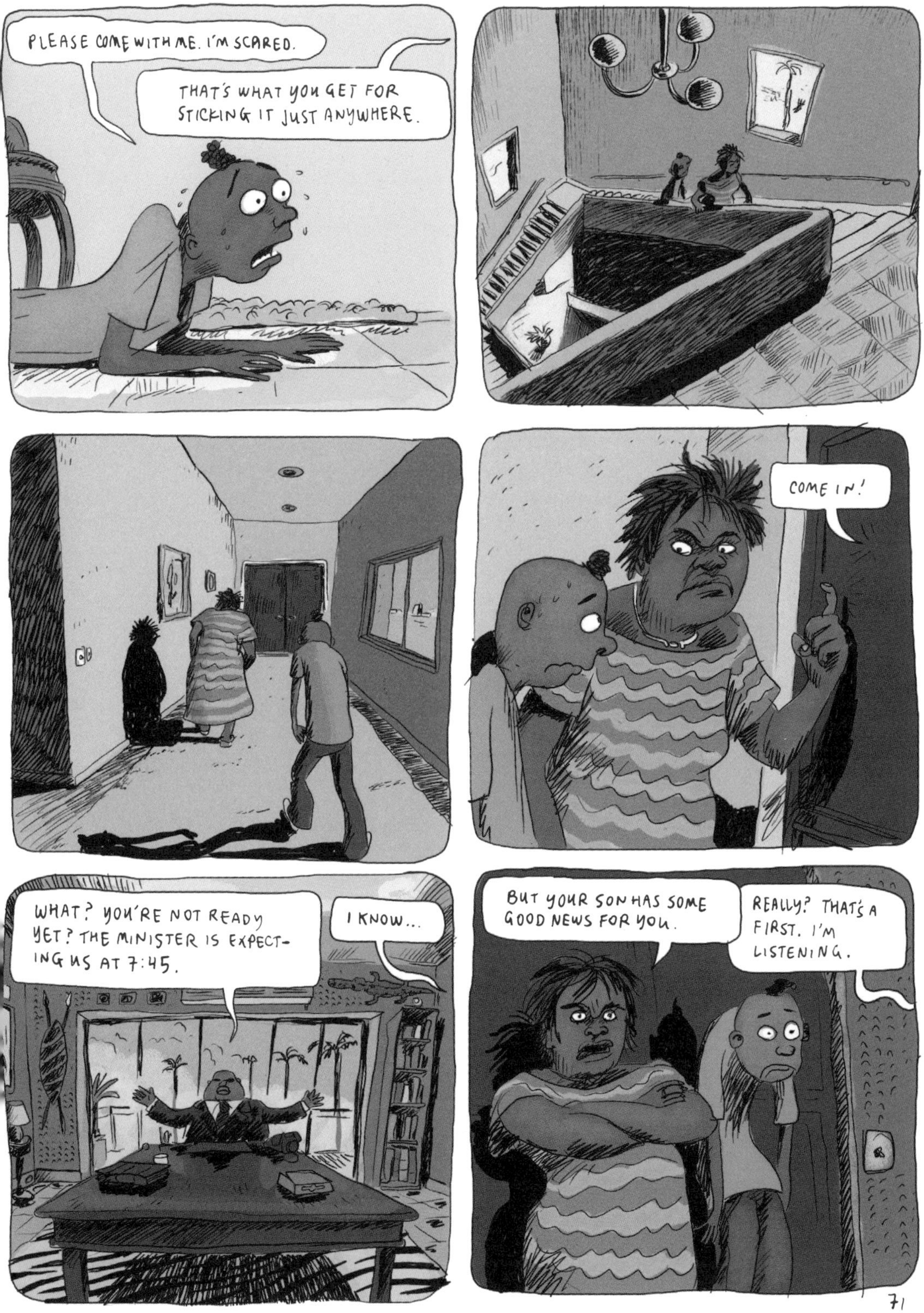
PLEASE COME WITH ME. I'M SCARED.
THAT'S WHAT YOU GET FOR STICKING IT JUST ANYWHERE.
COME IN!
WHAT? YOU'RE NOT READY YET? THE MINISTER IS EXPECTING US AT 7:45.
I KNOW...
BUT YOUR SON HAS SOME GOOD NEWS FOR YOU.
REALLY? THAT'S A FIRST. I'M LISTENING.

UH, PAPA, IT'S REALLY NOT THAT GREAT...
...IT'S THAT...
OK ENOUGH. YOUR WORTHLESS SON KNOCKED UP A GIRL!
WHAT?!
HOW DID HE DO THAT?
I WONDER. WHAT DO YOU THINK?
MOTHER, PAPA, I CAN EXPLAIN IT ALL.
SHUT UP, NOBODY WANTS TO KNOW.
IT GETS WORSE.
WHAT IS IT?
THEY'RE PEASANTS. FROM YOPOUGON.
no, they...
...HER FATHER IS A JOURNALIST AT CALAMITY MORNING.

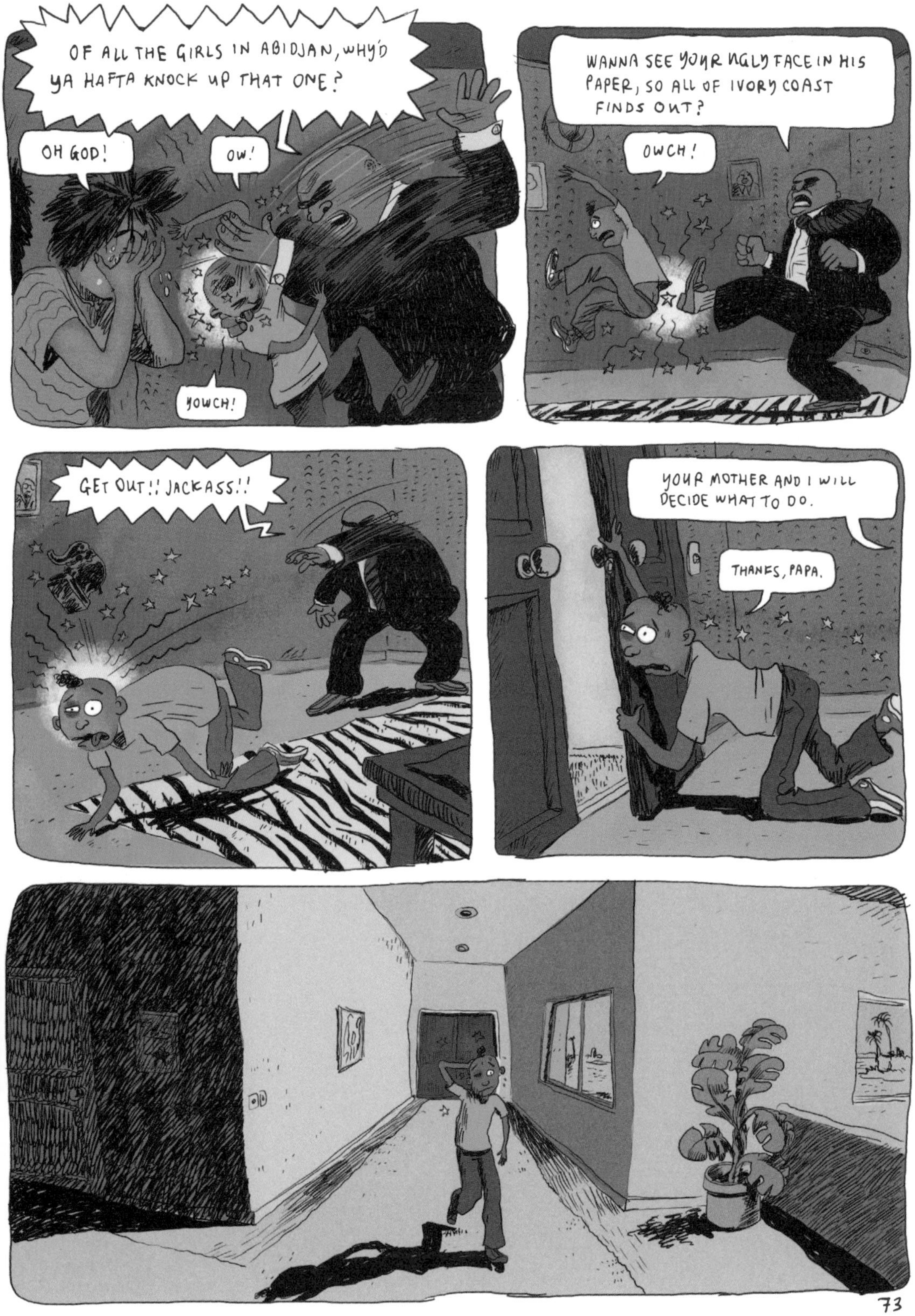
OF ALL THE GIRLS IN ABIDJAN, WHY'D YA HAFTA KNOCK UP THAT ONE?
OH GOD!
OW!
YOWCH!
WANNA SEE YOUR UGLY FACE IN HIS PAPER, SO ALL OF IVORY COAST FINDS OUT?
OWCH!
GET OUT!! JACKASS!!
YOUR MOTHER AND I WILL DECIDE WHAT TO DO.
THANKS, PAPA.

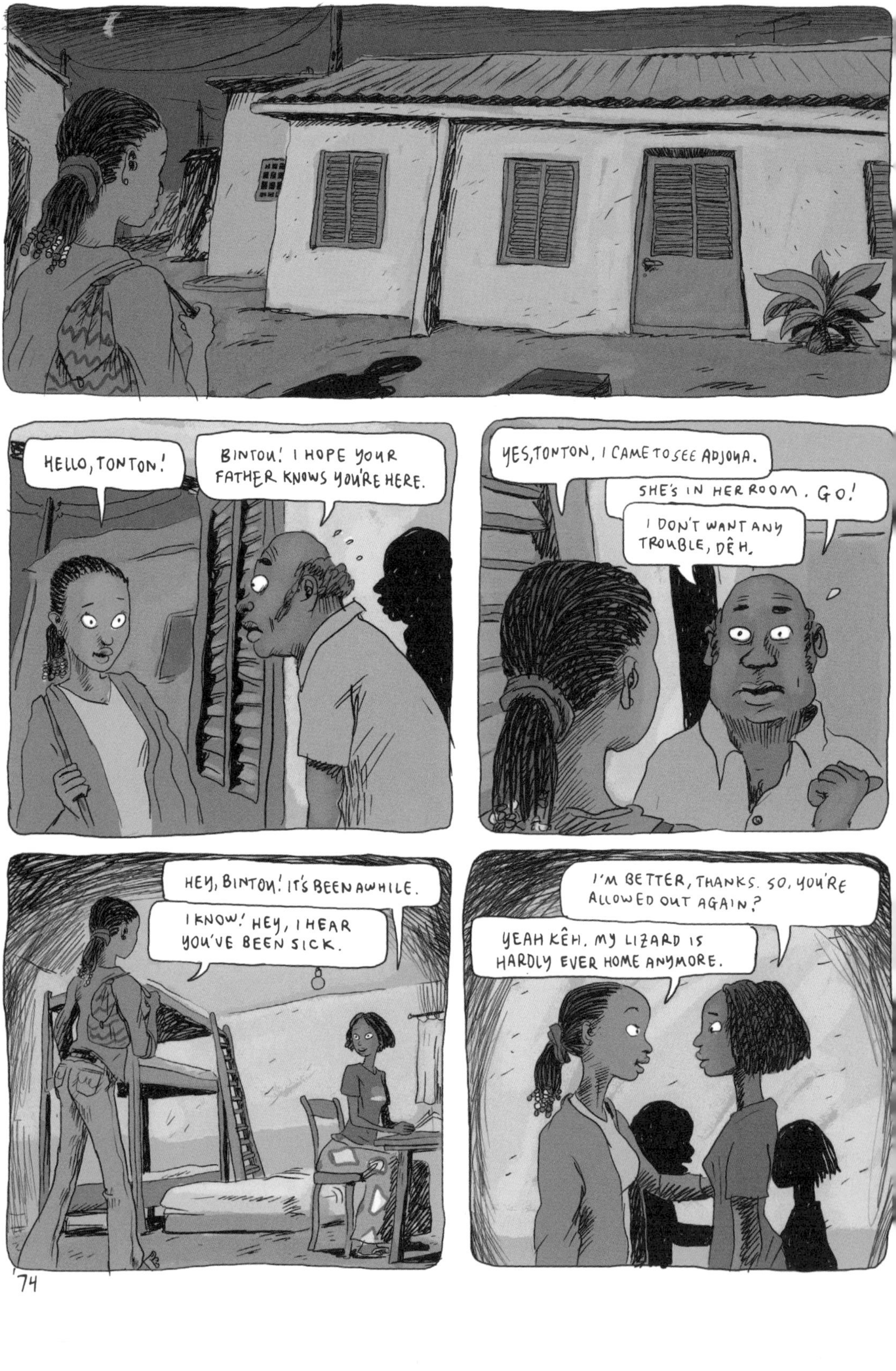
HELLO, TONTON!
BINTOU! I HOPE YOUR FATHER KNOWS YOU'RE HERE.
YES, TONTON, I CAME TO SEE ADJOUA.
SHE'S IN HER ROOM. GO!
I DON'T WANT ANY TROUBLE, DÊH.
HEY, BINTOU! IT'S BEEN A WHILE.
I KNOW! HEY, I HEAR YOU'VE BEEN SICK.
I'M BETTER, THANKS. SO, YOU'RE ALLOWED OUT AGAIN?
YEAH KÊH. MY LIZARD IS HARDLY EVER HOME ANYMORE.

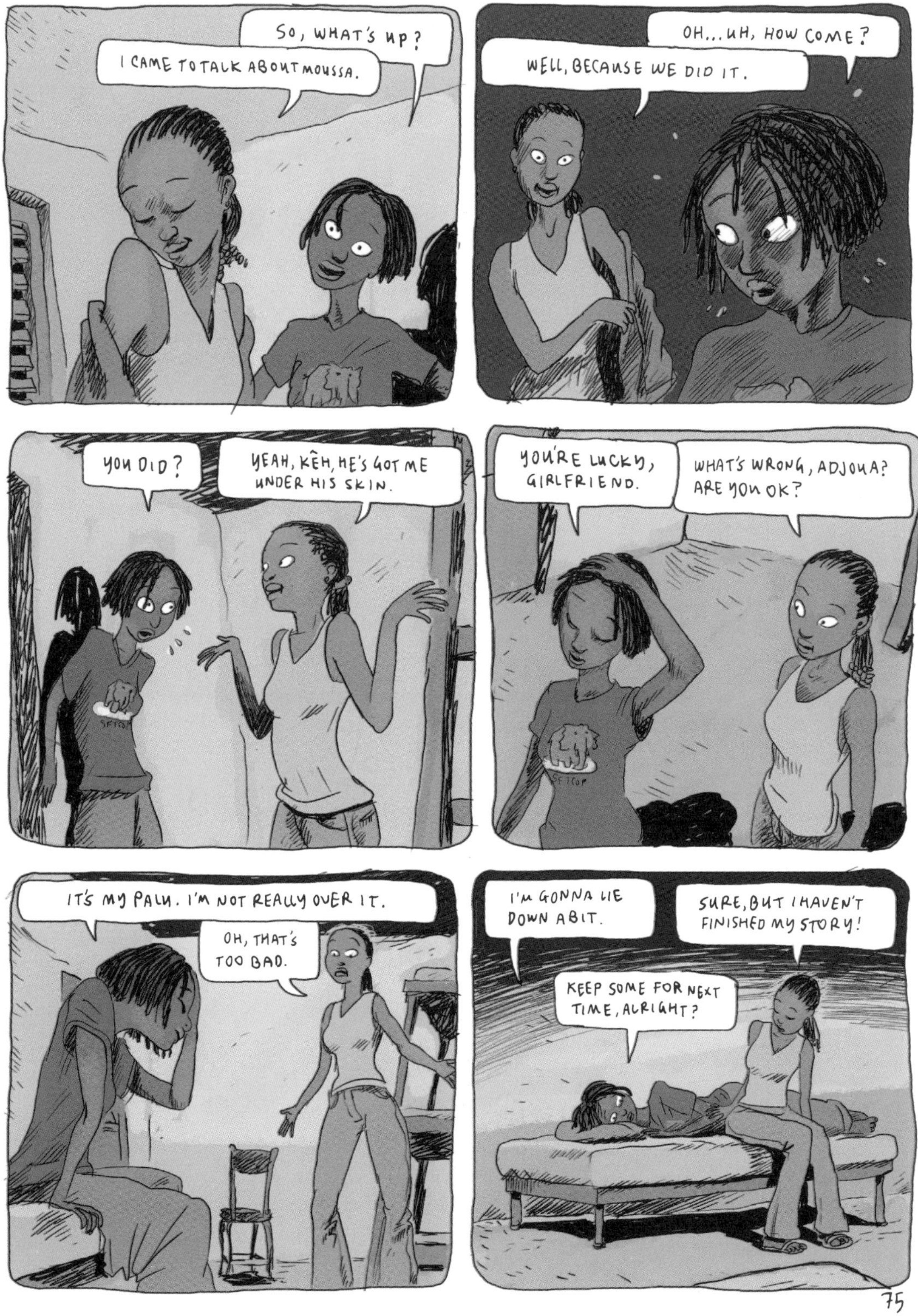
I CAME TO TALK ABOUT MOUSSA.
SO, WHAT'S UP?
WELL, BECAUSE WE DID IT.
OH... UH, HOW COME?
YOU DID?
YEAH, KÊH, HE'S GOT ME UNDER HIS SKIN.
YOU'RE LUCKY, GIRLFRIEND.
WHAT'S WRONG, ADJOUA? ARE YOU OK?
IT'S MY PALU. I'M NOT REALLY OVER IT.
OH, THAT'S TOO BAD.
I'M GONNA LIE DOWN A BIT.
SURE, BUT I HAVEN'T FINISHED MY STORY!
KEEP SOME FOR NEXT TIME, ALRIGHT?

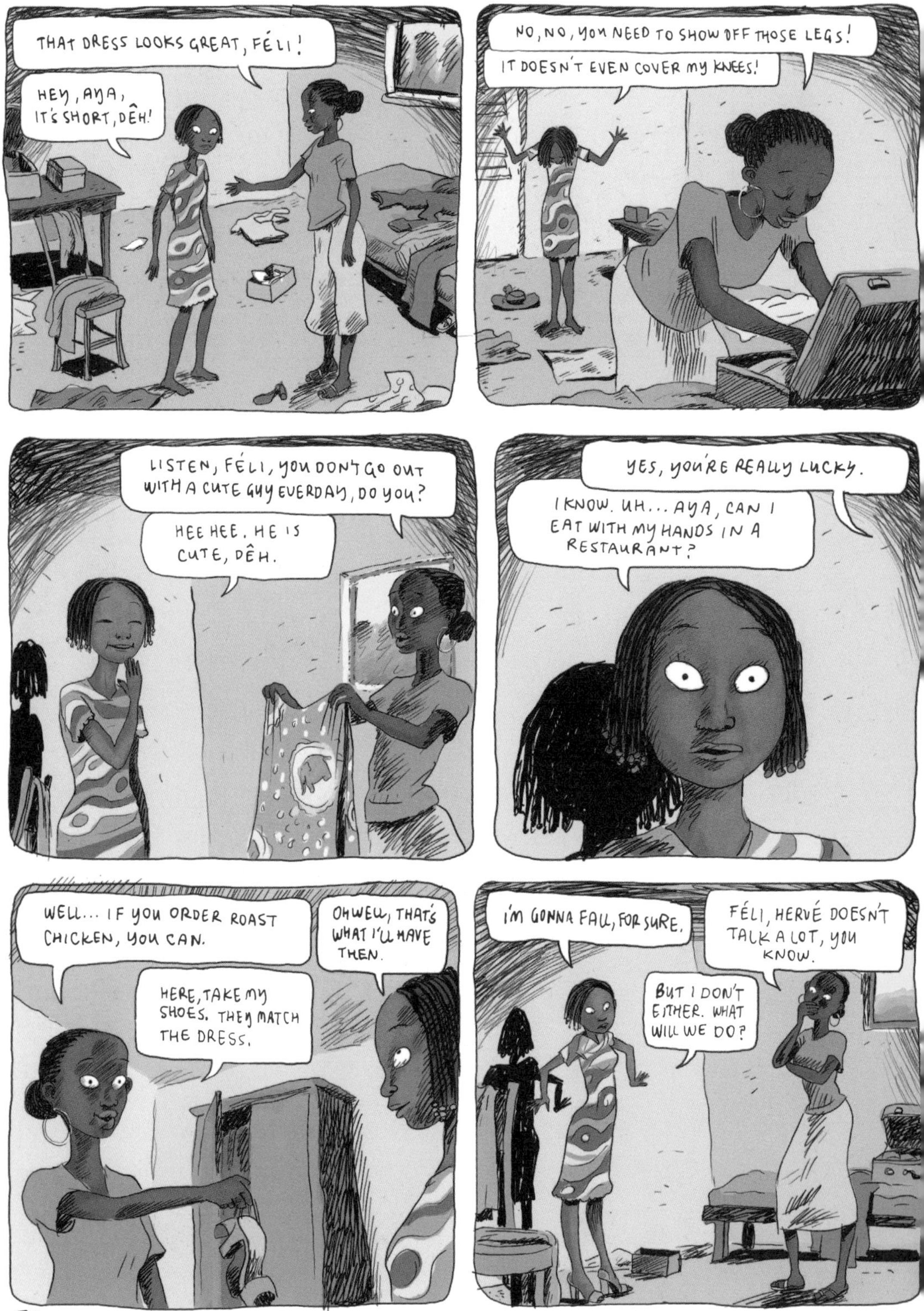
THAT DRESS LOOKS GREAT, FÉLI!
HEY, AYA, IT'S SHORT, DÊH!
NO, NO, YOU NEED TO SHOW OFF THOSE LEGS!
IT DOESN'T EVEN COVER MY KNEES!
LISTEN, FÉLI, YOU DON'T GO OUT WITH A CUTE GUY EVERDAY, DO YOU?
HEE HEE. HE IS CUTE, DÊH.
YES, YOU'RE REALLY LUCKY.
I KNOW. UH... AYA, CAN I EAT WITH MY HANDS IN A RESTAURANT?
WELL... IF YOU ORDER ROAST CHICKEN, YOU CAN.
OH WELL, THAT'S WHAT I'LL HAVE THEN.
HERE, TAKE MY SHOES. THEY MATCH THE DRESS.
I'M GONNA FALL, FOR SURE.
FÉLI, HERVÉ DOESN'T TALK A LOT, YOU KNOW.
BUT I DON'T EITHER. WHAT WILL WE DO?

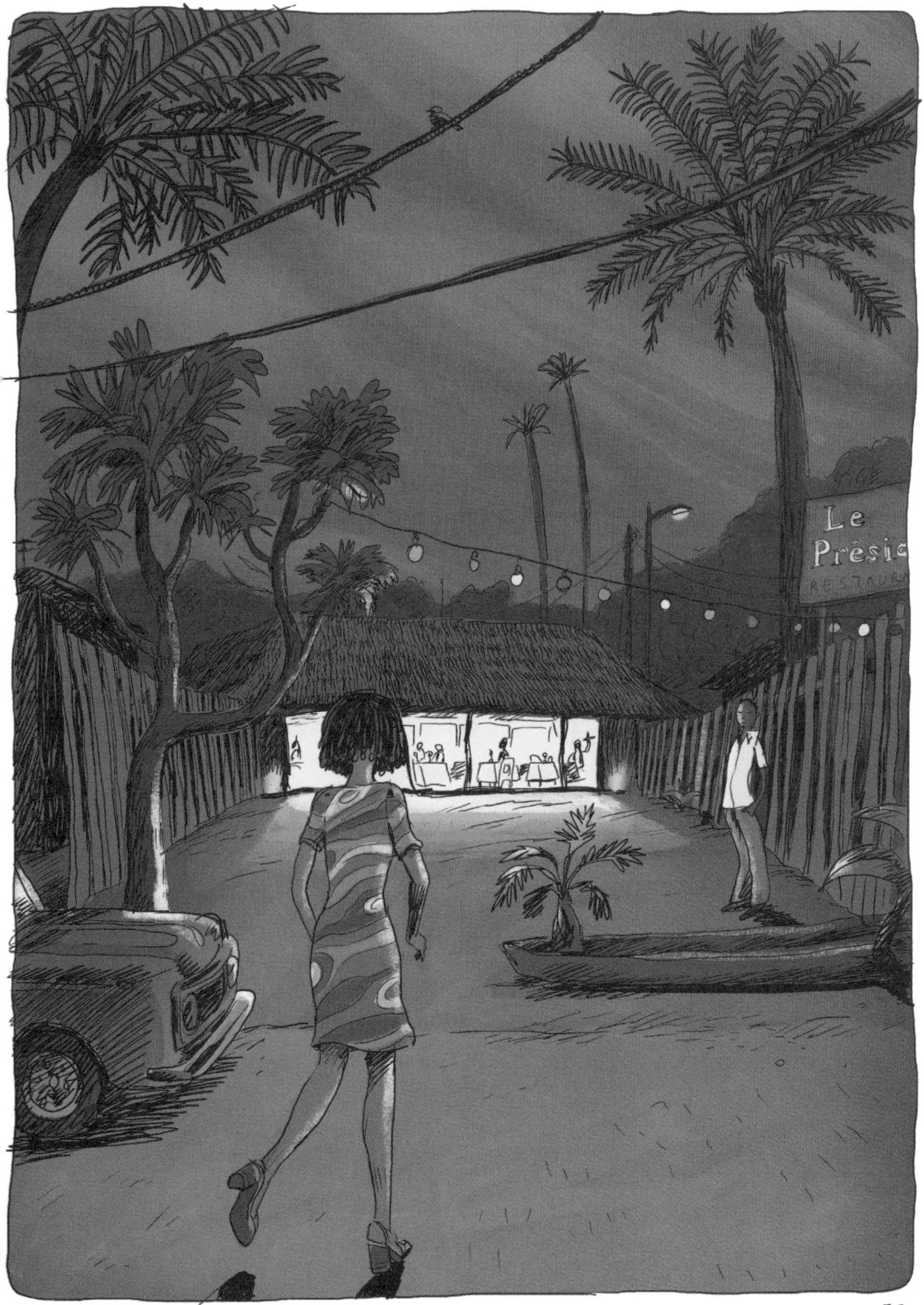
Le

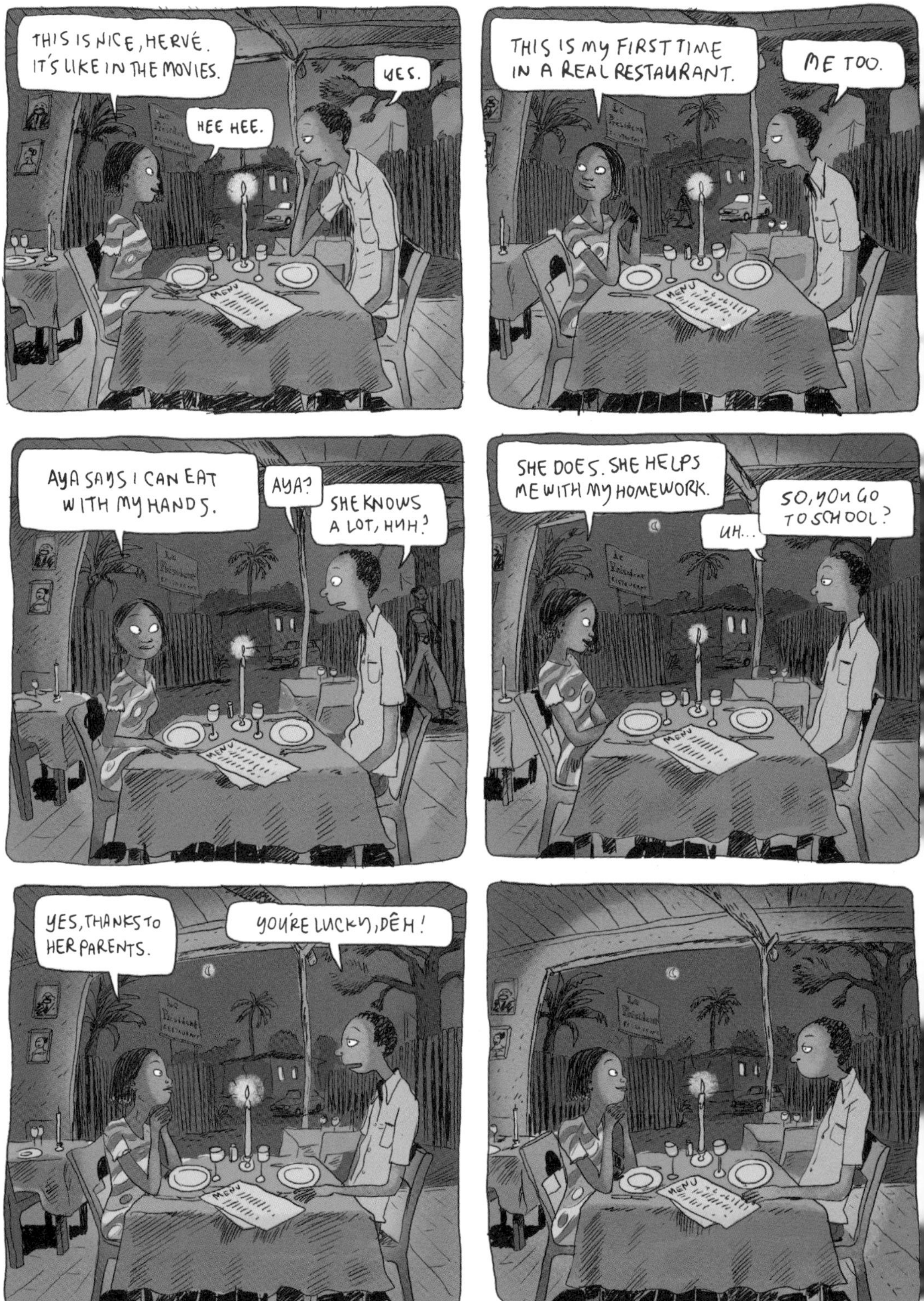
THIS IS NICE, HERVÉ. IT'S LIKE IN THE MOVIES.
HEE HEE.
YES.
THIS IS MY FIRST TIME IN A REAL RESTAURANT.
ME TOO.
AYA SAYS I CAN EAT WITH MY HANDS.
AYA?
SHE KNOWS A LOT, HUH?
SHE DOES. SHE HELPS ME WITH MY HOMEWORK.
UH...
SO, YOU GO TO SCHOOL?
YES, THANKS TO HER PARENTS.
YOU'RE LUCKY, DÊH!
MENU

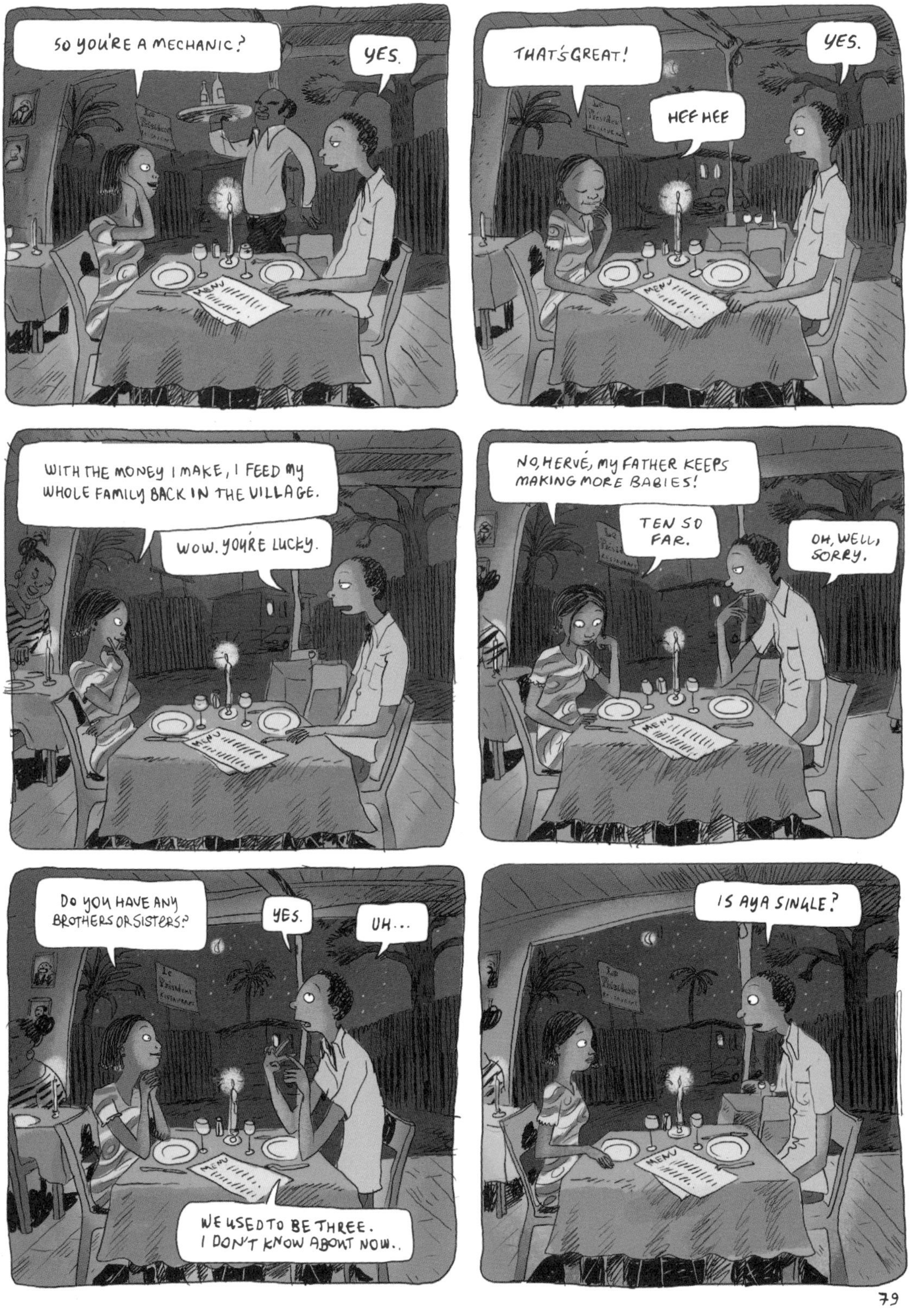
SO YOU'RE A MECHANIC?
YES.
THAT'S GREAT!
YES.
HEE HEE
WITH THE MONEY I MAKE, I FEED MY WHOLE FAMILY BACK IN THE VILLAGE.
WOW. YOU'RE LUCKY.
NO, HERVÉ, MY FATHER KEEPS MAKING MORE BABIES!
TEN SO FAR.
OH, WELL, SORRY.
DO YOU HAVE ANY BROTHERS OR SISTERS?
YES.
UH...
WE USED TO BE THREE. I DON'T KNOW ABOUT NOW..
IS AYA SINGLE?

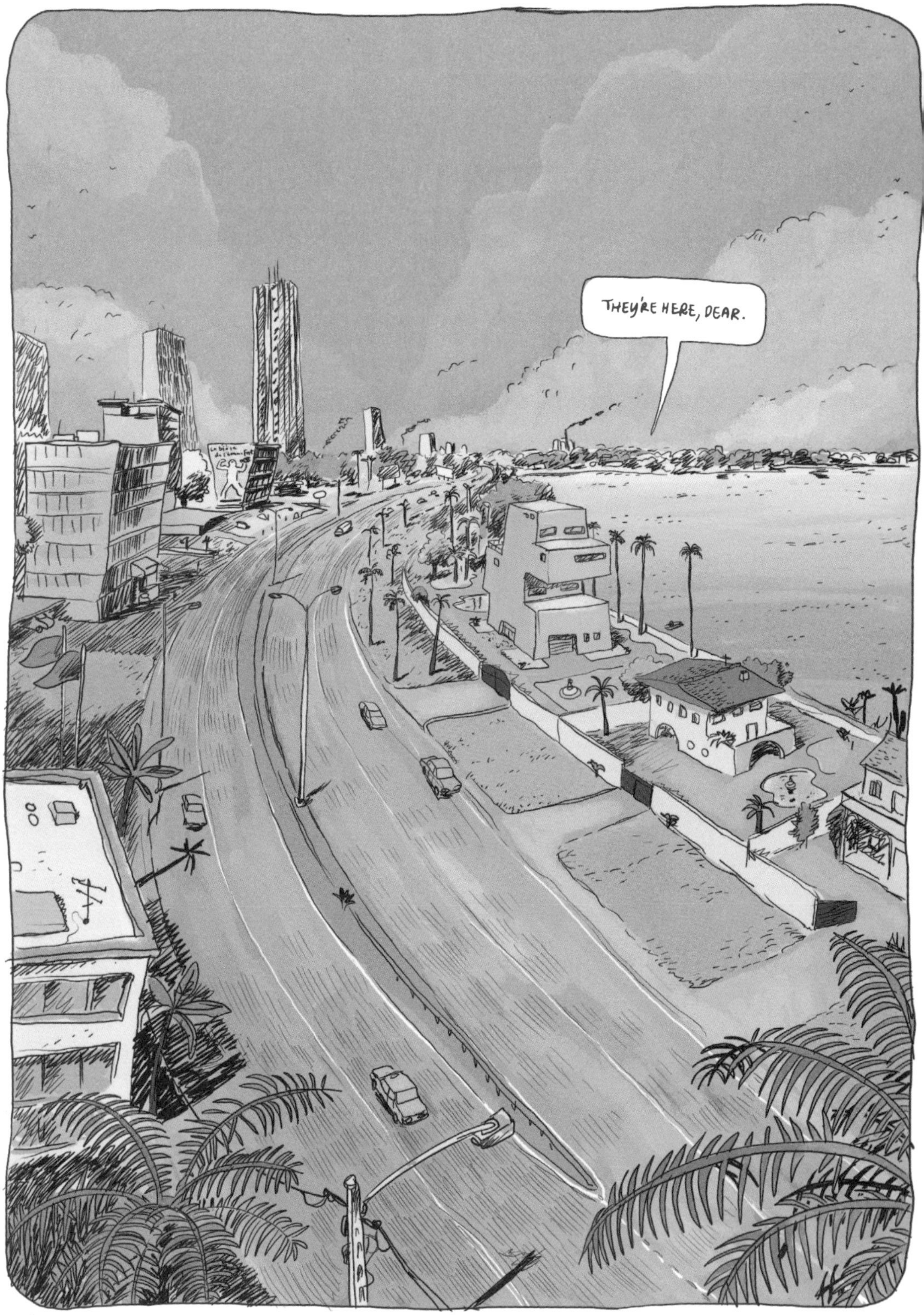
THEY'RE HERE, DEAR.

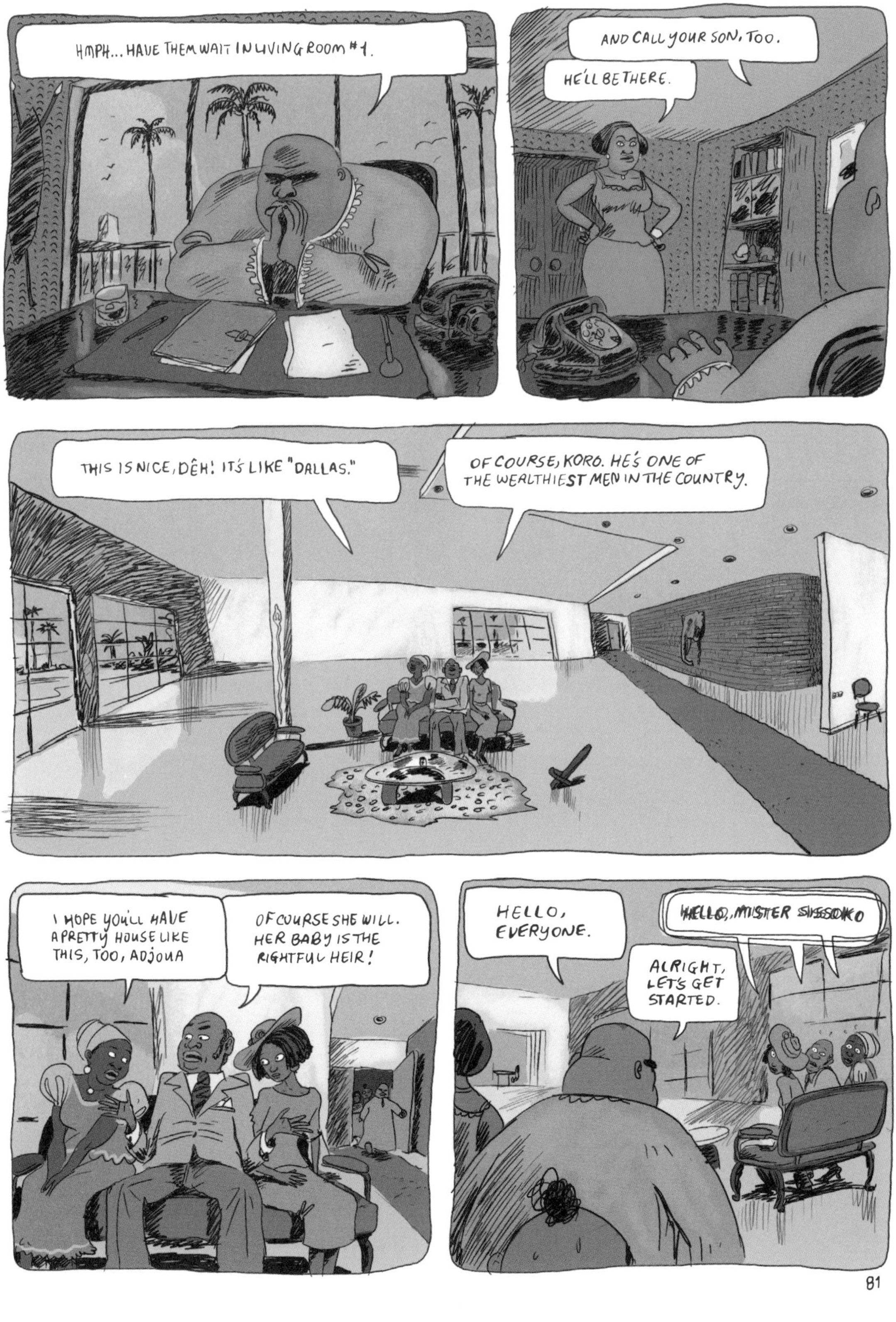
HMPH... HAVE THEM WAIT IN LIVING ROOM #1.
AND CALL YOUR SON, TOO.
HE'LL BE THERE.
THIS IS NICE, DÊH! IT'S LIKE "DALLAS."
OF COURSE, KORO. HE'S ONE OF THE WEALTHIEST MEN IN THE COUNTRY.
I HOPE YOU'LL HAVE A PRETTY HOUSE LIKE THIS, TOO, ADJOUA
OF COURSE SHE WILL. HER BABY IS THE RIGHTFUL HEIR!
HELLO, EVERYONE.
HELLO, MISTER SISSOKO
ALRIGHT, LET'S GET STARTED.

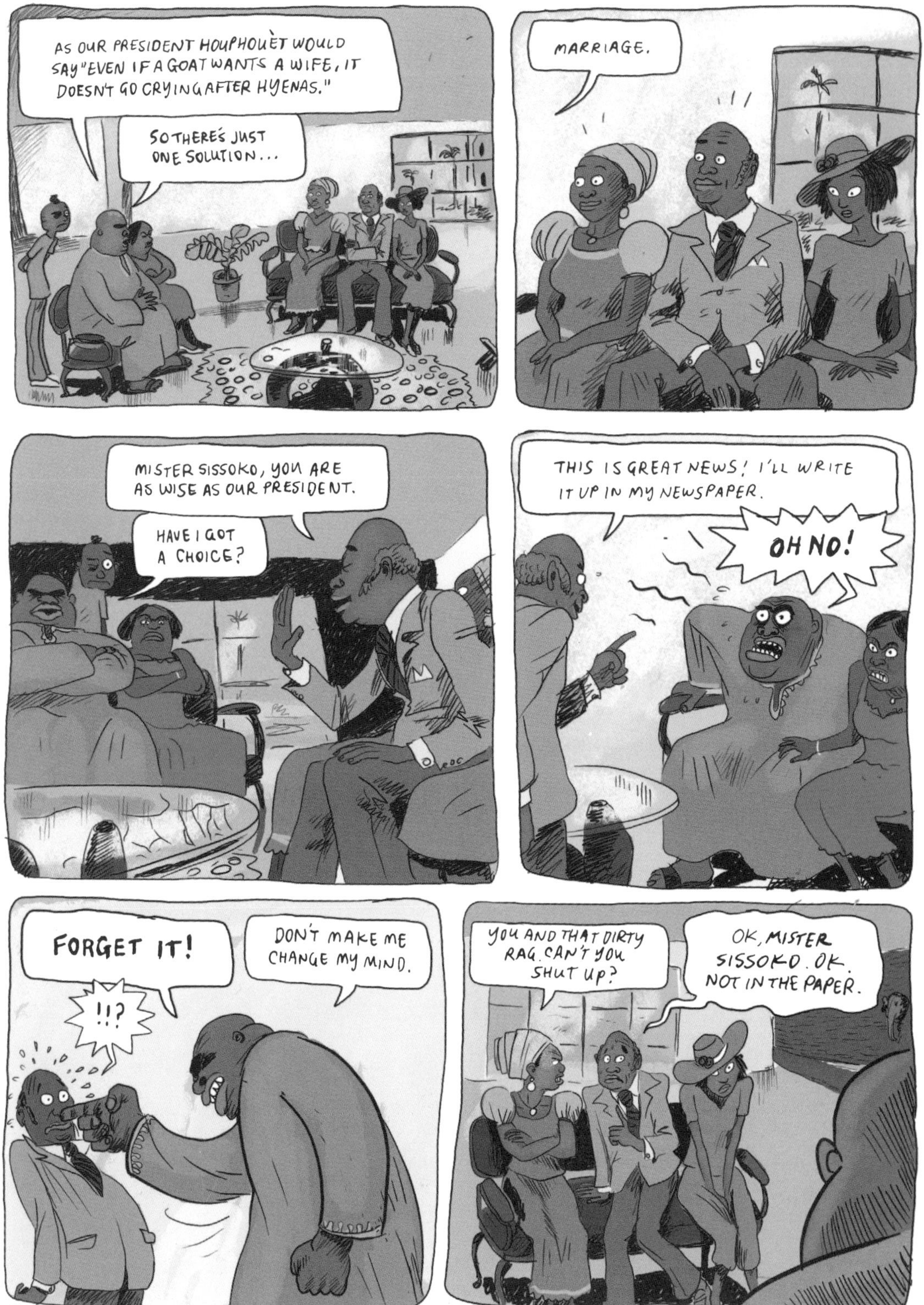
AS OUR PRESIDENT HOUPHOUËT WOULD SAY "EVEN IF A GOAT WANTS A WIFE, IT DOESN'T GO CRYING AFTER HYENAS."
SO THERE'S JUST ONE SOLUTION...
MARRIAGE.
MISTER SISSOKO, YOU ARE AS WISE AS OUR PRESIDENT.
HAVE I GOT A CHOICE?
THIS IS GREAT NEWS! I'LL WRITE IT UP IN MY NEWSPAPER.
OH NO!
FORGET IT!
!!?
DON'T MAKE ME CHANGE MY MIND.
YOU AND THAT DIRTY RAG. CAN'T YOU SHUT UP?
OK, MISTER SISSOKO. OK. NOT IN THE PAPER.

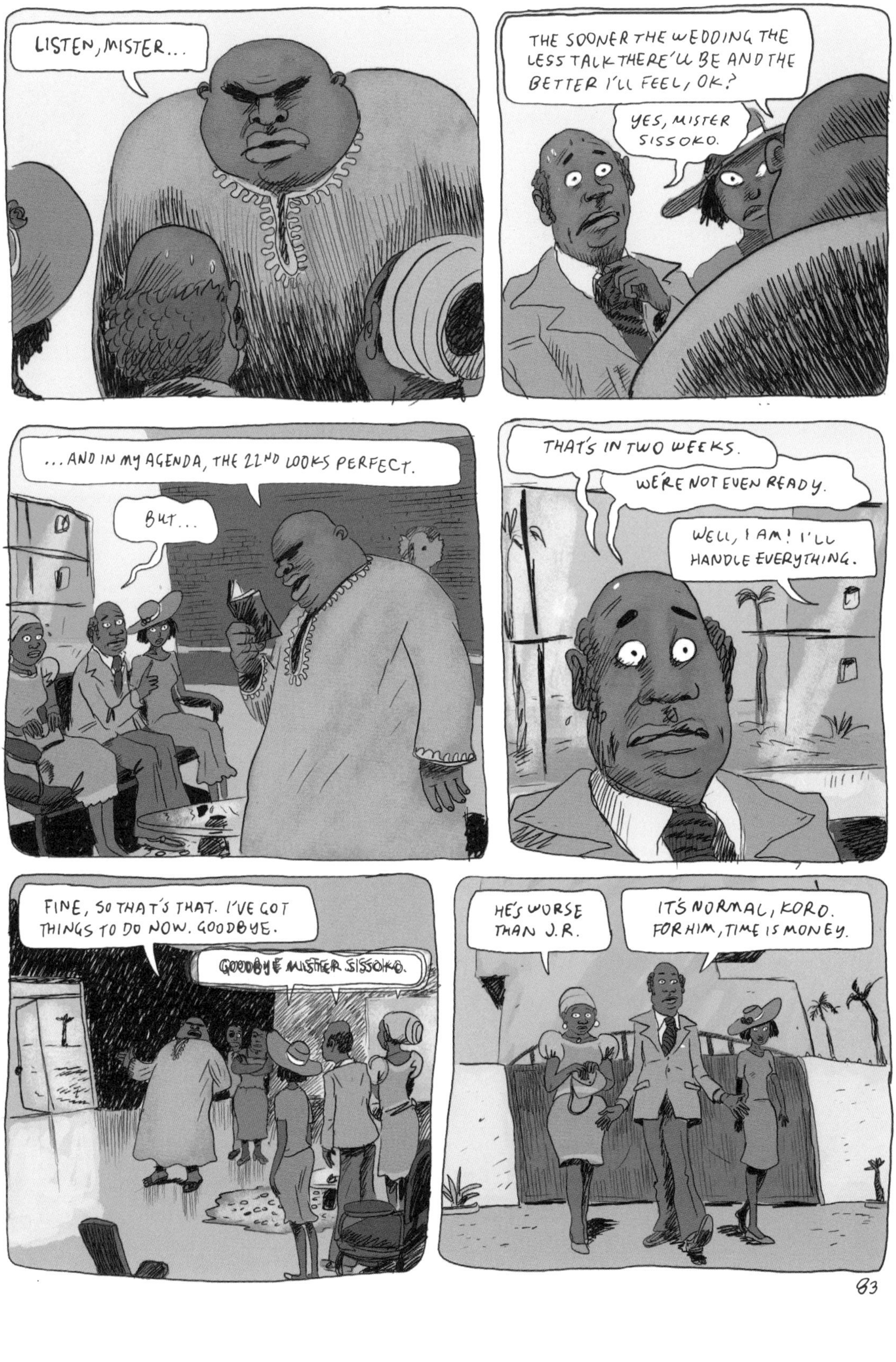
LISTEN, MISTER...
THE SOONER THE WEDDING THE LESS TALK THERE'LL BE AND THE BETTER I'LL FEEL, OK?
YES, MISTER SISSOKO.
...AND IN MY AGENDA, THE 22ND LOOKS PERFECT.
BUT...
THAT'S IN TWO WEEKS.
WE'RE NOT EVEN READY.
WELL, I AM! I'LL HANDLE EVERYTHING.
FINE, SO THAT'S THAT. I'VE GOT THINGS TO DO NOW. GOODBYE.
GOODBYE MISTER SISSOKO.
HE'S WORSE THAN J.R.
IT'S NORMAL, KORO. FOR HIM, TIME IS MONEY.

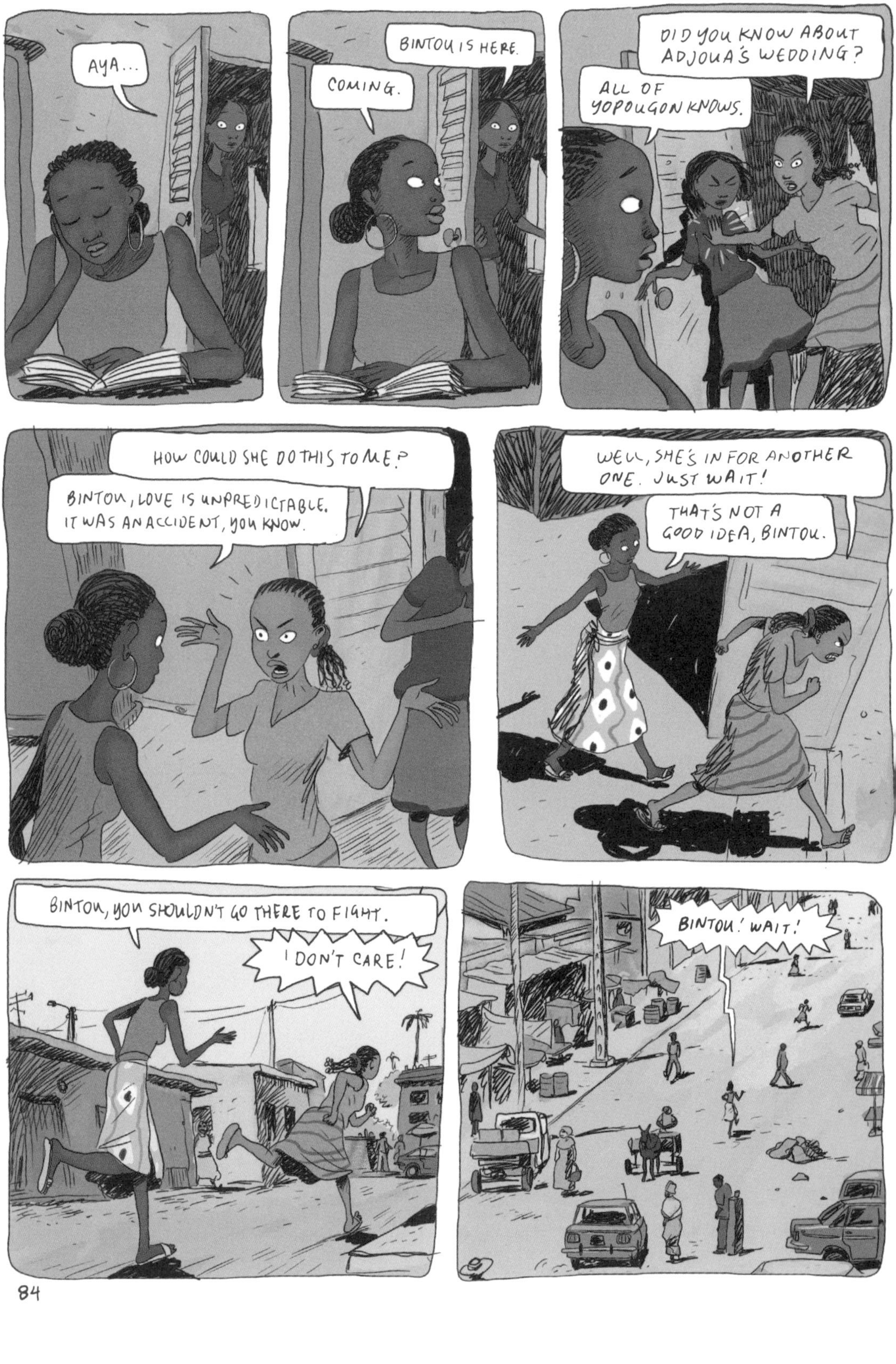
AYA...
BINTOU IS HERE.
COMING.
DID YOU KNOW ABOUT ADJOUA'S WEDDING?
ALL OF YOPOUGON KNOWS.
HOW COULD SHE DO THIS TO ME?
BINTOU, LOVE IS UNPREDICTABLE. IT WAS AN ACCIDENT, YOU KNOW.
WELL, SHE'S IN FOR ANOTHER ONE. JUST WAIT!
THAT'S NOT A GOOD IDEA, BINTOU.
BINTOU, YOU SHOULDN'T GO THERE TO FIGHT.
I DON'T CARE!
BINTOU! WAIT!

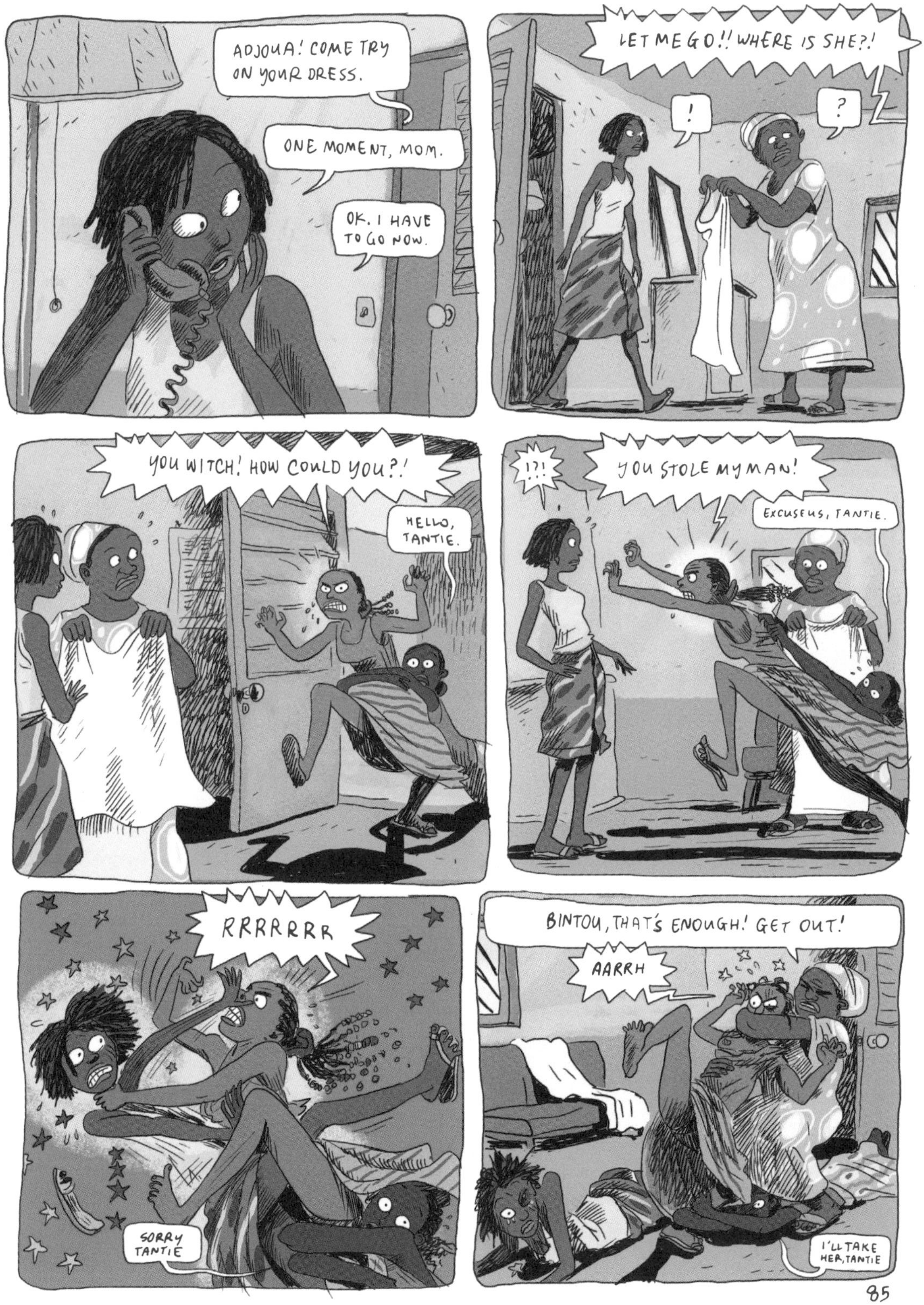
ADJOUA! COME TRY ON YOUR DRESS.
ONE MOMENT, MOM.
OK. I HAVE TO GO NOW.
LET ME GO!! WHERE IS SHE?!
!
?
YOU WITCH! HOW COULD YOU?!
HELLO, TANTIE.
!?!
YOU STOLE MY MAN!
EXCUSE US, TANTIE.
RRRRRRR
SORRY TANTIE
BINTOU, THAT'S ENOUGH! GET OUT!
AARRH
I'LL TAKE HER, TANTIE

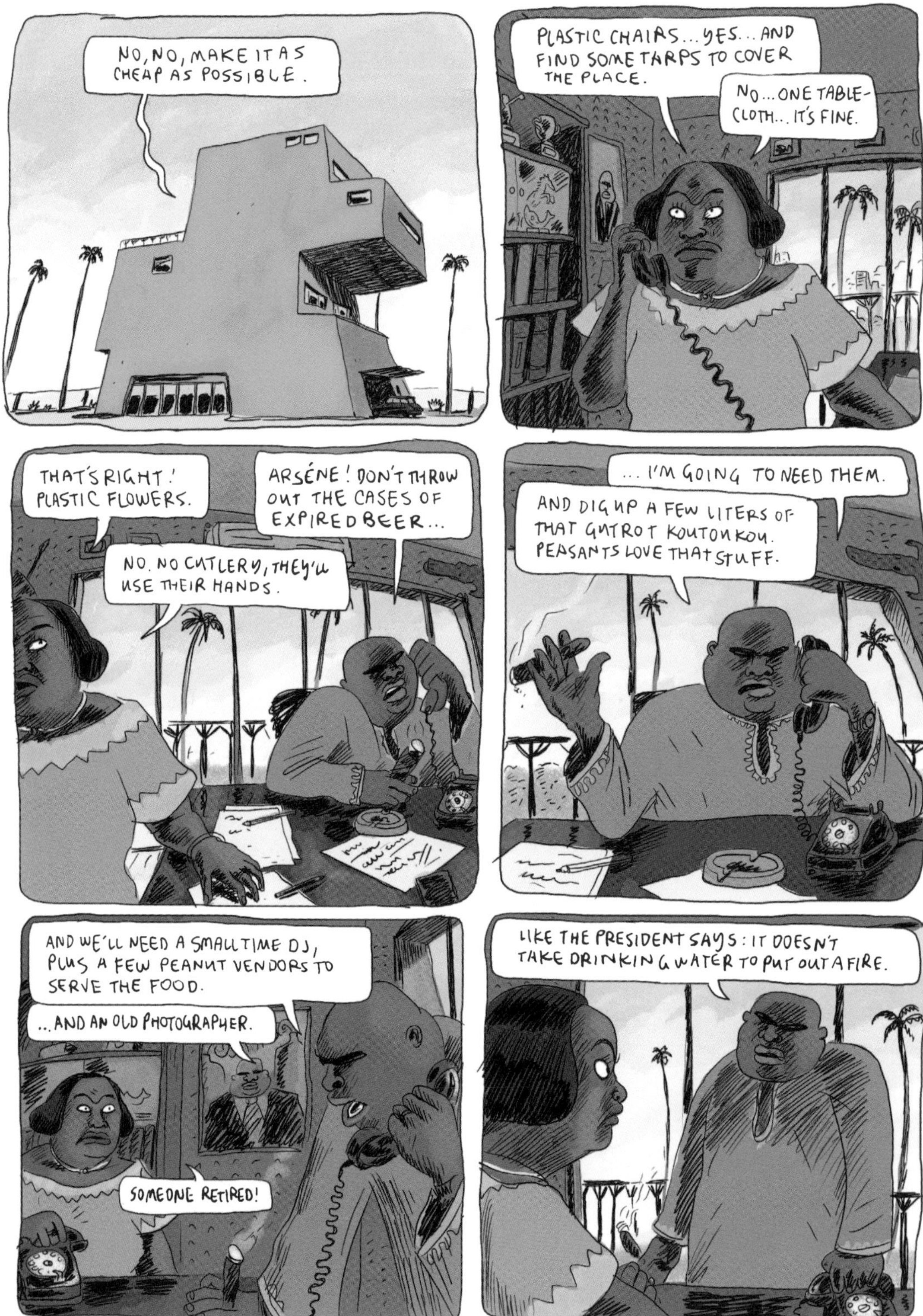
NO, NO, MAKE IT AS CHEAP AS POSSIBLE.
PLASTIC CHAIRS... YES... AND FIND SOME TARPS TO COVER THE PLACE.
NO... ONE TABLE-CLOTH... IT'S FINE.
THAT'S RIGHT! PLASTIC FLOWERS.
ARSÉNE! DON'T THROW OUT THE CASES OF EXPIRED BEER...
NO. NO CUTLERY, THEY'LL USE THEIR HANDS.
... I'M GOING TO NEED THEM.
AND DIG UP A FEW LITERS OF THAT GUTROT KOUTONKOU. PEASANTS LOVE THAT STUFF.
AND WE'LL NEED A SMALLTIME DJ, PLUS A FEW PEANUT VENDORS TO SERVE THE FOOD.
...AND AN OLD PHOTOGRAPHER.
SOMEONE RETIRED!
LIKE THE PRESIDENT SAYS: IT DOESN'T TAKE DRINKING WATER TO PUT OUT A FIRE.

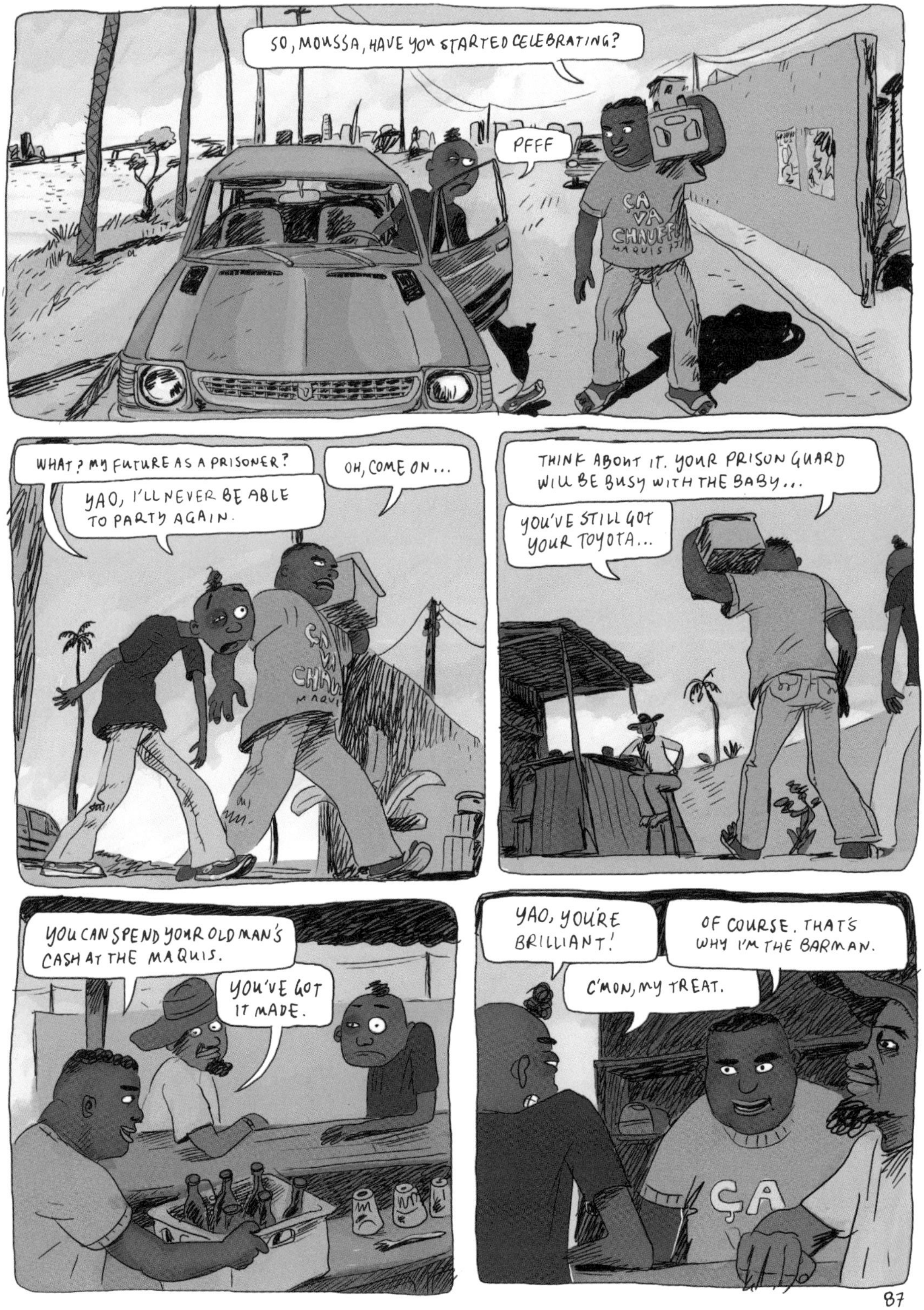
SO, MOUSSA, HAVE YOU STARTED CELEBRATING?
PFFF
ÇA VA CHAUFFE MAQUIS
WHAT? MY FUTURE AS A PRISONER?
YAO, I'LL NEVER BE ABLE TO PARTY AGAIN.
OH, COME ON...
THINK ABOUT IT. YOUR PRISON GUARD WILL BE BUSY WITH THE BABY...
YOU'VE STILL GOT YOUR TOYOTA...
YOU CAN SPEND YOUR OLD MAN'S CASH AT THE MAQUIS.
YOU'VE GOT IT MADE.
YAO, YOU'RE BRILLIANT!
OF COURSE. THAT'S WHY I'M THE BARMAN.
C'MON, MY TREAT.
ÇA

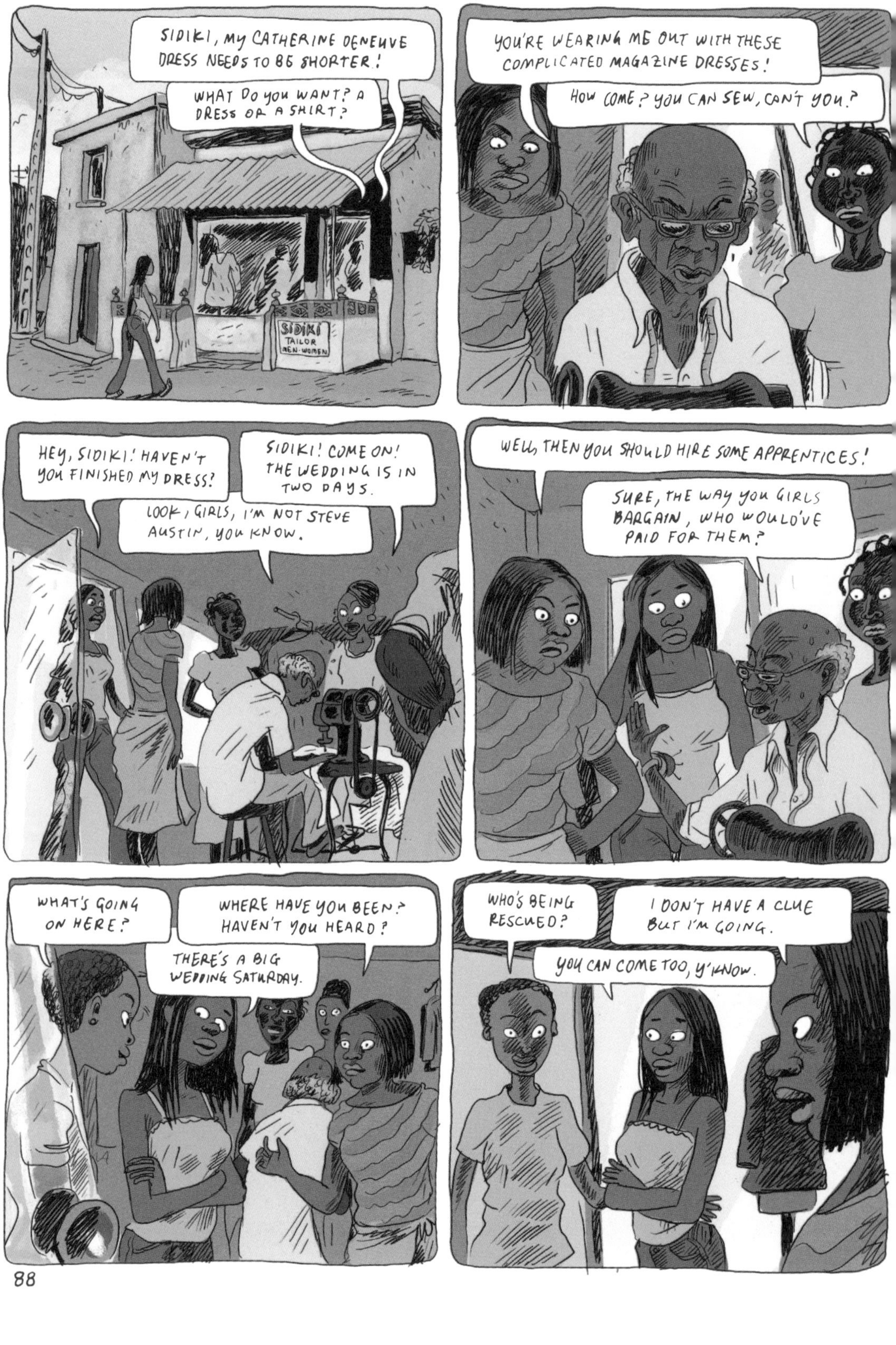
SIDIKI, MY CATHERINE DENEUVE DRESS NEEDS TO BE SHORTER!
WHAT DO YOU WANT? A DRESS OR A SHIRT?
YOU'RE WEARING ME OUT WITH THESE COMPLICATED MAGAZINE DRESSES!
HOW COME? YOU CAN SEW, CAN'T YOU?
SIDIKI TAILOR MEN·WOMEN
HEY, SIDIKI! HAVEN'T YOU FINISHED MY DRESS?
SIDIKI! COME ON! THE WEDDING IS IN TWO DAYS.
LOOK, GIRLS, I'M NOT STEVE AUSTIN, YOU KNOW.
WELL, THEN YOU SHOULD HIRE SOME APPRENTICES!
SURE, THE WAY YOU GIRLS BARGAIN, WHO WOULD'VE PAID FOR THEM?
WHAT'S GOING ON HERE?
WHERE HAVE YOU BEEN? HAVEN'T YOU HEARD?
THERE'S A BIG WEDDING SATURDAY.
WHO'S BEING RESCUED?
I DON'T HAVE A CLUE BUT I'M GOING.
YOU CAN COME TOO, Y'KNOW.

And on Saturday the 22nd, despite everything, Yopougon got to see its biggest wedding ever, thanks to all the surprise guests who came.

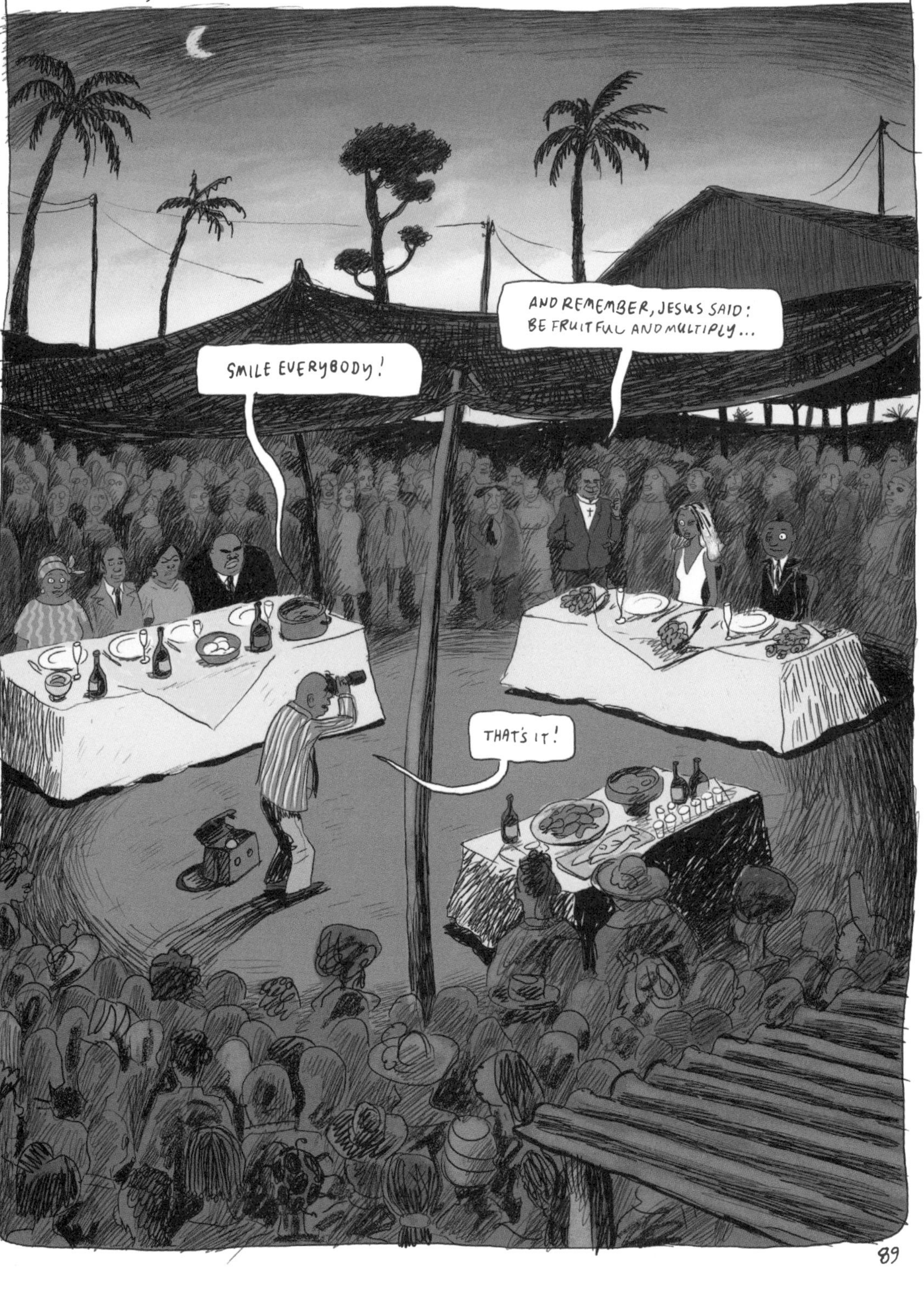
AND REMEMBER, JESUS SAID: BE FRUITFUL AND MULTIPLY...
SMILE EVERYBODY!
THAT'S IT!

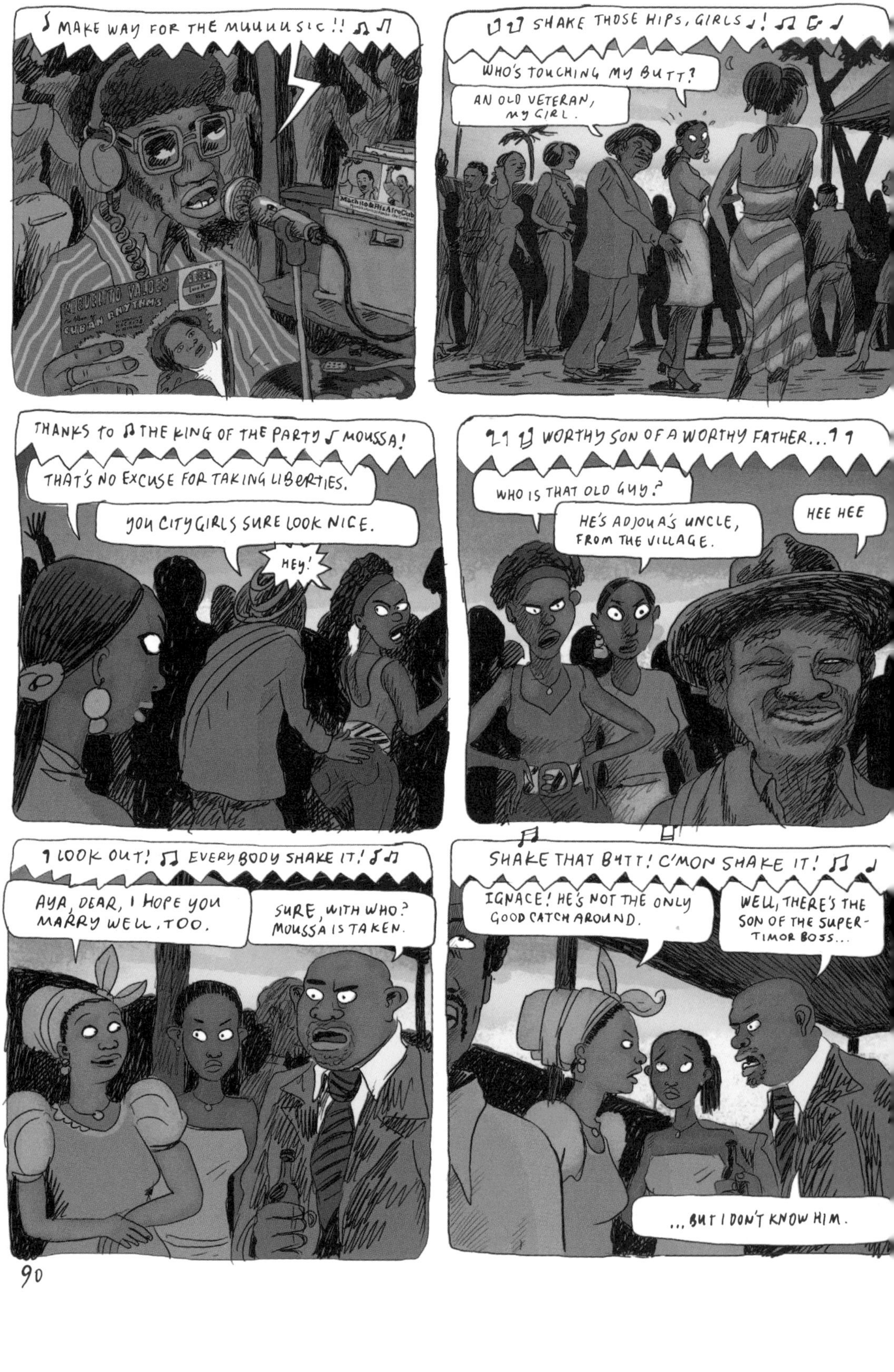
MAKE WAY FOR THE MUUUUSIC!!
SHAKE THOSE HIPS, GIRLS!
WHO'S TOUCHING MY BUTT?
AN OLD VETERAN, MY GIRL.
THANKS TO THE KING OF THE PARTY MOUSSA!
THAT'S NO EXCUSE FOR TAKING LIBERTIES.
YOU CITY GIRLS SURE LOOK NICE.
HEY!
WORTHY SON OF A WORTHY FATHER...
WHO IS THAT OLD GUY?
HE'S ADJOUA'S UNCLE, FROM THE VILLAGE.
HEE HEE
LOOK OUT! EVERYBODY SHAKE IT!
AYA, DEAR, I HOPE YOU MARRY WELL, TOO.
SURE, WITH WHO? MOUSSA IS TAKEN.
SHAKE THAT BUTT! C'MON SHAKE IT!
IGNACE! HE'S NOT THE ONLY GOOD CATCH AROUND.
WELL, THERE'S THE SON OF THE SUPER-TIMOR BOSS...
...BUT I DON'T KNOW HIM.

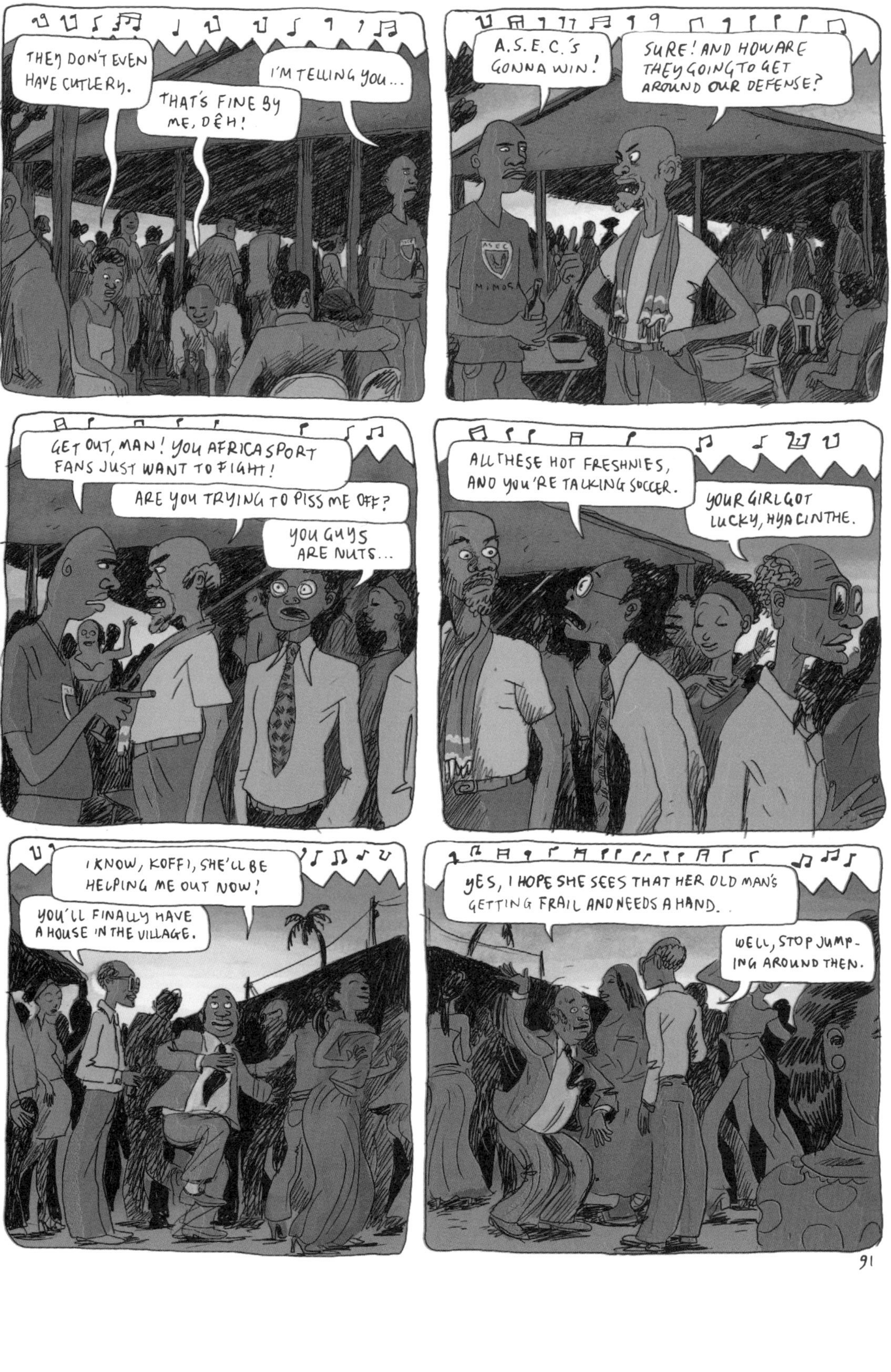
THEY DON'T EVEN HAVE CUTLERY.
THAT'S FINE BY ME, DÊH!
I'M TELLING YOU...
A.S.E.C.'S GONNA WIN!
SURE! AND HOW ARE THEY GOING TO GET AROUND OUR DEFENSE?
A.S.E.C. MIMOSA
GET OUT, MAN! YOU AFRICA SPORT FANS JUST WANT TO FIGHT!
ARE YOU TRYING TO PISS ME OFF?
YOU GUYS ARE NUTS...
ALL THESE HOT FRESHNIES, AND YOU'RE TALKING SOCCER.
YOUR GIRL GOT LUCKY, HYACINTHE.
I KNOW, KOFFI, SHE'LL BE HELPING ME OUT NOW!
YOU'LL FINALLY HAVE A HOUSE IN THE VILLAGE.
YES, I HOPE SHE SEES THAT HER OLD MAN'S GETTING FRAIL AND NEEDS A HAND.
WELL, STOP JUMPING AROUND THEN.

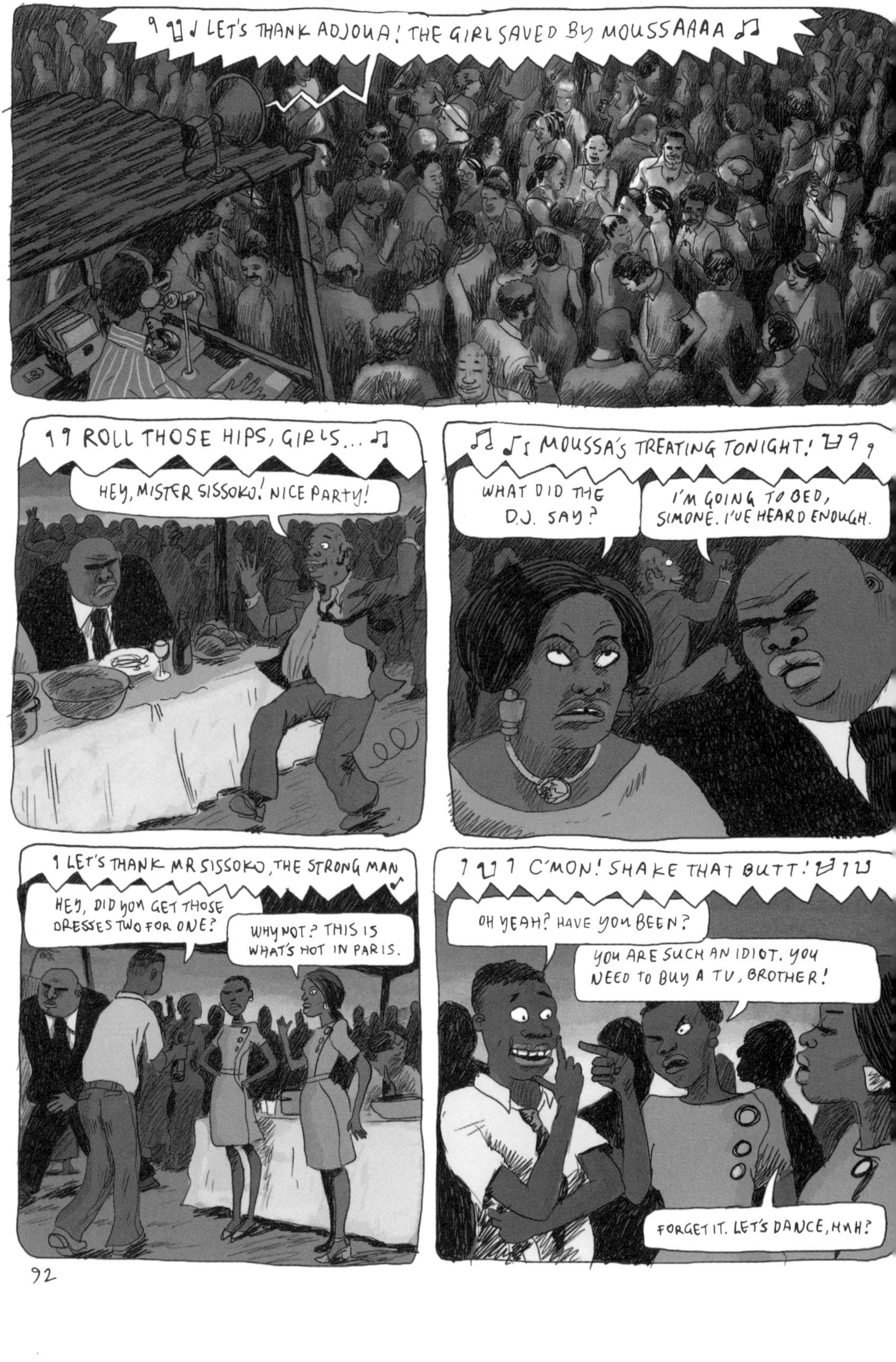
LET'S THANK ADJOUA! THE GIRL SAVED BY MOUSSAAAA
ROLL THOSE HIPS, GIRLS...
HEY, MISTER SISSOKO! NICE PARTY!
MOUSSA'S TREATING TONIGHT!
WHAT DID THE D.J. SAY?
I'M GOING TO BED, SIMONE. I'VE HEARD ENOUGH.
LET'S THANK MR SISSOKO, THE STRONG MAN
HEY, DID YOU GET THOSE DRESSES TWO FOR ONE?
WHY NOT? THIS IS WHAT'S HOT IN PARIS.
C'MON! SHAKE THAT BUTT!
OH YEAH? HAVE YOU BEEN?
YOU ARE SUCH AN IDIOT. YOU NEED TO BUY A TV, BROTHER!
FORGET IT. LET'S DANCE, HMH?

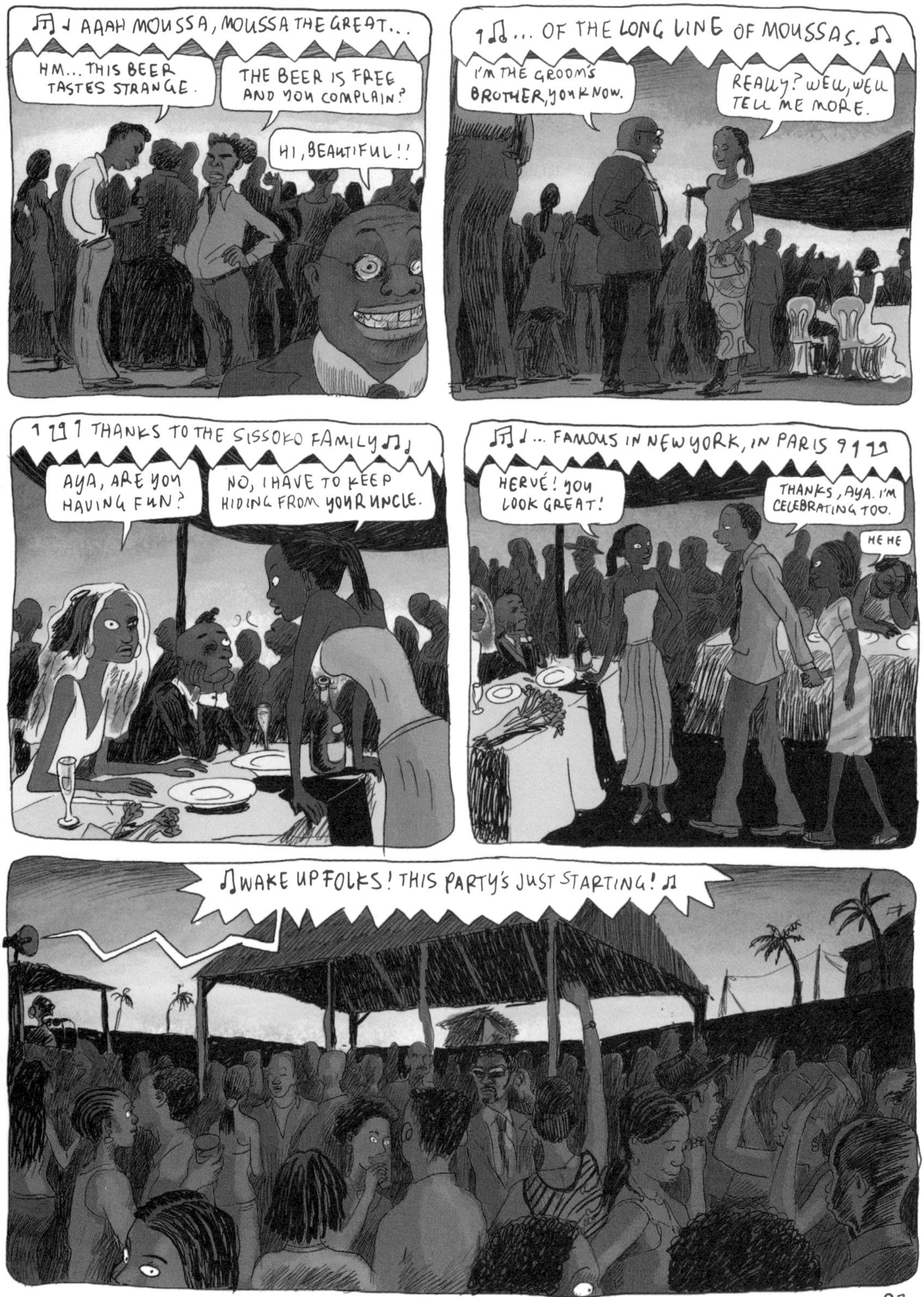
AAAH MOUSSA, MOUSSA THE GREAT...
HM... THIS BEER TASTES STRANGE.
THE BEER IS FREE AND YOU COMPLAIN?
HI, BEAUTIFUL!!
... OF THE LONG LINE OF MOUSSAS.
I'M THE GROOM'S BROTHER, YOU KNOW.
REALLY? WELL, WELL TELL ME MORE.
THANKS TO THE SISSOKO FAMILY
AYA, ARE YOU HAVING FUN?
NO, I HAVE TO KEEP HIDING FROM YOUR UNCLE.
... FAMOUS IN NEW YORK, IN PARIS
HERVÉ! YOU LOOK GREAT!
THANKS, AYA. I'M CELEBRATING TOO.
HE HE
WAKE UP FOLKS! THIS PARTY'S JUST STARTING!

Adjoua's baby came along eight months later, at the start of the rainy season.

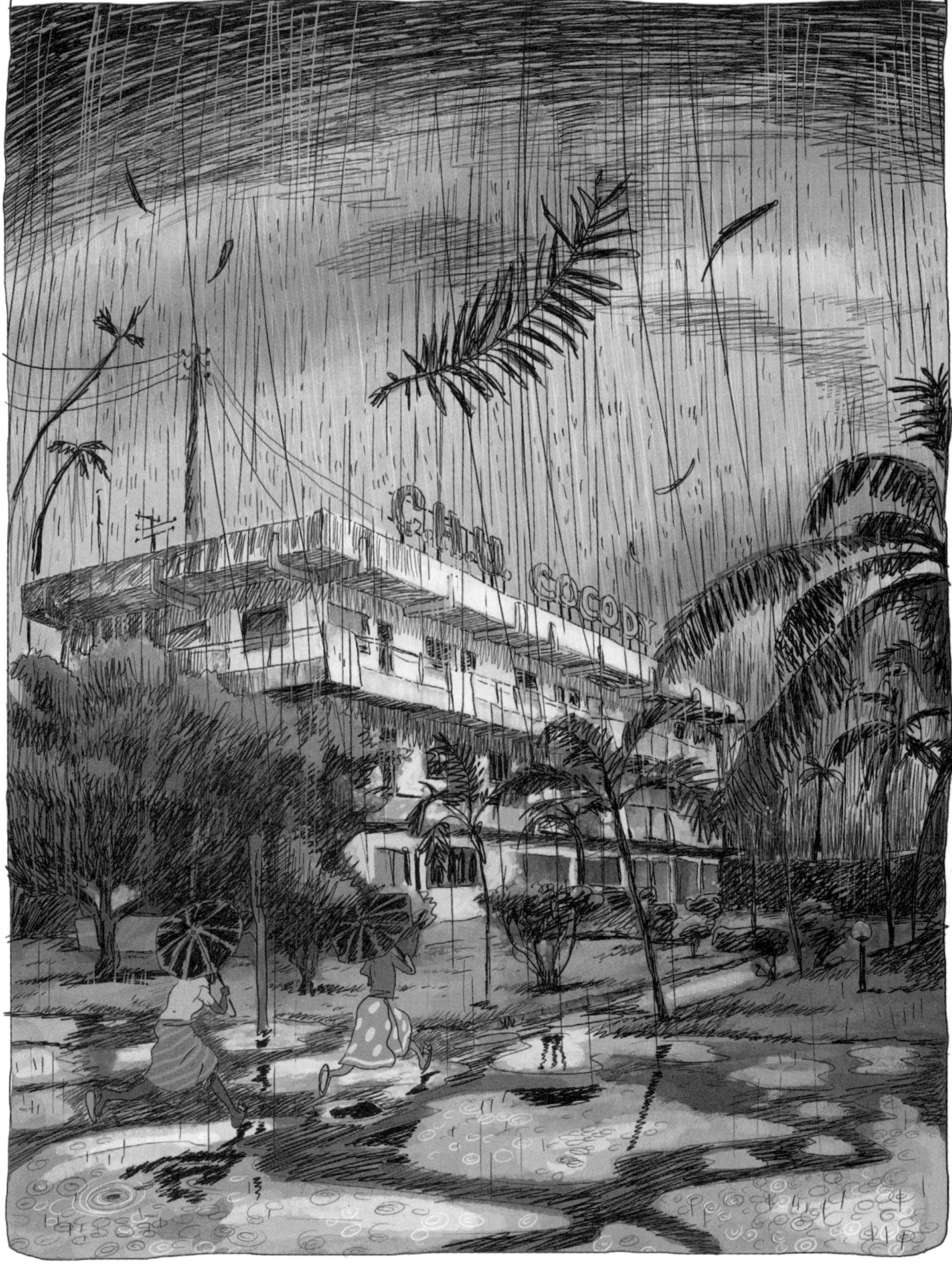
C.H.U. COCODY

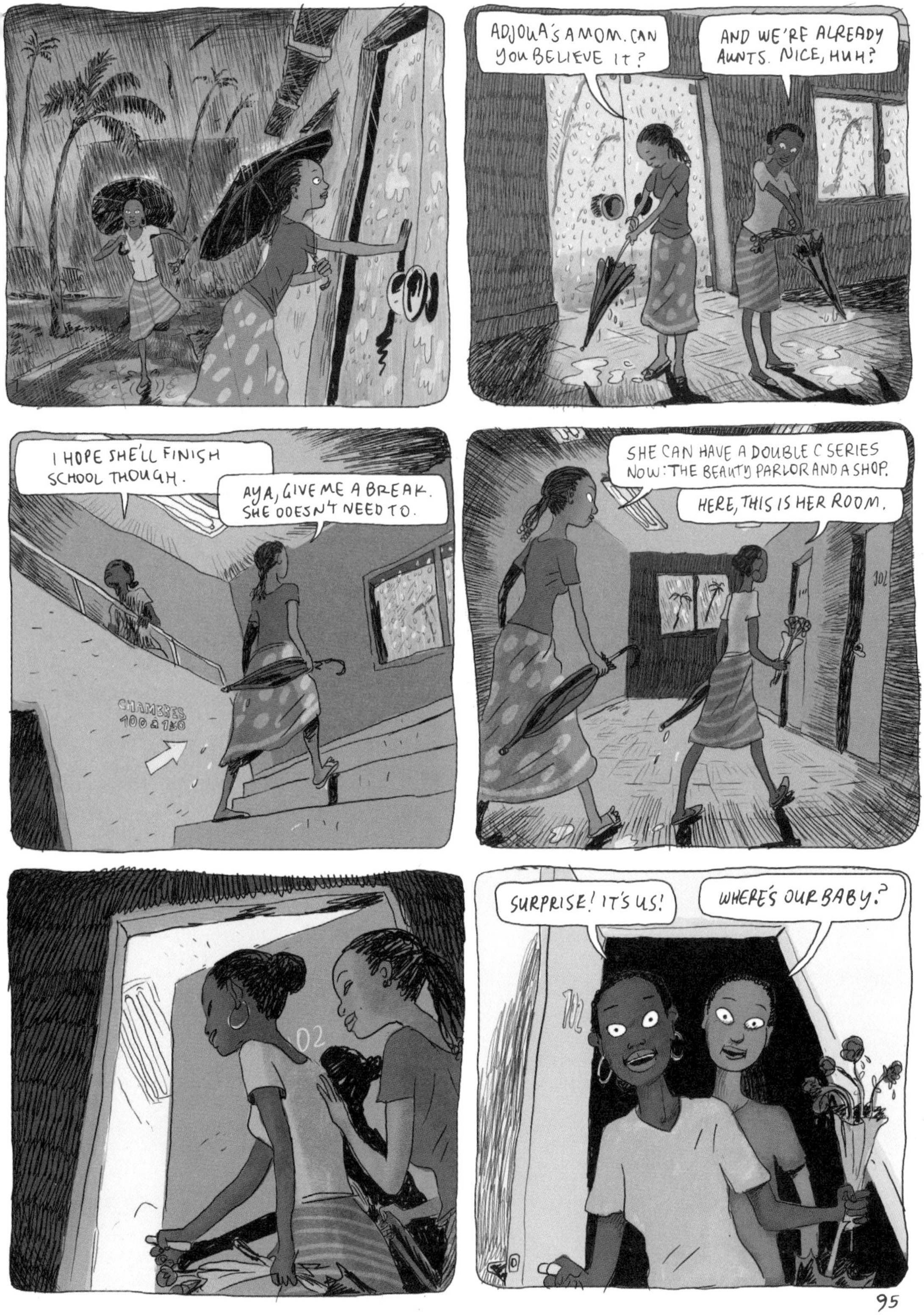
ADJOUA'S A MOM. CAN YOU BELIEVE IT?
AND WE'RE ALREADY AUNTS. NICE, HUH?
I HOPE SHE'LL FINISH SCHOOL THOUGH.
AYA, GIVE ME A BREAK. SHE DOESN'T NEED TO.
CHAMBRES 100 à 130
SHE CAN HAVE A DOUBLE C SERIES NOW: THE BEAUTY PARLOR AND A SHOP.
HERE, THIS IS HER ROOM.
SURPRISE! IT'S US!
WHERE'S OUR BABY?

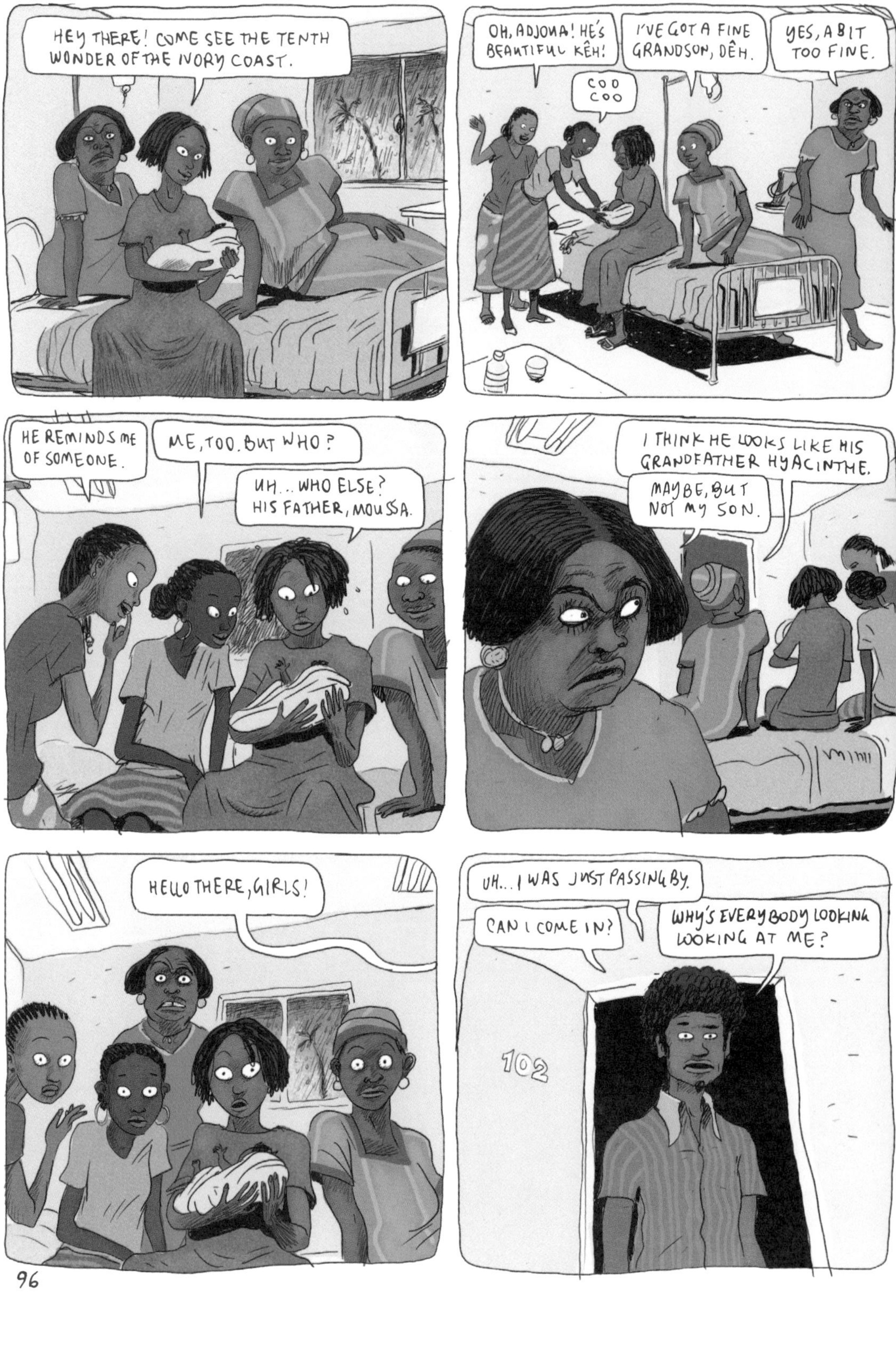
HEY THERE! COME SEE THE TENTH WONDER OF THE IVORY COAST.
OH, ADJOUA! HE'S BEAUTIFUL KÊH!
COO COO
I'VE GOT A FINE GRANDSON, DÊH.
YES, A BIT TOO FINE.
HE REMINDS ME OF SOMEONE.
ME, TOO. BUT WHO?
UH... WHO ELSE? HIS FATHER, MOUSSA.
I THINK HE LOOKS LIKE HIS GRANDFATHER HYACINTHE.
MAYBE, BUT NOT MY SON.
HELLO THERE, GIRLS!
UH... I WAS JUST PASSING BY.
CAN I COME IN?
WHY'S EVERYBODY LOOKING LOOKING AT ME?
102

IVORIAN BONUS

AFRICA
IVORY COAST

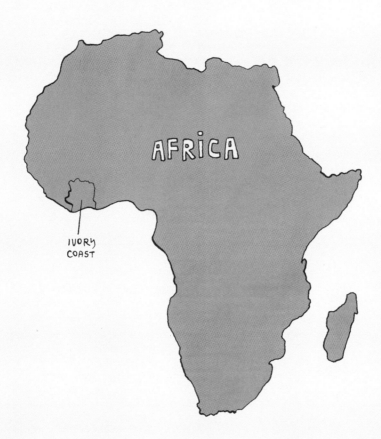

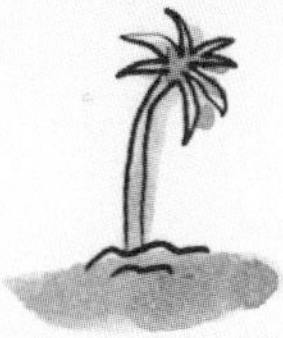

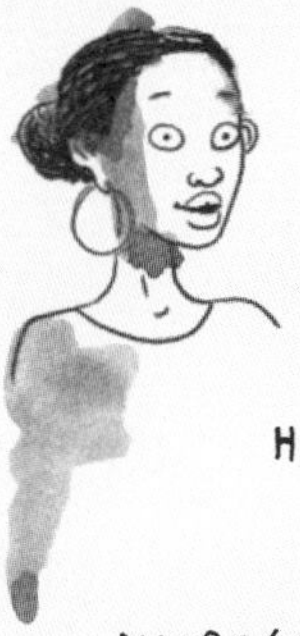

HERE'S A LITTLE **GLOSSARY** TO HELP YOU BETTER UNDERSTAND THE STORY:

- ALLOCO (A-LO-CO): DEEP FRIED SLICES OF PLANTAIN, A FAVORITE STREET FOOD.
- BANGALA (BAWN-GA-LA): SLANG, MALE REPRODUCTIVE ORGAN - YOU KNOW.
- DÊH (DEH): AN EXCLAMATION THAT INTENSIFIES MEANING. "SHE'S BEAUTIFUL, DÊH!" (SHE IS SOOO BEAUTIFUL!)
- FRESHNIE (FRESH-NEE): A NICE LOOKING GIRL.
- GAZELLE (GA-ZEL): A REAL BEAUTY.
- KAKABA (KA-KA-BA): SOMETHING TINY; AN INSECT. ALSO USED AS AN INSULT TO MEAN INSIGNIFICANT OR RIDICULOUS.
- KÊH (KEH): A CLIPPED EXCLAMATION ADDED TO THE END OF A WORD OR PHRASE FOR EMPHASIS, LEAVING NO ROOM FOR AMBIGUITY.
- KOUTOUKOU (KOO-TOO-KOO): AN ALCOHOLIC BEVERAGE MADE FROM FERMENTED PALM JUICE.
- MAMAN (MA-MAW): INFORMAL, MOTHER
- MAQUIS (MA-KEE): AN INEXPENSIVE OPEN-AIR RESTAURANT WITH MUSIC AND ROOM TO DANCE.
- PALU (PA-LU): SHORT FOR THE FRENCH "PALUDISME," MEANING MALARIA. "PALU" IS ALSO USED MORE GENERALLY TO REFER TO INFECTIONS INVOLVING FEVER, CHILLS, AND ACHES.
- TANTIE (TAWN-TIE): INFORMAL, AUNT. ALSO USED TO SHOW RESPECT OR AFFECTION WHEN TALKING TO AN OLDER WOMAN.
- TASSABA (TA-SA-BA): SLANG, BEHIND. "MOVE YOUR TASSABA!" (MOVE YOUR BUTT!)
- TONTON (TAWN-TAW): INFORMAL, UNCLE.

BACK HOME, WE HAVE A SAYING THAT GOES:

" YOU CAN ALWAYS TELL A WOMAN BY HER **PAGNE**."

A PAGNE (PA-NYE) IS A PIECE OF BRIGHTLY COLORED, WAX-PRINTED CLOTH. EVERY PATTERN HAS A MEANING, SO YOU NEED TO WATCH WHAT YOU WEAR. FOR EXAMPLE, NOW THAT I'M A RESPECTABLE, MARRIED WOMAN, I WOULD CHOOSE "CAPABLE HUSBAND" OR "SORRY, TAKEN."

- BINTOU, WHO IS SINGLE AND LOOKING FOR LOVE, MIGHT CHOOSE "FREE AS A BIRD" OR " YOU DON'T KNOW WHAT YOU'RE MISSING."

- AYA, WHO IS SINGLE AND PREFERS TO KEEP MEN AT A DISTANCE, WOULD CHOOSE "WATCH MY BITE!" OR "GO PLAY SOMEWHERE ELSE."

- A JEALOUS OR POSSESSIVE WOMAN WOULD WEAR A PAGNE THAT SAYS "MY ENEMY IS WATCHING" OR "YOUR FOOT, MY FOOT, IF YOU GO OUT, I'LL GO OUT TOO" - A CLEAR MESSAGE THAT SHE INTENDS TO KEEP A CLOSE EYE ON HER HUSBAND.

A PAGNE CAN BE SEWN INTO A SKIRT, A DRESS, OR A PAIR OF PANTS.

①

②

③

④

YOU CAN ALSO TAKE A SMALLER PAGNE AND WRAP IT AROUND YOUR HEAD. VERY CLASSY!

①

②

③

④

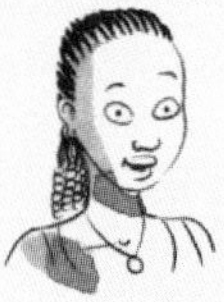

WHEN THEY SEE ME ROLL MY TASSABA, MEN FALL AT MY FEET. I'LL TELL YOU MY TRICK, BUT IT'S JUST ONE OF THE SPECIAL SECRETS I'VE GOT. AFTER ALL, I'M LOOKING FOR A GOOD CATCH, TOO. FIRST, YOU NEED TO LET YOUR HIP JUT OUT A BIT, AND YOU DON'T NEED A BIG BEHIND. NO, EVEN GIRLS WITH A SMALL OR FLAT BOTTOM CAN DO THIS.

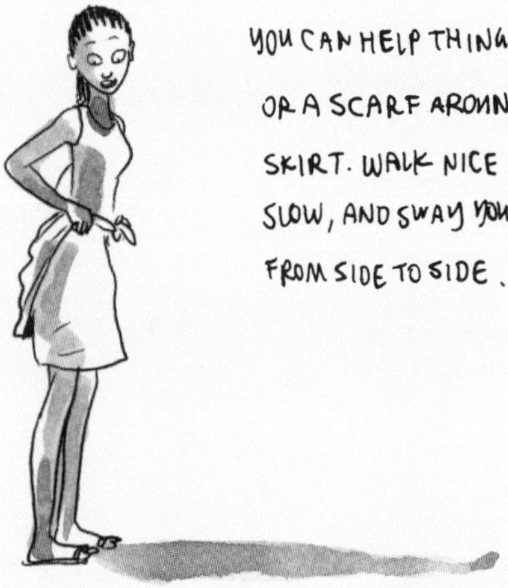

YOU CAN HELP THINGS ALONG BY WEARING A BELT ON YOUR PANTS, OR A SCARF AROUND YOUR DRESS OR SKIRT. WALK NICE AND SLOW, AND SWAY YOUR BUTT FROM SIDE TO SIDE.

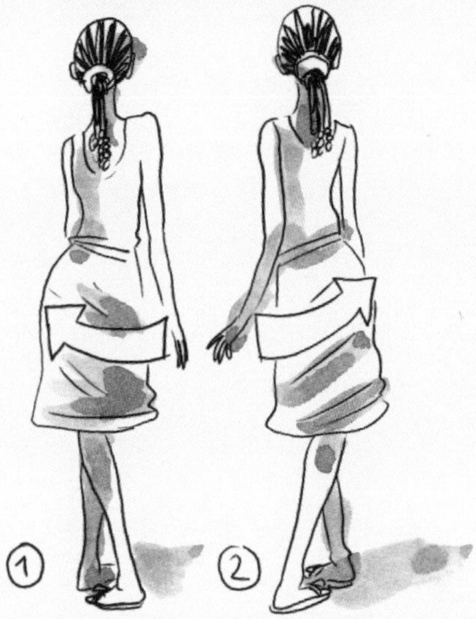
1
2

SAME THING ON THE DANCE FLOOR, BUT FASTER; YOU NEED TO REALLY SHAKE YOUR BEHIND. IT'S A MOVE WE CALL THE BUTT ROLL OR BUTT SHAKE.

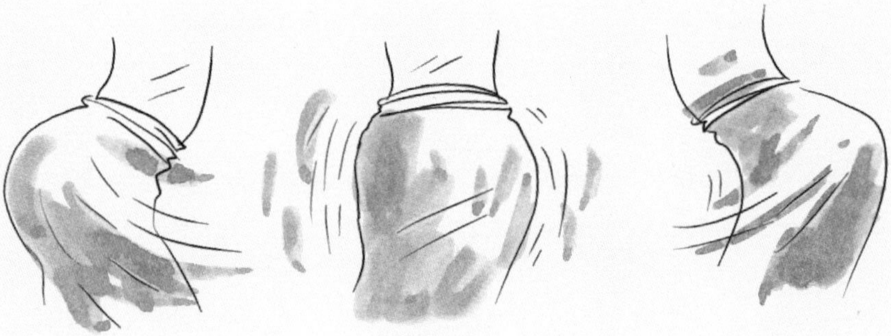

GOOD LUCK!

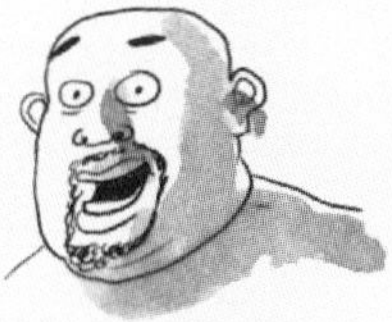

THERE'S SOMETHING I'VE GOT TO TELL YOU: I DON'T REALLY LIKE BEER.

MY FAVORITE DRINK IS "**GNAMANKOUDJI**," ALSO KNOWN AS GINGER JUICE. IT TASTES GREAT, OF COURSE, AND IT'S ALSO... A LOVE POTION.

HERE'S THE RECIPE:

PEEL 4 POUNDS OF FRESH GINGER.

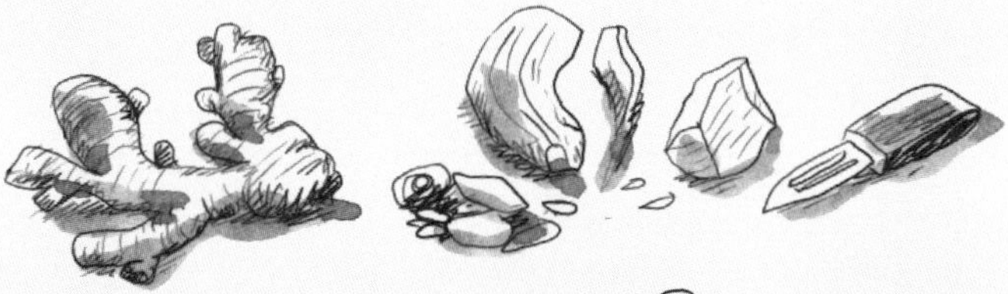

CRUSH OR POUND THE GINGER TO EXTRACT THE JUICE.

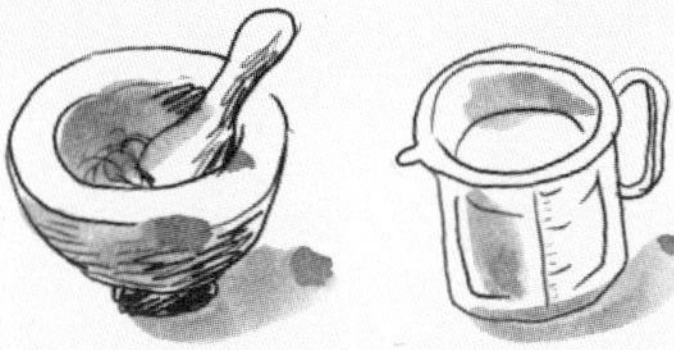

ADD WATER (A HALF OR WHOLE GALLON, DEPENDING ON HOW SPICY YOU WANT IT.)

LET THE MIXTURE REST FOR A WHILE, UNTIL THE STARCH SETTLES.

ADD SUGAR TO TASTE AND A FEW VANILLA BEANS.

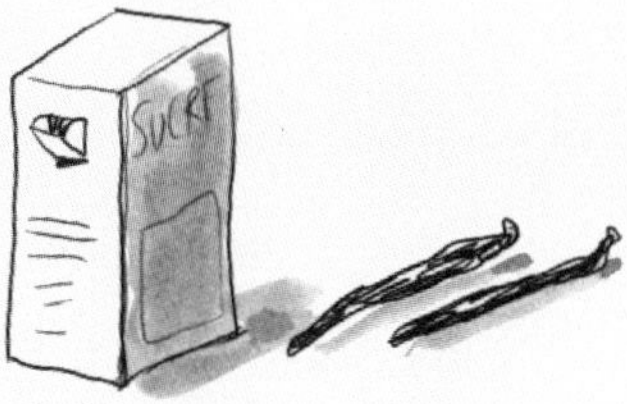

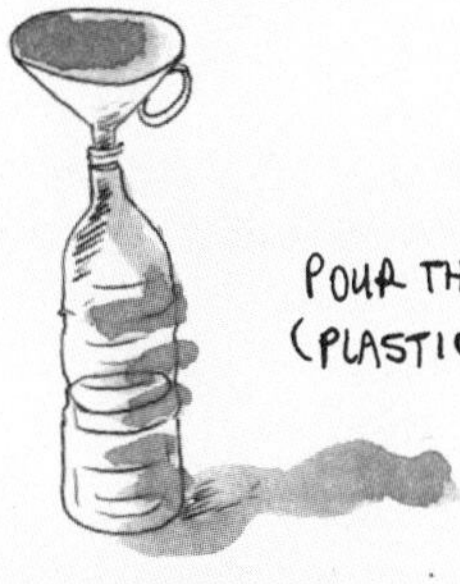

POUR THE JUICE INTO BOTTLES (PLASTIC IS FINE) AND REFRIGERATE.

YOU'RE DONE!

THE BEST ADVICE COMES LAST: YOU CAN MAKE FABULOUS COCKTAILS BY ADDING... YUM YUM... RUM, VODKA... WHATEVER YOU LIKE.

BELIEVE ME, YOU ARE IN FOR A GREAT TIME.

SEE YOU AROUND SOON!

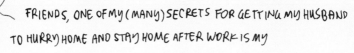

FRIENDS, ONE OF MY (MANY) SECRETS FOR GETTING MY HUSBAND TO HURRY HOME AND STAY HOME AFTER WORK IS MY

FAMOUS **PEANUT SAUCE**, ALSO KNOWN AS "BACK AND FORTH"-

TASTE IT AND YOU'LL BE BACK FOR MORE. HERE'S THE RECIPE.

TO SERVE 6 PEOPLE:

- 2 LBS BEEF (OR 1 FREE RANGE CHICKEN)

    - 4 LARGE TOMATOES

- 1 CAN OF TOMATO PASTE

- 2 LARGE ONIONS

- 1/4 LB JAR OF UNSWEETENED PEANUT BUTTER (DAKATINE OR BONMAFE' BRANDS IF YOU CAN FIND THEM)

- 1 HOT PEPPER

- SALT

- 2 MAGGI CUBES (OR OTHER BOUILLON)

1) START BY TRIMMING AND CUBING THE MEAT.

  DICE 1 ONION.

BROWN THE MEAT AND ONION IN A HEAVY POT (A CROCKPOT OR SKILLET), ADD A BIT OF SALT, COVER AND SIMMER FOR 15 MINUTES.

2) WHEN ALL THE LIQUID HAS EVAPORATED, ADD 4 TOMATOES, CUT INTO QUARTERS, THE SECOND ONION, CUT IN HALF, AND A CAN OF TOMATO PASTE.

3) AFTER 10 MINUTES, ADD WATER TO COVER THE MEAT. STIR IN THE PEANUT BUTTER, A PINCH OF SALT AND THE HOT PEPPER (DON'T SLICE OR CRUSH — THE PEPPER IS MEANT TO PERFUME THE SAUCE.) REMOVE THE PEPPER AFTER A WHILE (SERVE IT SEPARATELY) FOR PEOPLE WHO LIKE THEIR FOOD SPICY), COVER, AND SIMMER FOR HALF AN HOUR.

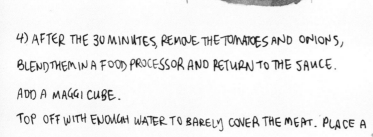

4) AFTER THE 30 MINUTES, REMOVE THE TOMATOES AND ONIONS, BLEND THEM IN A FOOD PROCESSOR AND RETURN TO THE SAUCE.
ADD A MAGGI CUBE.
TOP OFF WITH ENOUGH WATER TO BARELY COVER THE MEAT. PLACE A LID ON THE POT AND SIMMER. FOR ANOTHER 30 MINUTES.

5) WHEN A FILM OF OIL APPEARS ON THE SURFACE OF YOUR SAUCE, IT'S DONE.

SKIM OFF THE OIL IF YOU LIKE AND SEASON TO TASTE. ADD THE SECOND MAGGI CUBE. YOUR SAUCE SHOULD BE RICH AND FLAVORFUL. SERVE WITH RICE.

LET ME KNOW WHAT YOU THINK! ENJOY!

Marguerite Abouet was born in Abidjan in 1971. At the age of 12, she was sent with her older brother to study in France under the care of a great uncle. She now lives in Romainville, a suburb of Paris, where she works as a legal assistant and writes novels she has yet to show to publishers. *AYA* is her first graphic novel. It taps into Abouet's childhood memories of Ivory Coast in the 1970s, a prosperous, promising time in that country's history, to tell an unpretentious and gently humorous story of an Africa we rarely see— spirited, hopeful and resilient.

Clément Oubrerie was born in Paris in 1966. After a stint in art school he spent two years in the United States doing a variety of odd jobs, publishing his first children's books and serving jail time in New Mexico for working without papers. Back in France, he went on to a prolific career in illustration. With over 40 children's books to his credit, he is also co-founder of the 3-D animation studio, Station OMD. A drummer in a funk band in his spare time, he still travels frequently, especially to the Ivory Coast. In *AYA*, his first graphic novel, Oubrerie's warm colors and energetic, playful line connect expressively with Abouet's vibrant writing.

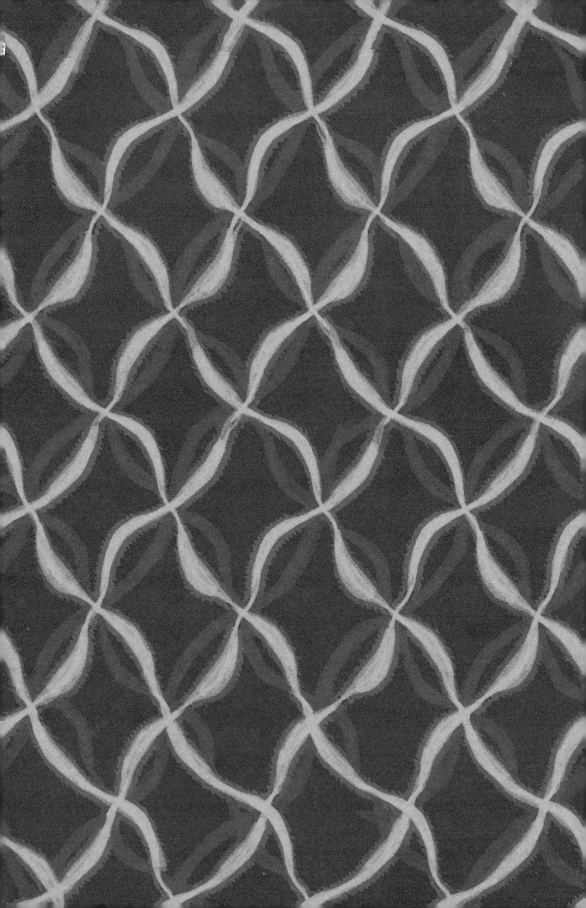